T5-DID-314

The New Americans
Recent Immigration and American Society

Edited by
Steven J. Gold and Rubén G. Rumbaut

A Series from LFB Scholarly

Uprooting Children

Mobility, Social Capital, and Mexican American Underachievement

Robert Ketner Ream

LFB Scholarly Publishing LLC
New York 2005

Library of Congress Cataloging-in-Publication Data

Ream, Robert Ketner, 1966-
Uprooting children : mobility, social capital, and Mexican American underachievement / Robert Ketner Ream.
p. cm. -- (The new Americans)
Includes bibliographical references and index.
ISBN 1-59332-063-9 (alk. paper)
1. Student mobility--United States. 2. Academic achievement--United States. 3. Social capital (Sociology)--United States. 4. Mexican American students. 5. Minority students--United States. I. Title. II. Series: New Americans (LFB Scholarly Publishing LLC)
LB3064.2.R4 2005
371.2'91--dc22

2004019387

ISBN 1-59332-063-9

Printed on acid-free 250-year-life paper.

Manufactured in the United States of America.

To Gary Kersey Hart, Founder of the California State University Institute for Education Reform

TABLE OF CONTENTS

TABLES AND FIGURES

ACKNOWLEDGMENTS

This book is both the subject and in many ways the product of social capital, an example of how not only *what* you know, but *who* you know, can lead to productive ends. I completed my PhD, under the direction of Russell W. Rumberger, in Fall 2001 at the Gevirtz Graduate School of Education at UC Santa Barbara. It was then my good fortune to have professor Barbara Schneider of the University of Chicago introduce me to Marta Tienda, director of Princeton University's Office of Population Research. Upon professor Tienda's invitation, I traveled cross-country to New Jersey that fall, where I enjoyed the postdoctoral freedom to fortify the idea-foundation underlying this book. I am greatly indebted to all these wonderful scholars, especially Russ Rumberger, who, as my intellectual mentor and friend, has generously encouraged me to partake of (and perhaps make a small contribution to) the "paradise of knowledge."

There are others who have made significant contributions to my development as a researcher; I have benefited from many excellent teachers. None have been more instrumental to my scholarly growth, however, than professor Rumberger, UC Santa Barbara political scientist Lorraine M. McDonnell, and education professor Richard P. Durán, who have consistently modeled a standard of research excellence I strive to live up to. Gevirtz School Dean Jules Zimmer also deserves special thanks for reminding me that "it's a good life!" we lead in pursuit of understanding.

Preparation of this manuscript would not have been possible without the combined assistance of The Spencer Foundation and the RAND Corporation. I am especially indebted to Spencer Foundation Senior Program Officer Margaret Jay Braatz, as well as RAND Education Director Dominic Brewer and Associate Director Charles Goldman, for their steadfast support of the work reflected here. I owe a similar debt to the American Educational Research Association (AERA) and its staff, in particular Jeanie Murdock. Two AERA fellowships in different years provided core support of important data collection and analysis phases of this project. In addition, I am grateful for the financial assistance that has been provided in successive stages by the UC Institute for Mexico and the United States, the UC Linguistic Minority Research Institute, and the UC Santa Barbara Center for Chicano Studies. I am also indebted to professors Steven

J.Gold and Rubén G. Rumbaut who saw promise in the early stages of this manuscript and subsequently recommended its publication in *The New Americans* book series where it now appears.

Securing the field data analyzed in this book largely depended on the school-based knowledge and invaluable biliteracy skills of three talented graduate students: Mariana Pacheco, Kimberly Barraza-Lawrence, and Jose Prado. Marta Acevedo, a high school counselor, also helped by translating interview protocols from English to Spanish. My younger sister, Kary Ream—herself a skilled social worker—contributed to this study by interviewing adolescent girls in Los Angeles. And Michael Vorhaus graciously offered the shelter of his home while I was conducting fieldwork away from mine. I am also grateful to many others in my family of friends who carefully read portions of this work, including Salvador Castillo, Lisa Chan, Derrick Chau, Michelle Cho, Patricia Fernández, Dawn Umemoto Houston, Sandraluz Lara-Cinisomo, Joe Luker, Nancy Nicosia, William Perez, Paula Razquin, Anne Ream, Lucrecia Santibañez, Sandra Way, and Elizabeth Yvon. Christopher Dirks deserves special recognition for applying his considerable technical skill to the process of taking this manuscript to publication.

Without the crucial assistance of three others I would not have finished this book. R. Clifton Spargo is a brilliant writer and editor with a critical eye that never ceases to amaze me. His red-line recommendations helped to make even my driest musings much more readable than they otherwise would have been. Julie McNall read and commented on earlier drafts of this book, and her meticulous attention to detail is greatly appreciated. Ana Inés Heras Monner Sans offered invaluable critiques of portions of the manuscript, encouraging me near the journey's end to articulate even more carefully the findings in this book. Working with Cliff, Julie, and Ana has reminded me of W.E.B. Du Bois' assertion that honest and earnest criticism is "the soul of democracy." I am a more thoughtful citizen for having been embraced by all three of them as a colleague and friend. The data analyses and interpretations expressed in this book are mine, however, and do not necessarily reflect the views of those who have helped me along the way, or of the granting agencies who funded this work.

Finally, I want to thank all the young people who shared their compelling stories with us. It is my hope that this work will somehow be of service to them.

CHAPTER 1

Introduction

> *The study of Latinos can only begin by charting unsuspected encounters, with full awareness that the task is bound to find unsuspected mirrors bound to reflect the researcher's unguarded gaze.*
>
> — Roman de la Campa, *Latinos and the Crossover Aesthetic*

Among the wide-ranging challenges facing American educators and the divergent theories and methods we employ to redress inadequacies in our educational system, perhaps no other issue is more pressing than the disparity in educational achievement among racial/ethnic groups.[1] However it is measured, whether by school grades, standardized test scores, course selection, or high school and college completion rates, the fact that there is a persistent history of group-level achievement differences in American education is not debatable. Nevertheless, the *reasons* we give for this problem—as well as the theoretical presuppositions and research techniques on which many past explanations have been premised—can be strongly contested. This was dramatically illustrated by the explosive reaction to publication of Herrnstein and Murray's *The Bell Curve* (1994), which by linking genetic characteristics to group achievement differences marked the troubling re-emergence of a line of research most scholars in the field thought was obsolete. Herrnstein and Murray's thesis has been largely discredited by other works (Jencks, et al., 1972; Bowles & Gintis, 1972; Thompson, Detterman, & Plomin, 1991; Valencia & Solorzano, 1997; Jencks & Phillips, 1998) and debunked by "anti-essentialist" arguments (Loury, 2002), all of which leave little doubt that so-called innate differences between "races" are actually the shameful product of a long history of discriminatory political and cultural practices, as well as continued ethnocentric biases in the contemporary political and economic structures of American society (Du Bois, 1903; Wilson, 1987; Massey & Eggers, 1990; Kozol, 1992; Menchaca, 1995; Vernez & Abrahamse, 1996; Trueba, 1999; Valencia, 2002; Villenas & Foley, 2002; National Research Council, 2004). It is precisely because some student groups have consistently performed at higher levels than other groups of students, and because the causes of this phenomenon tend to be naturalized (instead of being more reasonably understood as the culmination of problematic historical, economic, cultural, and sociopolitical factors), that social scientists must continue steadfastly in their efforts to illuminate a problem that is now commonly designated as the "achievement gap."

Sociologist James Coleman's controversial 1966 report to the U.S. Congress, *Equality of Educational Opportunity*, was the first national study to describe racial/ethnic differences in academic achievement among children of various ages (Phillips, 2000). For years prior to the *Coleman Report*, investigations of this nature had been largely focused on educational inputs; school quality had been measured by the resources that went into schools, not the quality of the students who came out of them (Coleman, Hoffer & Kilgore, 1982). Since the publication of Coleman's report, empirical research on the achievement gap has emerged in fits and starts. Indeed, nearly two decades passed before U.S. Secretary of Education Terrel Bell's 1983 report to Congress, *A Nation at Risk*, inspired a renewed focus on the persistent educational underachievement of minority students in the United States (Miller, 1995).[2]

Eleven years later, *The Bell Curve* sparked a firestorm of debate that catalyzed more research discrediting insidious claims about the genetic inevitability of group-level achievement differences. Most pointedly, the authors of *The Black-White Test Score Gap* (Jencks & Phillips, 1998) boldly asserted that eliminating the gap was not only within reach, but would do more to promote racial equality than any other strategy now under serious political consideration. In response to changing demographics and a new economy in which employment prospects and wages are more highly correlated with educational attainment than ever before, many policymakers have redoubled efforts to achieve group-level equality of educational outcomes. At the federal level, the Clinton administration's final budget plan called for a symbolic gesture with real consequences, allotting $50 million to reward states that make significant gains in closing the achievement gap between high- and low-performing students (Robelen, 2000). A new law in North Carolina now requires the state board of education to include "closing the achievement gap" in its statewide accountability scheme. That state's *Advisory Commission on Raising Achievement and Closing Gaps* also orchestrates an annual conference that has raised national awareness of the issue (Public Schools of North Carolina, 2004). In a similar spirit, the preamble to the 2001 version of the 1965 Elementary and Secondary Education Act signed into law (PL 107-110) by President George W. Bush, explicitly states that the purpose of the federal No Child Left Behind Act (NCLB) is to bring an end to group-level differences in student achievement (Thernstrom & Thernstrom, 2003). And in May 2004, the National Education Association Foundation, the philanthropic arm of the NEA, announced a substantial grant program aimed at closing the achievement gap between minority and low-income students and their more affluent peers (*Education Week*, 2004).

To keep pace with these new initiatives and to reach a point where the programs they inspire might have the desired consequences, researchers must continually account for the ever-shifting demographics in student populations. Until recently, scholars have focused primarily on the achievement gap between Blacks and Whites (e.g., Jencks & Phillips, 1998; Hallinan, 2001) simply because more research had been conducted about testing performance among African American students than among other groups, and also because, until fairly recently, Blacks were far more numerous in the United States than other minority groups (Jencks & Phillips, 1998). But rapid Hispanic/Latino[3] population growth has altered the racial and ethnic landscape in America. At the same time the growth of the standards movement since the late 1980s, with its link to state assessments and K-12 test scores (Carnoy, Elmore & Sisken, 2003; McDonnell, 2004), has illuminated glaring achievement differences between groups, making educators specifically aware of the low average educational achievement and attainment patterns in the U.S. Latino population. As a result, the public's concerns about the gap have broadened and also newly concentrated on U.S. Latinos.

Changing Demographics in the United States

With more than one-third of the U.S. Latino population still under eighteen, Latinos are projected to be the largest minority group in the United States by 2005.[4] The number of U.S. Latinos is growing eight times more rapidly than the population as a whole (Vernez & Mizell, 2002), and after 2020, the Latino population is projected to add more people to the United States every year than all other racial/ethnic groups combined (U.S. Department of Commerce, Bureau of the Census, 2000a). At this pace, there will be 16 million more U.S. Latinos (59 million) than Blacks (43 million) by the year 2025 (Davis, 2001). In short, no other group will do more to change the nation's schools in the next quarter century than the new ethnic mosaic of Latinos, whose student population is expected to increase more than 50 percent between 1985 and 2025 when nearly one-quarter of the U.S. population (and its K-12 students) will be Latino (White House Initiative, 1998; U.S. Census Bureau, 2000a; Tienda, 2001).

While the highest concentration of Latino school-age children will continue to be in the southwest, many other regions of the country will share in the large percentage increase in Latino students. Illinois and Missouri are among the midwestern states that can expect a 30 to 40 percent increase in their Hispanic school-age population between 2000 and 2015. Hispanics constitute nearly 30 percent of the population in Chicago and hold the balance of power in most city elections. Even higher increases are projected for various eastern states including Massachusetts and Virginia (see Figure 1.1): Arlington is now more than 20 percent Hispanic (Davis, 2001).

Figure 1.1. Projected Percent Increase in Hispanic School-Age Population (ages 5-17), 2000 to 2015

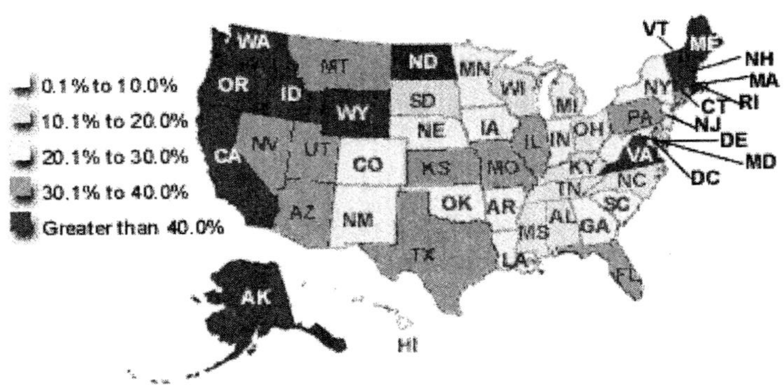

SOURCE: *Population projections for states by age, sex, race, and Hispanic origin: 1995 to 2025*. U.S. Bureau of the Census, population division, PPl-47.

Nature and Extent of the Achievement Gap

Although some gaps in the academic performance of Latino and non-Latino White students have narrowed over the past two decades,[5] various studies point to the persistence of large achievement differences distinguishing the two groups at all educational levels.[6] Perhaps the best evidence comes from the National Assessment of Educational Progress (NAEP), widely known as "the nation's report card." For at least the past thirty years, Latino test scores in NAEP reading and mathematics have lagged behind those of non-Latino Whites (U.S. Department of Education, National Center for Education Statistics, 1998b). In fact, by the time children are nine, performance differences have emerged in all academic subjects, and thirteen-year-old Latinos are approximately two years behind White students of the same age in both reading and math. These trends continue at the secondary education level. At age seventeen, Latino twelfth-graders are reading at levels similar to thirteen-year-old White eighth-graders (NCES, 1998b). Figures 1.2a and 1.2b illustrate the nature and persistence of the Latino-White test score gap among seventeen-year-old adolescents as measured by standardized reading and mathematics test scores from the mid 1970s to 1999.[7]

Figure 1.2a. Trends in Average Reading Scores by Race/Ethnicity

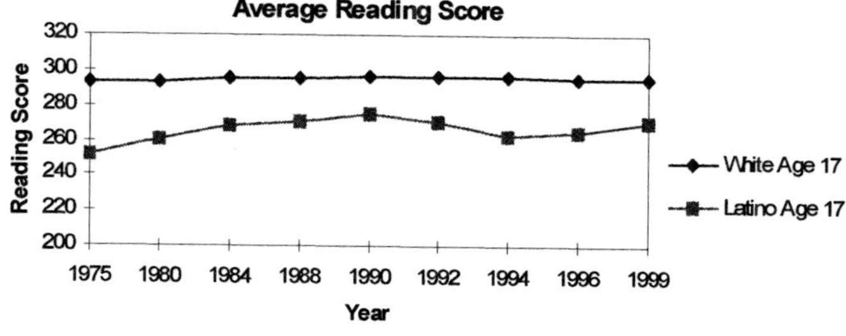

Figure 1.2b. Trends in Average Math Scores by Race/Ethnicity

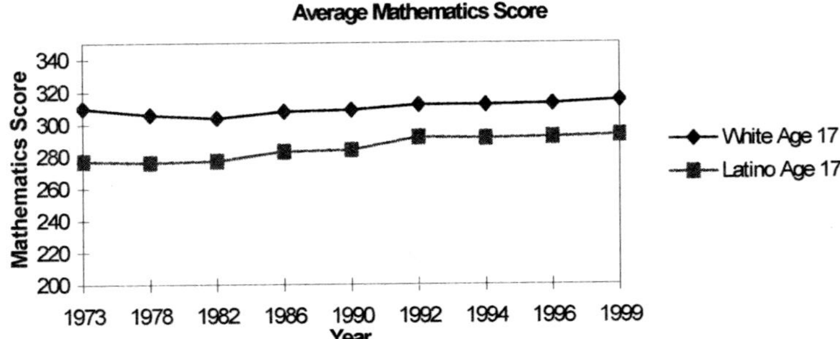

SOURCE: U.S. Department of Education, National Center for Education Statistics, National Assessment of Educational Progress (NAEP), 1999 Long-Term Trend Assessment.

While standardized achievement data reveal students' relative mastery of specific knowledge and skills, other data, such as high school and college completion rates, demonstrate differences in group-level educational attainment. Although the gap in high school completion rates between Blacks and Whites has narrowed significantly in the past twenty-five years (NCES, 1998a), double-digit disparities in the graduation rates of Latino and non-Latino White high school students have persisted (NCES, 1998c). As a corollary to this phenomenon, numerous studies demonstrate that Latino students are much more likely to drop out of school than non-Latino Whites (Fernández, Paulsen & Hirano-Nakanishi, 1989; Trueba, Spindler & Spindler 1989; Rumberger, 1995; Rumberger & Rodríguez, 2002). The alarmingly high Latino high school dropout rate—1.4 million Latinos between the ages of 16 and 24 were dropouts in 2001 (U.S. Census Bureau, 2002b)—is, in fact, twice that of Blacks and more than three times that of non-Latino Whites (see Figure 1.3).[8]

Not surprisingly, these numbers prefigure similar trends in educational attainment at the college level, where Latinos are about half as likely as their non-Latino White peers to complete four years of college—a gap that has not shown signs of diminishing over time (NCES, 1995b; Vernez & Mizell, 2002). Whereas 25 percent of non-

Latino Whites and almost 15 percent of African Americans have completed a bachelor's degree or advanced degree, only 11 percent of Hispanics have done so (U.S. Department of Commerce, 1998). Significantly, Latinos who do finish college also take longer than their non-Latino peers and are more likely than either African American or White students to require upward of six years to secure a bachelor's degree (NCES, 1996). Such findings, coupled with dramatic Latino demographic shifts, suggest that the gap in educational achievement will persist and grow in significance if its causes are left unresolved.[9]

Figure 1.3. Status Dropout Rates of 16- to 24-Year-Olds by Race/Ethnicity, 1981-2001

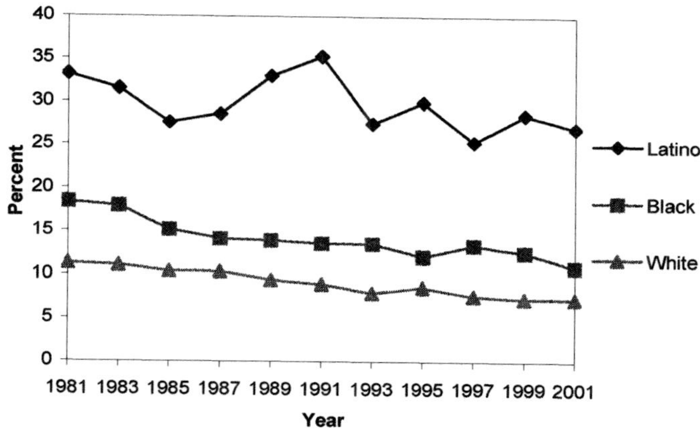

SOURCE: U.S. Department of Commerce, Bureau of the Census, Current Population Survey, unpublished data; and U.S. Department of Education, National Center for Education Statistics, Dropout Rates in the United States, Prepared October, 2002.

While achievement differences between Latinos and non-Latinos are pronounced, they may not be as disparate as within-group differences in student performance among Latino sub-populations (Miller, 1995; Valencia, 2002). Students of Mexican descent are dropping out of school at nearly three times the rate of their Cuban American counterparts (NCES, 1995b), while also scoring significantly lower on Stanford achievement tests than Cuban, Nicaraguan, and Colombian Americans (Portes & Rumbaut, 2001). Indeed, Latino underachievement is particularly pronounced for Mexican Americans, who as illustrated in Figure 1.4 constitute approximately 67 percent of U.S. Latinos, compared to the 14 percent from Central and South America and the Caribbean, the 9 percent from Puerto Rico, and the 4 percent of Cuban descent (U.S. Census Bureau, 2002a).

Figure 1.4. Percentage Breakdown by Latino Sub-Population in the United States

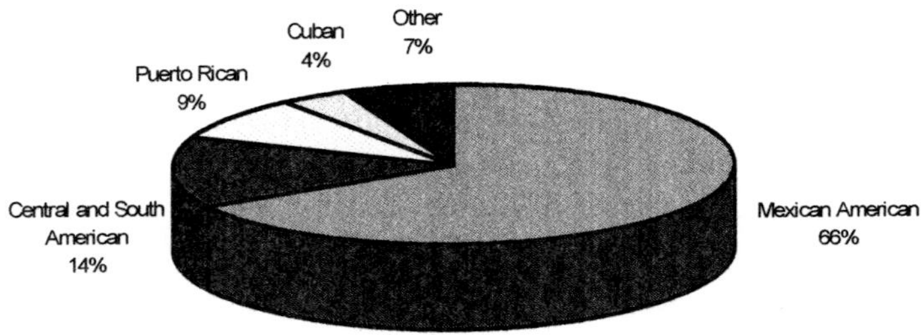

SOURCE: U.S. Department of Commerce, Bureau of the Census, Annual Demographic Supplement to the March 2002 Current Population Survey. Issued June 2003.

In terms of college preparedness, SAT verbal scores among Mexican American college-bound students actually fell by nine points from 1989-1999, while scores for U.S. Puerto Ricans increased eighteen points on the SAT's 800-point scale (College Entrance Examination Board, 1999). Once admitted to college, students of Mexican origin demonstrate the lowest college completion rate among Latino sub-groups (Chapa & Valencia, 1993). From such information, it is not hard to conclude that Mexican American students face the greatest immediate educational challenge among all Latino subgroups in the United States (De la Rosa & Maw, 1990; Aguirre & Martinez, 1993; Vigil, 1997; Valenzuela, 1999; Stanton-Salazar, 2001; Grogger & Trejo, 2002; Valencia, 2002; Gibson, Gándara & Koyama, 2004).

Explaining Mexican American Underachievement

Most studies designed to explain low average levels of Mexican American student achievement and educational attainment appeal to theoretical notions involving three interrelated kinds of capital—specifically, human capital, cultural capital and physical/economic capital. Neo-classical economists originally introduced human capital theory (Schultz 1961; Becker, 1964) to explain how altering people's knowledge and skill levels will set in motion a more efficient use of economic capital (Coleman, 1990). What French sociologist Pierre Bourdieu termed "cultural capital" (Bourdieu, 1979) has been employed in a variety of ways (Lareau, 1987; Lamont & Lareau, 1988; Spillane et al., 2003), from explaining educational and consumptive tastes across social classes (DiMaggio, 1982; Bourdieu, 1984), to investigating the cultural underpinnings of the achievement gap (Gándara, 1994). Framed at the intersection of human and cultural capital, language barriers are most frequently cited in association with Mexican American underachievement, with the result that most of the federal and state activity aimed at increasing the achievement of Latino youth throughout the 1970s and 1980s focused on English language acquisition and development for students with limited English proficiency (Gándara, 1994; Valdés, 1998; Gibson et al., 2004).[10] Other studies have focused more broadly on the explanatory power of culture, noting for example that youth of Mexican descent often attend schools where teachers have little knowledge of the students' cultural backgrounds, which can lead to students' alienation and disengagement from school (Matute-Bianchi, 1986; Trueba, 1988; Menchaca, 1989; Valenzuela, 1999; Gibson et al., 2004). Not surprisingly, socioeconomic disadvantage is also a well-researched contributor (Lareau, 1989; Velez, 1989; Miller, 1995; Brooks-Gunn & Duncan, 1997; Trejo, 1997; Valencia, 2002) to a problem only exacerbated by inequitable schooling and substandard educational facilities (Shields et al., 1999; Rumberger & Gándara, 2000; Pearl, 2002).

Where Traditional Explanations Fall Short

Although contemporary research offers various reasons for low average levels of student achievement among Mexican origin youth, some of the explanatory pieces are still missing from the puzzle. For example, socioeconomic disadvantage does not prove to be as consistent a predictor of educational underachievement as one might expect. Studies based on human and economic capital do not explain why some middle-class minority student groups consistently perform below non-Latino Whites with similar family and school backgrounds (Miller, 1995; Phillips et al., 1998; Jencks & Phillips, 1998). Nor has research yet explained why racial disparities in educational achievement prove to be greater among students whose parents are college educated than among students whose parents lack even a high school degree (College Entrance Examination Board, 1999).[11] And while primary cultural differences, such as language, do distinguish many minorities from the mainstream, considerable debate has continued among researchers as to the significance of such factors (Cook & Ludwig, 1997; Darder, Torres & Gutierrez, 1997). Thus, some studies have begun to question "secondary cultural difference" theories (Ogbu 1978; 1992) by showing that many minority students, regardless of the terms of their incorporation into the U.S. mainstream, share perceptions about their educational experiences that are similar to—if not more optimistic than—those of their non-minority peers (Cook & Ludwig, 1997; Ainsworth-Darnell & Downey, 1998).

Society's Interest in Eliminating the Achievement Gap

Why should we care about group inequality? As the 1983 congressional report *A Nation at Risk* re-emphasized, a fundamental determinant of a nation's productivity is the educational level of its population. The relation of literacy to the efficiency of workers has been highlighted by a recent employment study in the United States, which found that as many as one-half of all job seekers are seriously limited in the kinds of work for which they are eligible as a direct consequence of their own extremely low levels of literacy. These problems are even more acute for Latinos and Blacks who obtained a high school education or less (Loury, 1987; Kirsch, Jungeblut, & Campbell, 1992). While social policy has made workplace discrimination less of a career barrier than it was thirty years ago,[12] the question of educational attainment nevertheless continues to severely limit minority advancement in the marketplace. As affirmative action programs have been drawn increasingly into question, especially with regard to admission standards for state universities, we should also admit that active educational policies addressing gaps in educational achievement need to remain a priority, since eliminating racial/ethnic differences in test-score performance not only offers to improve employment and earnings prospects for minorities, but also promises to help us end divisive debates over racial preferences in the workplace and in education. If colleges and universities could achieve student population diversity without making race an explicit factor in their admissions decisions, much of the fury around the politics of affirmative action would likely be diffused (Jencks & Phillips, 1998).

Given the obvious national economic and social benefits that would follow if group-level educational achievement were more evenly distributed—including increased tax revenues and contributions to Medicare and Social Security, as well as revenues saved in public welfare, health and law enforcement programs (Vernez & Mizell, 2002)—it is perhaps surprising that the research and policy communities have not been even more focused on efforts to put an end to the achievement gap.[13] Certainly the sensitive nature of the subject plays a part in explaining the apparent reluctance of the scholarly community to research the gap or grapple with it in the policy arena (Phillips, 2000). Even so, and according to only the most pragmatic calculus of political decision-makers, the likelihood the population base of U.S. workers will increasingly come to be made up of persons drawn from groups whose amount of education and whose actual educational performance is significantly below the achievement levels of the remainder of the nation's populace prefigures a future in which work force conditions will prove increasingly to be an impediment to U.S. economic productivity (Baumol et al., 1989). It may be that those of us who are presently affected by the educational handicaps of Latinos only in an indirect way will end up deeply regretting our lack of foresight if we are not able to provide the vision, planning and resources required to deal effectively with Latino and, more specifically, Mexican American underachievement (Miller, 1995; Baumol et al., 1989; Portes & Rumbaut, 2001; Vernez & Mizell, 2002).[14]

The Current Study

What I have set out to do in this study is to link an emergent literature on social capital with research on residential and student mobility in order to show that Mexican American underachievement is at least in part the result of the social network instability accompanying high rates of transience among this particular group of students. Broadly defined, social capital is the aggregate of the actual or potential resources embedded in social networks that may be converted, *via* social exchange, into other manifestations of capital, including physical/economic capital (Bourdieu, 1986), human capital (Coleman, 1988) and healthy civic participation and community cohesion (Putnam, 2000). Since it has recently been acknowledged that we know quite little about the relative importance of social capital across different spatial and cultural domains (Rothstein, 2000; Fuller & Hannum, 2002; Ream, 2003), in this study I focus specifically on social capital inhering in family, peer, community, and school social networks.

Like the frequent repotting of plants, mobility tends to disrupt social root systems, limiting the capacity of students and their interlocutors to develop and maintain social capital by (a) disrupting family cohesion, (b) inhibiting students' efforts to make new friends and adjust socially to a new school situation, and (c) impinging on the development of reciprocal relations between students and institutional agents within the broader community (Jason et al., 1992; Pribesh & Downey, 1999; Putnam, 2000; Ream, 2003). In turn, this process is often detrimental to adolescents' self-confidence and their overall well-being (Munton 1990; Wood et al., 1993; Rumberger et al., 1999). It follows that, insofar as mobility impacts the resources that inhere in social networks, holding sway over group stability and academic achievement, the *mobility/social capital dynamic* merits our close attention (Mehan at al., 1994; McLanahan & Sandefur, 1996; Olsen 1997).

If mobility were not so commonplace, such concern about its potential association with declining stocks of social capital (Putnam 2000) and educational underperformance among mobile student groups (Wood et al., 1993; Pribesh & Downey, 1999, Rumberger et al., 1999) might seem unwarranted. There is no getting around the fact, however, that mobility is widespread (GAO 1994; Hudis & Rathnam 1994; Rumberger, 2003; U.S. Census Bureau, 2004), and it is probably not realistically solved by telling parents, in an increasingly mobile and fragile marketplace, that for the sake of their children, they aught not to move. The majority of U.S. school children make at least one non-promotional school change by the twelfth grade, and many transfer schools much more frequently (Rumberger et al., 1999; Swanson & Schneider 1999; Rumberger, 2003; Offenberg, forthcoming). A survey of more than fifty local education agencies throughout the United States revealed that in many districts the proportion of students enrolled in a school for less than the entire academic year exceeded 30 to 40 percent (Ligon & Paredes 1992). Another study of immigrant children reported that turnover rates in a majority of schools in three California school districts exceeded 50 percent per year (McDonnell & Hill 1993). Choosing up sides in a kickball game when students have yet to even learn the names of roughly half their classmates is only the most trivial of playground problems. It is not surprising then that mobility is particularly pronounced among U.S. Latinos (Rumberger 2003; U.S. Census Bureau, 2004) who constitute by far the most significant of recently immigrated communities and thus the very population most susceptible to various kinds of economic and social instability (Rumberger 2003). Nevertheless, student and residential mobility among Mexican origin youth has remained a largely unexplored area of study (Ream & Castillo, 2001).

James Coleman (1988, 1990) was perhaps the first to address the *mobility/social capital dynamic*, and others have followed suit (Tienda, 1991; Hagan, MacMillan & Wheaton, 1996; Pribesh & Downey 1999; Pettit & McLanahan, 2003; Ream, 2003). In this book I build upon Coleman's research and take it a step further by suggesting the impact of mobility on social capital development may be particularly detrimental to Mexican origin youth, per the following hypothesis: *Mexican Americans learn less in school than non-Latino Whites, in part because they have less access to social capital due to the fact that they are more mobile during their school careers.* It is a rather axiomatic notion that some groups of people have more ample resources embedded in their social networks than others; but it has rarely been investigated whether different *forms* of social capital, like different kinds of currency, give evidence of differential exchange value.[15] So just as newly minted *Euros* are good for *paella* in Valencia but won't buy a hotdog at Wrigley Field no matter how international the Chicago Cubs' fan base may now be, the convertibility of certain forms of social capital may also be conditioned by the people who possess it and the places where they attempt its exchange. Are, for example, some forms of social capital more convertible into test score performance than others? To answer that question and others like it, I apply the notion that the convertibility of resources embedded in social networks may differ between racial/ethnic groups to the broader context of *the mobility/social capital dynamic* in order to test a second hypothesis: *Different forms of social capital, like different forms of currency, have differential exchange value—hence the process of academic achievement differs for the two groups in a manner that disadvantages Mexican origin youth.*

In short, this investigation pursues two hypotheses. The first posits that Mexican Americans learn less in school than non-Latino Whites because they have less access to social capital, a condition which is at least partly contingent upon the fact that they are more mobile during their school careers. The second draws a distinction between the *availability* of social capital and its *convertibility* by considering whether different forms of social capital give evidence of differential exchange value that works to the disadvantage of Mexican origin youth. These hypotheses are examined *via* the following research questions:

- To what extent do mobility rates and the availability of various forms of social capital differ between Mexican Americans and non-Latino Whites of varying socioeconomic and/or nativity status?
- What is the relationship between mobility, social capital, and twelfth grade academic achievement among Mexican American and non-Latino White adolescents?
- Do group-level differences in the relationships between these factors contribute to Mexican American underachievement?

Beyond its contributions to understanding the achievement gap and low average test score performance among Mexican Americans in particular, this study makes two additional contributions to the current state of research on this subject—one theoretical and the other methodological. First, by employing social capital theory, I investigate whether social capital and mobility interact to influence adolescents' academic achievement and their experiences in specific social institutions. Second, by employing a mixed-methods research design rather than the more common single-method research technique, I attempt to combine the strengths of survey and field research, demonstrating that methodological cross-pollination can be used to triangulate findings and increase confidence in research conclusions.

The findings from this investigation suggest that the *mobility/social capital dynamic* is particularly detrimental to Mexican origin youth. When we ask what it is about the dynamic that causes differential educational outcomes between Mexican Americans and non-Latino Whites, the survey analyses show that Mexican Americans are more mobile than their non-Latino White counterparts and are over-represented among the highly mobile. If we juxtapose the reactive and the strategic reasons behind student transience, the interview analyses also suggest that the reasons students change school may have bearing on the educational impacts of mobility. Moreover, in spite of the potential utility of various forms of social capital, Mexican Americans may face a comparable disadvantage in terms of its availability as well as its convertibility into valued educational outcomes.

Reduced stocks of social capital may be partly explained by the economic, social, and political challenges faced by the growing percentage of Mexican American youth who are immigrants or whose parents are immigrants. Language barriers and employment-related demands appear to be particularly challenging for the immigrant and second-generation populations who constitute the majority of Mexican Americans in the United States (Portes & Rumbaut, 2001). Even though building and fortifying social networks across domains has the potential to improve the quality of life for individuals and their broader community, findings in this study illustrate that social capital does not always work to the benefit of those who tap it (Portes & Landolt, 1996). In fact, students of Mexican origin in possession of what appears on the surface to be a valued form of social currency in schools may actually be the unwitting recipients of a form of *counterfeit* social capital that impinges on their school success (Ream, 2003). So alongside the many beneficial manifestations of social capital noted throughout this book, this study shows that relationships are also fraught with subtractive elements. Under the best circumstances, social capital is exchanged in the production of socially desirable outcomes. In the wrong proportion or in less than desirable circumstances, however, its negative manifestations can hamper productivity. It is in part the enigmatic relation between the social capital postulate and some of these more perplexing results that makes a careful examination of the theory and its relevant research worthwhile—not only for its potential to influence student performance, but also for the light it may shed on suspected group-level differences in the way it does so.

Overview

In the opening chapters of this study, Chapters 2 and 3, I elaborate the theoretical model in some detail and assess the data and methods I employ to investigate the *mobility/social capital dynamic*. Chapter 2 summarizes the theoretical and empirical work that weaves this study together, focusing primarily on (a) social capital as the theoretical basis for this investigation, and (b) mobility as a primary independent factor under study. I open the chapter by addressing various theoretical approaches that have been employed to investigate the achievement gap, along with the strengths and weaknesses of the empirical research borne of those theories. Considering social capital theory, including its origins and applications, I offer a more thorough explication of the theory as a logical next-step in the process of deductive research, with my own research designed to address the gap, especially as it pertains to Mexican American underachievement. This chapter concludes with a summary of existing research on the incidence, consequences and causes of student and residential mobility. In Chapter 3, I turn to more pragmatic concerns relevant to the methods I use in this study, offering a thorough review of the research design employed herein, and introducing my approach to mixed-methods data collection and analysis.

Over the course of Chapters 4 through 7, I present the survey and field research results I have obtained. Chapter 4 offers a closer look at the nature of the achievement gap between Mexican Americans and non-Latino Whites, further exploring the degree to which the gap remains intact even when the comparison groups are considered according to socioeconomic and nativity status. I then study the incidence and consequences of student mobility among the two groups, again taking into account the demographic characteristics of their members. As Chapter 5 delves at greater depth into social capital—discussing, for example, the ways in which, as an enigmatic resource, social capital remains difficult to measure by empirical techniques—I consider this postulate in a domain-specific fashion, which is to say, among families, between peers, and within communities and schools. The question of the availability of social capital among Mexican Americans and non-Latino Whites within each of these arenas is also considered, setting the stage for further exploration of its impact on student achievement in the two subsequent chapters. In Chapters 6 and

7, I attempt to interweave the survey and interview data in a manner designed to illuminate the *mobility/social capital dynamic* with regard to its contributions to Mexican American underachievement.

Throughout my study, the mixed-methods approach links the emergent social capital literature with research on student mobility so as to investigate student performance among Mexican American and non-Latino White adolescents. Most immediately, the research results suggest that low average test scores among Mexican American adolescents are at least in part dependent upon high rates of student mobility, since mobility may impinge on students' social networks. Moreover, disadvantages in the availability of certain forms of social capital, as well as measurable differences in its convertibility, may additionally contribute to low achievement among Mexican origin youth. What such results should encourage in researchers is an increased focus on the reasons students change schools and a greater sensitivity to inter- and intra-ethnic aspects of the socialization process that may well contribute to group-level differences in the availability and utility of various social capital resources. The concluding discussion in Chapter 8 addresses the broader implications of these findings, encouraging policymakers to consider mobility *and* social capital as related factors conducive to policy manipulation when designing programs intended to mitigate low average educational achievement and attainment among youth of Mexican descent, and when designing accountability schemes used to measure school and student performance.

---

[1] I use the term "racial/ethnic" to refer to the major racial and ethnic groups in the United States—namely Hispanics/Latinos, non-Latino Whites, African Americans, Asian Americans and Native Americans. It should be acknowledged, however, that "race" is a particularly problematic categorization, fraught with ethical and philosophical problems that have been eloquently set forth in deliberations in philosophy and cultural studies about the ontological status of "race" (Du Bois, 1903; Appiah, 1992; Gilroy, 2000; Loury, 2002; National Research Council, 2004).

[2] See, for example, *One-Third of a Nation* (Commission on Minority Participation and American Life, 1988).

[3] On the west coast the meta-categorical term *Latino* is generally preferred to *Hispanic*—the latter adopted in the 1970s and first employed in the 1980 U.S. Census (Bean & Tienda, 1987). I tend to employ the term *Latino*, although both labels are used synonymously throughout this book. Likewise, within the diverse Latino/Hispanic population, the terms *Mexican American*, *Mexican origin*, *Mexican descent* and *Chicano* are interchanged to reference individuals of Mexican ancestry who were either born in the United States or Mexico (Valencia, 2002). As mere labels, however, none of these terms adequately acknowledge the diverse ethnic and cultural heritage in the populations they describe (Macías, 1993; Miller, 1995).

[4] According to Census 2000 figures, the U.S. Latino population may already exceed the U.S. Black population (12.5 percent compared to 12.3 percent, respectively). But these figures are subject to interpretation, since more than three-quarters of a million Americans identify themselves as both Latino *and* Black (U.S. Bureau of Census, 2000b).

[5] For example, in 1975 average reading proficiency among 17-year-old Latinos was far below that of 17-year-old Whites, and even below that of 13-year-old Whites. By 1992, however, the achievement gap had fallen by one-third, such that 17-year-old Latinos were reading at about the same level as 13-year-old Whites (NCES, 1995b).

[6] For a thorough review of group-level achievement differences as measured by standardized test scores for elementary and secondary school populations, college-bound high school students, and for those planning to pursue education beyond the bachelor's degree, see *An American Imperative* (Miller, 1995) and also *No Excuses: Closing the Racial Gap in Learning* (Thernstrom & Thernstrom, 2003).

[7] Standardized test data should be interpreted with caution, particularly since they are limited in what they can assess (Heubert & Hauser, 1999; McDonnell, 2004). For example, most standardized tests employ multiple choice questions rather than open-ended essay questions that might more thoroughly explore students' range of skills and creativity. And standardized tests can be particularly problematic when making between-group achievement comparisons. That lack of English proficiency can inhibit student performance on standardized *mathematics* tests (Durán, 1987, pp., 119-121) underscores this point.

---

[8] Disproportionately high dropout rates are partly attributable, however, to significantly greater dropout rates among Latino immigrants. For example, the dropout rate for Latino 16 to 24-year-olds born outside the United States (44 percent) was double the rate for those born in the U.S. (21 percent) (NCES, 1998a). In fact, foreign-born Latinos are the only immigrants in the United States who have a lower level of education than their native-born counterparts (Vernez & Mizell, 2002).

[9] It should be noted, however, that Latinos are also making real educational gains over generations—improvements that are obscured by the continuing influx of new immigrants. A recent longitudinal study employing U.S. Census and *Current Population Survey* data demonstrates impressive Latino advances in educational *attainment* across generations. Illustratively, Mexican immigrants born during 1905-1909 averaged but 4.3 years of schooling. Their American-born sons, averaging 9.3 years, doubled the years of schooling. And their grandsons were high school graduates, averaging 12.2 years of schooling (Smith, 2003).

[10] In 1974, The Supreme Court ruled in a major legal case, *Lau v. Nichols*, that public schools must provide an education that is comprehensible to students who do not speak English. When Chinese-Americans in San Francisco filed the case, English was the only language of instruction in American public schools. Thus, English language learners (ELLs) were precluded from a meaningful educational experience (Valencia et al., 2002). After the *Lau* decision, policymakers and educators began to search for better ways to instruct ELLs. In 1976, for example, California passed a law (Assembly Bill 1329) that required schools with specific numbers of ELLs to be offered bilingual education. Other states followed suit (Crawford, 1989). By the late 1980s, however, bilingual education had become contentious and politicized. And by the late 1990s, anti-bilingual education sentiment reached a tipping point with the 1998 passage of a California initiative, Proposition 227, designed to severely limit public schools from using native language instruction to teach (García & Wiese, 2002; Guerrero 2002).

[11] This finding is particularly troubling since the gaps in achievement appear to be greatest at the top of the achievement spectrum—the pool from which our nation's leaders are drawn.

---

[12] This point is partially illustrated in *The Black-White Test Score Gap* (1998), where Christopher Jencks and Meredith Phillips analyze Black-White earnings as a function of test performance across time. They do so by comparing the Black-White test performance/earnings ratio in 1964 and then again in 1993. Most tellingly, among men who scored above the 50th percentile on the Armed Forces Qualification Test (AFQT), Black average earnings rose from 65 percent of White average earnings in 1964 to 96 percent of White average earnings in 1993 (Jencks & Phillips, 1998, p. 4-6).

[13] In the wake of the Supreme Court's unanimous 1954 desegregation ruling in *Brown v. Board of Education* and the subsequent Civil Rights movement, the decades of the 1960s and 1970s witnessed targeted initiatives to improve schooling for disadvantaged children, including minority groups that were disproportionately poor. Although these efforts led to a reduction in the achievement gap, particularly between African-Americans and non-Latino Whites, the gap remains a stubbornly persistent educational problem.

[14] These concerns were echoed by former President Clinton's Advisory Commission on Educational Excellence for Hispanic Americans, which went so far as to warn that educational opportunity for Latinos has become "a matter of economic and national security" (Gewertz, 2000).

[15] *Forms* of social capital conjure notions of the density of social networks including relationship depth and levels of commitment, their range across socioeconomic, racial/ethnic and generational borders, and the personal or public domains in which relationships are made manifest (McNeal 1999; Meier, 1999). Different forms of relationships may lead to different benefits, including information, influence, and social solidarity (Sandefur & Laumann, 1998).

CHAPTER 2

The Achievement Gap, Social Capital and Mobility: An Overview

To the extent that current theoretical frameworks prove unequal to the task of dealing with some of the newly emerging key questions, there develops a pressure within the discipline for new or revised frameworks.

— Robert K. Merton, *Three Fragments from a Sociologist's Notebooks*

Given the magnitude and persistence of an achievement gap that our society has direct interest in eliminating, it comes as no surprise that scholars across various disciplines have deployed or developed a wide range of theories to help explain this phenomenon. From the explicit ways that parents invest knowledge and talent into their children's skill-development, to the implicit means by which governmental institutions sometimes reproduce educational inequalities, and from the manner in which culture shapes educational tastes across social classes, to the stereotypes that threaten success in any domain where such stereotypes are prevalent, the continuing saga of educational inequality has stimulated an ecumenical body of research over the past four decades. The arc of this work has encouraged a growing interest in social networks and the ways that person-to-person interaction directly facilitates and/or obstructs the capacity for people to utilize the resources that can be made available through their social relationships. By linking the emergent literature on social capital (arguably the most influential concept to emerge from economic sociology in the last decade) with research on residential and student mobility, I attempt to show that Mexican American underachievement does depend in part upon the network instability that accompanies high rates of student transience. While there is as yet no specific body of work that might be categorized as mobility theory *per se*, studies focusing on the incidence, consequences, and causes of mobility are also discussed in this chapter in order that they might be explicitly related to students' educational performance.

Theories Employed to Investigate the Achievement Gap

In the 1960s, *human capital theory* surfaced as the initial theoretical perspective guiding investigations of differential academic achievement. Neo-classical economists originally introduced human capital theory (Schultz, 1961; Becker, 1964) as a guide to the study of economic growth. They asserted that just as physical capital (i.e., assets that generate income) is created by transforming materials into tools that enable production, human capital is created by changing people in such a way as to give them unique skills and capabilities that enable the most efficient use of physical capital (Coleman, 1990). As a result of interdisciplinary cross-pollination between economists and their colleagues in the emergent field of educational sociology, human capital theory emerged as an effective hypothesis for investigating the family background factors that influence educational outcomes among students.

The widely read *Coleman Report* marked the onset of a large body of research adhering closely to human capital theory in its investigations of family background (Rumberger, 1983; Velez, 1989), household socioeconomic status (Brooks-Gunn & Duncan, 1997; Miller, 1996), and parent education levels and parenting practices (Furstenberg & Nord, 1985; Garfinkel & McLanahan, 1986; Astone & McLanahan, 1991)—all of which were shown to influence educational outcomes. In short, human capital theory suggests that parents are uniquely positioned to invest their own talents into the skill-development of their children, fostering in them tastes and preferences for schooling (Haveman & Wolfe, 1994). But some parents are more willing or simply more capable of making those investments than others, and this may contribute to the achievement gap.

In contrast to human capital theory, neo-Marxist *reproduction theories* have been employed to explain the achievement gap by focusing on macro-level institutional factors including government, the marketplace (Bowles, 1971; Carnoy, 1974; Bowles & Gintis, 1976; Karabel & Halsey, 1977) and mainstream culture (Bourdieu, 1973; Bourdieu, 1977; Bourdieu & Passerson, 1977; Willis, 1981). Directly influenced by the economist philosopher Karl Marx and subsequent social theorist Max Weber, reproduction theory suggests that through implicit control of the education system, governmental institutions and the marketplace contribute to the reproduction of existing social and educational inequalities. More specifically, different levels of education regularly correspond to and may also predict different levels reached by laborers within the workforce, so that we can also read the stratified division of labor back upon the internally organized differential experiences of students under our education system. Thus, minorities are typically "concentrated in schools whose repressive, arbitrary, generally chaotic internal order, coercive authority structures, and minimal possibilities for advancement mirror the characteristics of inferior job situations" (Bowles & Gintis, 1976, p. 132). At the heart of reproduction theory is the assumption that inequitable resource distribution and subsequent educational stratification occur in large part by design—specifically, as a consequence of deliberate institutional praxis (Bourdieu, 1973).

Scholars who have concentrated on the mediating, yet influential force of culture in all of our lives suggest that educational stratification occurs less by deliberate institutional design than by a wider, implicit set of factors. The theories pertaining to culture, championed largely by anthropologists and sociologists, point to behavioral, sociopolitical and historical manifestations of the cultural domain (Bourdieu 1979; DiMaggio, 1982; Bourdieu, 1984; Lamont & Lareau, 1988) to account for the perpetuation of the achievement gap (Gándara 1993; 1994). During the 1960s, when the Civil Rights movement was making important policy gains, scholarly literature focused especially on the impact of cultural deprivation (Bereiter & Englemann, 1966; Deutsch et al., 1967) as a fundamental aspect of educational stratification (Gándara, 1993). By the 1970s, however, social scientists began to focus less on what one group might be lacking in its experience of a monolithic, normative culture and more on theories highlighting the significance of cultural difference (Baratz & Baratz, 1970). The line between cultural deprivation and cultural difference may seem a fine one, but what distinguishes the two terms is that cultural difference theorists were able to develop hypotheses that attributed value to cultural conditions outside the mainstream (Valdés, 1998), while yet investigating the potential cultural underpinnings of the gap in achievement. One refinement of this theory is the notion of primary cultural difference, which calls attention to collective behaviors—

particularly those pertaining to language use (Cummins, 1981) and speech styles (Labov, 1963; Hymes, 1974)—that existed before two different populations came into contact. Sociolinguists, drawing largely on the seminal work of Vygotsky (1962) and on subsequent studies of language and literacy practices in diverse communities, have thoroughly investigated the notion of *primary cultural difference*, identifying the very close relationship between culture, communicative process, and cognition (Trueba, 1988). Thus, ways of speaking (both verbal and non-verbal) among non-mainstream students act as cultural markers that, when misunderstood or devalued by teachers and school personnel, inhibit student performance in school (Gumperz, 1972; Au & Mason, 1981; Erickson & Mohatt, 1982; Erickson, 1993).

While differences in language and communication style often set minorities apart from the mainstream White majority, these factors do not account for the significant historical and sociopolitical aspects of minority group identity, which may help us explain why some minority students are more successful in schools than others. Addressing this issue from a compelling theoretical perspective, anthropologist John Ogbu (1978) focused on secondary *cultural* differences that emerge in the aftermath of contact between mainstream and non-mainstream groups. By emphasizing the historical terms of incorporation into the United States that mark minority identity within mainstream American society, Ogbu's theory calls attention to various collective and historical meanings associated with minority group status. It does so by juxtaposing minority groups classified as "voluntary/immigrant" with those which are "involuntary/caste-like."

Although voluntary minorities may actually benefit from a "dual frame of reference" (Suarez-Orozco, 1987), especially when the oppressive experiences of the immigrant's immediate past overshadow concerns regarding U.S. cultural hegemony, the involuntary (e.g., African American) minority experience is characterized by unfavorable terms of incorporation into the mainstream, a phenomenon that often serves to emphasize mainstream repression. Specifically, involuntary minorities often perceive acculturation to mainstream U.S. society as synonymous with "acting White," or "selling out." Minorities who carry these perceptions may shun academic success in the name of group fidelity, particularly when the terms of success in school correspond too neatly to other cultural behaviors that involve "selling out" (Fordham & Ogbu, 1986; Ogbu, 1992).

In spite of the many obstacles that inhibit educational achievement among minority students, many forge ahead to attain high levels of academic success (Cummins, 1981; Matute-Bianchi, 1986; Valencia, 1991; Hurtado & Garcia, 1994; College Board, 1999; Conchas, 2001; Valencia, 2002; Perry et al., 2003). Ironically, however, these minorities within the academic vanguard may encounter further minority-specific achievement barriers as a result of their identification with schooling. In his groundbreaking work on how stereotypes shape intellectual identity and educational performance, Claude Steele (1997) explains the link between domain identification—in this case, African Americans who find self identity in the domain of schooling—and what he calls "stereotype threat." According to Steele, stereotype threat arises when "one is in a situation or doing something for which a negative stereotype about one's group applies" (p. 614). Thus, stereotypes become particularly threatening for those who associate their identity and self-worth with success in a domain where their own group has been obviously stereotyped.

One illustrative finding first reported in Steele & Aronson (1995) involved Black and White Stanford University students who were administered a test composed of the most difficult items on the verbal GRE exam. Simply reporting their race on a demographic questionnaire immediately before taking the test was enough to depress the performance of Black students, so that, with the question of racial consciousness foregrounded, Whites outperformed Blacks according to mean test scores. Without the race prime, however, the results were reversed—Blacks outperformed Whites. These findings and others reported by Steele suggest that stereotype threat can even impair the standardized test performance of "domain-identified" students—those in the academic vanguard with the greatest confidence and skills.[16]

Where Traditional Explanations Fall Short

Although the research I have noted above has gone a long way in contributing to a growing body of literature explaining group-level achievement differences, many questions remain unanswered. That middle-class minority student groups consistently perform below non-Latino Whites with similar family and school backgrounds (Miller, 1995; Phillips et al., 1998; Jencks & Phillips, 1998), and that racial disparities are greater among students whose parents are college educated than they are for students whose parents lack even a high school degree (College Entrance Examination Board, 1999), are findings that suggest the explanatory limits of human capital theory. Reproduction theory also falls short as a guide for studying the achievement gap, since we now have ample evidence that a large number of minority students do succeed in schools. And while language and primary cultural differences clearly distinguish minorities from the mainstream, relevant research remains the subject of ongoing debate (NABE, 1995; Cook & Ludwig, 1997; Darder, Torres & Gutierrez, 1997). Even among anthropologists there are "those who discount incongruent communication styles as a bogus explanation of achievement differences" (Erickson, 1993, p. 33). Emergent studies are also beginning to undermine secondary cultural difference theories by showing that many "involuntary/caste-like" minority students hold even more optimistic perceptions about schooling than their mainstream peers (Cook & Ludwig, 1997; Ainsworth-Darnell & Downey, 1998). And while stereotype threat appears to impinge on the educational performance of African Americans, it has only recently been investigated for its applicability among other racial/ethnic groups, including U.S. Latinos (Massey et al., 2003)—and with inconclusive results.

Social Capital

Given the theoretical/empirical shortcomings noted above, social scientists have renewed the search for alternative perspectives that can better inform our understanding of the achievement gap. One such perspective, based on social capital theory, calls for researchers to consider more closely factors that distinguish the inter- and intra-ethnic socialization process among minorities from the socialization process typical of mainstream students (Stanton-Salazar, 1997; Fuller & Hannum, 2002; Ream, 2003). Social capital theory is beginning to encourage scientists to pay particular attention to the ways that social interaction facilitates and/or obstructs the conversion of resources, which, in turn, holds promise for demystifying the social dynamics of educational inequality.

An Overview of Social Capital

The social groups in which people interact are important for shaping identity, priorities, and values. Indeed, active participation in social life often facilitates access to personal, professional, and political power and resources. The *convertibility* of the actual or potential resources embedded in social networks, *via* social exchange, into other forms of capital is the subject of considerable attention among theorists who study relationships, social networks, and social exchange. Reflected in "the capacity of individuals to command scarce resources by virtue of their membership in networks or broader social structures" (Portes, 1995, p. 12), social capital is made up of resources that may be converted into physical/economic capital (Bourdieu, 1986; Bourdieu & Wacquant, 1992), human capital (Bourdieu, 1986; Coleman, 1988) and healthy civic participation and community cohesion (Fukuyama, 1995; Putnam, 2000). Moreover, the fungibility of social capital bridges the sociological and economic perspectives, thus capturing the attention of policymakers who are seeking creative solutions to social problems (Portes, 1998).

Just as human capital is brought about by changing people to give them skills and capabilities that make them able to act in new ways, social capital is created when the relations among people change in ways that facilitate action. While human capital is embodied in the skills and knowledge acquired by individuals, social capital is less tangible, inhering in the relations among persons (Coleman, 1990). The notion of social capital suggests that resources are "embedded" (Polanyi, 1957; Granovetter, 1985) within a network of social ties and relationships that both enable and limit a person's actions. Thus, social relationships affect behavior directly—through the exchange of emotional support, information, and material resources—and indirectly, through norms, expectations and social structures that form the basis for social interactions (Coleman, 1988; Croninger & Lee, 1996).

Social capital is considered a fundamental ingredient of healthy civic participation and community cohesion, in part because of group-enforced norms of trust and reciprocity that improve social productivity by facilitating coordinated action (Putnam, 1993; Fukuyama, 1995; Rahn & Transue, 1998; Orr, 1999). Coleman's (1988) reference to the efficiency of the New York City wholesale diamond market is perhaps the most often cited example of how frequent and sustained social interaction among merchants provides the insurance necessary to secure reciprocal relations that preclude malfeasance within the tightly knit community of Jewish diamond traders (Portes, 1998). Adding to the complexity of social capital are the various academic disciplines in which it has been employed, the numerous ways it has been taken up, and its relative novelty (Woolcock, 1998). Illustratively, the number of sociology and anthropology journal articles featuring social capital has more than doubled since 1990 (Wall et al., 1998). In fact, some suggest that with so many diverse interpretations, social capital is a theoretical construct on the verge of creating more confusion than clarity (Wall, et al., 1998; Astone et al., 1999). At the very least, a review of the origins of social capital and its most commonly recognized interpretations is in order.

Founding and Guiding Perspectives on Social Capital

Sociologists Pierre Bourdieu and James Coleman, along with political scientist Robert Putnam, are perhaps most commonly recognized for introducing the concept of social capital to the study of social phenomena (Wall et al., 1998; Astone et al., 1999).[17] It is their work, in fact, that largely shaped the theoretical and conceptual framework guiding this book. Bourdieu's (1986; 1990) conception of social capital, so frequently cited in sociological journals, bears the imprint of his earlier work addressing cultural reproduction (Bourdieu, 1973; 1977). According to Bourdieu, social capital contributes to the maintenance or alteration of one's position in the social hierarchy. My exploration of relational hierarchy in this study is influenced by Bourdieu's theoretical perspective, specifically in regard to the association between social network hierarchy and Mexican American underachievement.

For his part, Coleman (1988; 1990) finds an implicit connection to neoclassical economic thought as embodied in the theory of human capital (Schultz, 1961; Becker, 1964; Becker & Tomes, 1986). However, he does so in a reformist sense, emphasizing the ways that relationships among individuals, as well as between individuals and social structures, facilitate norms and rational pursuits (Portes & Sensenbrenner, 1993; Schneider, 2000). Coleman's social capital framework is most obviously influential in sociology and education journals, where he is frequently cited. This study takes up particularly his hypothesis that mobility is a contributor to social capital depletion, as I investigate whether the *mobility/social capital dynamic* has important implications for differential student outcomes and low average test score performance among adolescents of Mexican descent.

Finally, Putnam (1993; 1995; 2000) considers social capital on a broader, less individualistic scale. His initial work on social capital compared regional variations in the performance of local government in northern and southern Italy to illuminate the neighborhood, community, and societal implications of social capital (Putnam, 1993). By emphasizing the "vibrancy of associational life" as a fundamental component of healthy civic society, Putnam contends that the erosion of certain types of public social capital is particularly threatening to the foundations of democracy (Putnam, 2000); not surprisingly, he is frequently cited among political scientists and political psychologists. Since one might infer his insistence on parsing the impact of *formal* relationships fostered by adolescents in schools and government-sponsored networks in relation to the *informal* networks constituting family and peer relationships (Green & Brock, 1998), Putnam's ideas contribute to this study especially insofar as it seeks to probe the impact of mobility on those formal and informal relationships that are such important components of social capital.

Although Bourdieu's, Coleman's and Putnam's conceptions of social capital are distinct, there are common threads by which they are linked.[18] In particular, the *convertibility* of social capital into physical/economic capital (Bourdieu, 1986), or into behavioral norms and educational performance (Coleman, 1988), or into community cohesion (Putnam, 2000) must be foregrounded by an explanation of the social underpinnings of productivity. Table 2.1 summarizes the underlying assumption of each theorist's view of social capital, charts the domain in which empirical work might be guided by the assumption, and provides the operational focus suggested by both the assumption and the domain.

A view of the theoretical underpinnings of the social capital construct helps tease out the various domains across which it is posited to be available and useful. In turn, these domains serve as a framework for this study, as I examine the relative importance of social capital within families, among peers, within the communities where students and their families reside, and—perhaps most notably—in schools, with not altogether expected findings that reveal some of the intricacies of the postulate.

Table 2.1. Founding Perspectives on Social Capital

	Bourdieu	Coleman	Putnam
Underlying Assumption	Social capital at once a tool for individual advancement and a tool to reproduce existing class, cultural, racial inequalities	Family structures/ social relationships enable exchange of social capital for physical and/or human capital	Social capital valued for strengthening civil society and democratic forms of government
Investigative Domain	Individual or group vis-à-vis class, culture and/or race considerations	Family, school and community	Community, region, state/nation
Operational Focus	Exchange value of social capital Social capital vis-à-vis group/class factions within mainstream culture	Exchange value of social capital Social capital manifested in trust, norms, sanctions, obligations and expectations	Exchange value of social capital Social capital manifested in civic participation, i.e., membership in community organizations Distinction between government-sponsored relationships (the state) and informal networks (civil society)

Family Social Capital

Within the *family*, parent/child and sibling relationships form the building blocks of social capital development (Coleman, 1990; Astone & McClanahan, 1991; Parcel & Menaghan, 1994; Boisjoly, Duncan & Hofferth, 1995; Furstenburg & Hughes, 1995; Brooks-Gunn & Duncan, 1997). There is by now an extensive literature on the implications of family social capital, especially in the form of parental involvement, for students' educational advancement (Marjoribank, 1995; Paulson, 1994; Sui-Chu Ho & Willms, 1996; Kao & Tienda, 1998). Some studies focus on education oriented parent-child relations—regarding, for example, course selection or homework—within the home (Sui-Chu Ho & Willms, 1996). Still others focus on parent-initiated educational activities that take place outside the home, such as visiting museums or attending concerts (Kao & Tienda, 1998).

Parent-initiated contact with other parents and with school personnel also reflects a form of family social capital in which the parent-as-advocate catalyzes student advancement (Stevenson & Baker, 1987; Carbonaro, 1998). For example, parents' participation in social networks that include the parents of other similarly aged school children may provide feedback on effective child-rearing strategies and make available crucial information about school policies, teachers, and many of the students' peers (Horvat, Weininger & Lareau, 2003). All of this empowers families to channel their resources as effectively as possible into children's educational success (Pong, 1998).

Although not all of the aforementioned studies are couched in the language of social capital, they nevertheless reflect Coleman's conception of family social capital as a convertible resource facilitating student achievement. Many researchers have begun to employ the concept of social capital more explicitly in their investigations of parental involvement by using variables that reflect parents' connections with their children's friends' parents (Carbonaro, 1998), parent involvement in children's schooling (Horvat et al., 2003), parent/child communication, and homework support as individual items contributing to the operationalization of composite measures of family social capital (White & Kaufman, 1997; McNeal, 1999). Close analysis of these studies suggests that the distinction in terminology (i.e., parental involvement vs. family social capital) may be more semantic than substantive. Indeed, McNeal (1999) argues that the parental involvement behaviors noted above fit nicely within the rubric of social capital in large part because parent/child interaction is the vehicle by which parents bestow human capital upon their children (Park & Palardy, 2004).

A fairly recent study measured parent-child interactions at the eighth grade level to predict tenth grade school performance among various ethnic groups, with the results suggesting that family social capital manifested in parent/child interaction has a positive impact on adolescents' school grades across racial/ethnic groups (Keith et. al., 1998). Arvizu (1996) found that "when parents are involved, children do better in school, and they go to better schools" (p. 814). Another study employed *NELS:88* base-year data to demonstrate the positive impact of parent/child interactions regarding course selection and school programs on children's reading and mathematics achievement (Sui-Chu Ho & Willms, 1996). This study also analyzed the school-level implications of family social capital in the form of parental involvement in schools. On the whole, it suggested that student achievement improves for those students attending schools with elevated levels of parental involvement, and that the children of parents who participate in school activities and are in frequent contact with teachers demonstrate elevated academic performance levels (Stevenson & Baker, 1987). Exploring the way that networks come into play when parents face problematic school situations, a recent ethnographic investigation found, for example, that middle-class parents are uniquely able to draw on social capital manifested in their contacts with other professionals to mobilize the information, expertise and authority needed to contest the judgments of school officials (Horvat et al., 2003).

Although the preponderance of evidence suggests the positive impact of family social capital on student and school achievement, differences in the availability of family social capital may also contribute to group-level differences in educational outcomes (Horvat et al., 2003). For example, if children have strained relationships with their parents or if parents are not available to supervise and interact with their children, parental influence may be undermined. This seems particularly common for the large percentage of children growing up in single-parent families (Bumpass, 1984). Research shows that children of single parents are not as close to their fathers as children living with both parents (Furstenberg & Nord, 1985; Amato, 1987) and thus are more susceptible to peer pressure to engage in antisocial behavior (Crane, 1991).[19] Furthermore, the convertibility of family social capital into academic success may be inhibited among immigrant families. While the children of immigrants are known to rely heavily on their parents and other family members for emotional and psychological support (Keefe et al., 1979; Becerra, 1988), immigrant parents' social capital investments in their children are commonly limited by the losses parents sustain through immigration, as a result of serious economic pressures (Trejo, 1996, 1997), and by the language barriers that alienate them from the schools their children attend (Olsen, 1988; Rogler, Cortes & Malgady, 1991; Delgado-Gaitan, 1991; Hauser & Thompson, 1995; Stanton-Salazar, 2001).

Peer Social Capital

Although it is clear that parents and families play a critical role in students' long-term educational plans and goals (Brittain, 1963; Steinberg, Dornbusch, & Brown, 1992), peers exhibit extraordinary influence on adolescents' day-to-day behaviors with regard to their education, including how much time they spend on homework, whether they enjoy coming to school each day, and how they behave in the classroom (Steinberg et al., 1992; Hurd, 2004; Gibson et al., 2004). In adolescence, the interplay of individuals and their peers becomes especially important (Berndt & Ladd, 1989; Claes, 1992; Carnegie Council, 1995; Schneider & Stevenson, 1999), since adolescents spend twice as much time with peers as with family (Larson & Richards, 1991). By all appearances, peers—including age mates, best friends, buddies and acquaintances—fulfill a developmental need that cannot be met by parents (Harris, 1998) or other adults (Hartup, 1993), and research suggests that this need for belonging may actually increase as children grow in age (Hymel et al., 1996). However one accounts for its increased prominence in the lives of older school children, peer social capital merits attention on the basis of its sway over attitudes and orientation toward schooling (Valenzuela, 1999) and academic development (Mehan et al., 1994; Olsen, 1997)—most specifically at the secondary school level (Oakes, 1985; Brantlinger, 1993; Vigil, 1997). For instance, Goodenow (1993) has demonstrated that peer support in middle school is a significant predictor of school motivation and overall expectations for academic success. Other studies provide evidence of a consistent link between social competence and student achievement (Vosk et al, 1982; Dishion, 1990).

While such findings point to the importance of peer social capital in academic advancement and educational performance, they also leave unanswered questions. In particular, we might ask what are the qualitative aspects of peer interaction that lead to these positive educational outcomes. Research shows that students who have friends who like school (Hinojosa & Miller, 1984), or who get good grades, are interested in school, or regularly attend classes (Ekstrom et al., 1986) are more likely to encounter educational success than those who have friends who do not exhibit this set of characteristics. Furthermore, analysis of *High School and Beyond* data demonstrates that out of several variables, it is peers' engagement in school that has the most powerful impact on students' own interest in school, which, in turn, has the largest direct influence on educational achievement (Pittman, 1991). In short, peer social capital and academic integration appear to be intertwined in important ways that influence educational outcomes.

While peer social capital merits attention for its positive impact on educational outcomes, we have also to observe the "downside" of peer social capital and its potential contribution to anti-school behaviors (see Gibson et al., 2004, Chapters 3-6).[20] Bourdieu readily acknowledged the struggle associated with efforts to maintain or improve social status within institutionalized social networks. Such a struggle may be reflected in schools where social sorting among students into high-status, middle-status, or "fringe groups" (Brantlinger, 1993) defines social boundaries determining who interacts with whom, and under what conditions. A recent ethnographic study at a southwestern high school illustrates the manner in which "subtractive" school practices often fan the flames of peer social de-capitalization among minority students (Valenzuela, 1999).[21] Such a conclusion is evidenced in strained relationships among Mexican Americans of different generational status:

> U.S.-born and Mexico-born youth routinely mistrust, misunderstand, and misuse one another. The more recent immigrants report being appalled by the attire and comportment of their roguish U.S.-born counterparts. They view this group as "americanizados" (Americanized), while the more culturally assimilated youth shun their immigrant counterparts as "un-cool," subdued, and "embarrassing" for embodying characteristics they wish to disclaim (Valenzuela, 1999, p. 19).

In light of these findings, Valenzuela and others (see Conchas, 2001; Gibson et al., 2004; Raley, 2004) assert that the institutional structure of schools can either contribute to or erode students' peer social capital accumulation. These studies also suggest that the presence or absence of supportive and/or academically oriented peer networks acts as a barometer reflecting schools' success or failure when it comes to sustaining social capital with a positive bearing on students' education.

Community Social Capital

Although social capital has traditionally been analyzed on the individual level, within the context of the family and among peers (Jessor, 1993), it is important to consider the role it may also play in the broader community, say, within the neighborhood or among religious groups (Greeley, 1997). Putnam's compelling thesis on the decline of social capital (Putnam, 2000) argues that government performance is based in part on the degree to which community life reflects the civic ideal as articulated by Alexis de Tocqueville—an ideal that includes factors such as basic elements of social capital, including trust, successful cooperation among community members, and networks of civic engagement (Tocqueville, 1969).

Other social scientists have studied social capital accumulation in neighborhoods and community settings by investigating immigrant assimilation (Portes & Sensenbrenner, 1993). Several distinct forms of assimilation can be understood in the context of social capital development taking place between immigrants and the communities into which they are enfolded. For example, immigrants who join well-established and diversified ethnic groups, such as Cuban immigrants in Miami, have access to a range of social and material resources far beyond those which are made available through official government assistance programs (Portes & Rumbaut, 2001). The social capital available to immigrants who join cohesive communities capable of enforcing external demands and exercising internal constraints stands in stark contrast to the lack of social capital afforded those who join communities experiencing what some have referred to as "epidemic social problems" (Crane, 1991, p. 122). Over-concentration of immigrants in the inner city often brings the children of immigrants into sustained contact with U.S.-born minority students who have developed an adversarial subculture that rejects the usefulness of education and discourages achievement in school (Rumbaut & Cornelius, 1995). In short, some groups receive enough of the forms of community social capital that can aid them in their academic and subsequent marketplace achievement, while others do not (Portes & Zhou, 1993).

Of course, immigrants are not the only ones who benefit from valuable forms of community social capital, nor are they the only ones who suffer from its absence in the face of social disorder (Wilson, 1987). Neighborhood studies demonstrate that positive social interaction—such as helping with childcare or borrowing—occurs more frequently in neighborhoods where trust is prevalent (Cochran & Riley, 1988; Croninger & Lee, 1996; Small, 2002). Conversely, in disadvantaged unsafe neighborhoods, families are unlikely to ask for assistance and therefore receive it less often. In such an environment, children suffer from limited contacts and from fewer positive relationships with non-kin adults, neighborhood children, and classmates (Cocharan & Riley, 1988; Jarrett, 1997), all of which may help explain differential community social capital and its potential to stratify academic achievement among school children.

While the indirect effect of community social capital on children's academic advancement can be inferred from the research reviewed above, few studies have investigated the postulate for its direct effects on students' performance in school. Following up on his early investigations of community social capital, Coleman (1971) studied church attendance as a predictor of school completion, finding attendance at religious services to be a measure of community social capital attained through "intergenerational closure" (i.e., members of the sect, both adults and children, who communicated shared norms and expectations of religious life). His findings show that church attendance is strongly related to school completion, with the non-churched students dropping out of public schools at nearly twice the rate of those public school students who regularly attended church services (Coleman, 1988).

Perhaps in response to research of this nature—and to concerns regarding the alleged disappearance of community social capital (Bellah, 1986; Etzioni, 1993; Putnam, 2000)—many schools have worked to develop strategies for building forms of neighborhood and community social capital that improve the educational performance of public school students. The Annie E. Casey Foundation's *New Futures Initiative* has made major investments in public schools that are working to facilitate institutional collaboration between public education, religious communities, and social service organizations (White & Wehlage, 1995). Efforts of this nature emphasize that public and private resources need to go directly into targeted areas as community social capital investments (Melaville & Blank, 1991; Rist, 1992). The available literature on service learning (Kurth, 1995; Kleiner et al., 2000) and other efforts encouraging student participation in community service activities also reflect the trend toward building community social capital for the betterment of public schools and the students they serve.

School Social Capital

Institutionalized teacher/student relationships are also important for social capital development. In fact, students' relations with school personnel, especially with teachers, are critical in determining the extent to which they find school to be a welcoming or an alienating place (Astone & McLanahan, 1991; Valenzuela, 1999; Stanton-Salazar, 2001). An extensive analysis of the best practices in school reform identified teacher/student conversation—in a word, "talking"—as the key component of effective advocacy on behalf of students, increasing students' engagement in school and their expectations for achievement (Snyder, Morrison & Smith, 1996). Another longitudinal study tracking the academic success of at-risk students in New York City found that their educational careers were distinguished by strong relationships with teachers and school personnel. School social capital of this nature can create pathways to emotional and social growth that are absolutely critical to at-risk students' subsequent educational success (Bensman, 1994). Other studies demonstrate that teacher support for and interaction with students predicts adolescents' school motivation, their expectations for academic success (Goodenow, 1993), and various other aspects of productive school functioning (Lee & Smith, 1999), including higher academic achievement and students' self-esteem (Crosnoe, Johnson & Elder, 2004; Ryan, Stiller & Lynch, 1994).

Again, we might ask for more specifics. What are the qualitative aspects of school social capital that effect the positive school-related outcomes noted above? The "caring literature" argues that trusting relationships between students and school personnel foster learning opportunities (Noddings, 1992; Valenzuela, 1997) that form the basis for social capital development within schools and among school children (Bryk & Schneider, 2002). Assent to school authority, however, involves trust on the part of students that authority will be exercised benignly. This involves "trust in the legitimacy of the authority and in the good intentions of those exercising it, trust that one's own identity will be maintained positively in relation to the authority, and trust that one's own interests will be advanced by compliance with the exercise of authority" (Erickson, 1993, p. 36).[22]

While trust between students and school personnel is an important factor in school social capital development, its absence can have egregious effects on students' school engagement and subsequent learning. School ethnographies have identified a superficial notion of caring deployed by many school personnel that stands in stark contrast to students' ideas about what a more "authentic" notion of caring should be (Noddings, 1984; Bowditch, 1993; Courtney & Noblit, 1994). Once again, Valenzuela's research among adolescent Mexican Americans is informative:

> Rather than moving toward another human being to grasp their subjective reality, the overriding concern in schools is with form and non-personal content.... When Mexican-American youth reject schooling, they do so because their teachers do not fully apprehend their ethnic, social-class and peer-group realities, including their culture of caring. (Valenzuela, 1997, pp. 324-25)

Valenzuela suggests that different conceptions of caring can lead to a breach of trust between mainstream school personnel and non-mainstream students. Other studies demonstrate similar patterns of distrust and social distance between mainstream institutional agents and minority youth (Fordham & Ogbu, 1986; Sánchez-Jankowski, 1991), which may result in part from a lack of overlap in subcultural values and norms (Gottlieb, 1975; Stanton-Salazar & Dornbusch, 1995; Gibson et al., 2004). A breakdown in trust can inhibit school social capital development, leading to students' disengagement from school and subsequent human capital depreciation. Thus, Wehlage & Rutter (1986) found that many students do not believe teachers are highly interested in their well-being, and this perception promoted their disengagement from school and, in many cases, students' subsequent dropout.

It becomes clear that the presence or absence of social capital, as viewed in a domain-specific fashion, has important implications for students' educational achievement and academic success. Yet it is also important to consider that even when available, social capital may be inequitably distributed, create stratifying effects, and pose as a drawback for certain students.

Emergent Research Based on Social Capital Theory

In their study of U.S. immigrants, Portes & Sensenbrenner (1993) were perhaps the first to take a close look at the links between social capital, culture, and social advancement, but their research—based in part on Granovetter's (1985) studies of "embeddedness"—remained focused on economic action. Ten years later, Stanton-Salazar & Dornbusch (1995) broke new ground by employing a social capital framework to connect social capital, culture, and the achievement gap. In his follow-up work addressing the fungibility of social capital, Stanton-Salazar (1997) posits that social capital can facilitate the *conversion* of culture-based funds of knowledge (Moll, Amanti & Gonzelez, 1992; Vélez-Ibañez & Greenberg, 1992; González et al., 1995) into mainstream educational achievement. Concomitantly he suggests—sounding not unlike Bourdieu—that social capital can inhibit the conversion of culture-based attributes (Portes & Landolt, 1996) perceived by certain "institutional agents" (i.e., teachers, counselors and social service workers) to be threatening to mainstream society. For example, social capital, as it bears specifically on minority students' relationships with mainstream school personnel, can facilitate the conversion of gifted students' biliterate Spanish/English skills into leadership positions and student engagement, but only when biliteracy is recognized by school personnel as being important (Valencia, 2002). According to another more recent study of the relationships between students and school personnel, which similarly introduces conditions that may qualify the beneficial effects of social capital, Mexican American adolescents sometimes share with school personnel a form of *counterfeit* social capital that can impinge on their test score performance (Ream, 2003).

Paying particular attention to school personnel, Stanton-Salazar and others take a step beyond acknowledging the importance of social capital to specify *formal* relationships in school settings (school social capital) as being especially instrumental in the process of social capital development and as having a direct impact on differential achievement between student groups. More specifically, working-class racial minority youth may be particularly beholden to school personnel (more so than their middle-class Euro-American counterparts) and yet, largely because of primary cultural differences, they appear to be less able to secure support. Such an assertion seems compelling, but it is only beginning to be put to empirical evaluation (Ream, 2003). As this line of research encourages new direction for research linking social capital and educational stratification, it also suggests the importance of investigating social capital in a domain-specific fashion so that its relative contribution to student achievement can be compared between groups and across domains.

From Social Capital to Mobility: An Inferential Leap

The aforementioned research offers a reasonable starting-point for linking the emergent literature on social capital with research on residential and student mobility. To whit, if racial minorities fortify social ties in ways that differ from their mainstream counterparts, and if these differences inhibit the accumulation and transmission of important resources embedded within social networks, then high rates of mobility may be particularly harmful for minorities who must constantly re-negotiate relationships, some of which have been especially difficult for them to establish in the first place. This *mobility/social capital dynamic* deserves further investigation for its potential stratifying effects. I wish first, however, to review the literature on mobility, including its incidence, consequences, and causes.

Mobility

The Incidence of Mobility

While all students make scheduled school changes—most commonly as the result of being promoted from one type of school to another, such as elementary school to middle school or from middle school to high school (Scott et al., 1995)—increasing numbers of students are moving from one school to another for reasons other than normal promotion (Plank et al., 1993; Swanson & Schneider, 1999). The practice of students making non-promotional school changes is herein referred to as student mobility. Student mobility, in this case, occurs when a student enrolls in the first grade level of a school and then transfers to another school before graduating from that school (Rumberger, 2003). While few studies on adolescent mobility have drawn the distinction between student mobility and residential mobility (Rumberger & Larson, 1998; Swanson & Schneider, 1999; Pribesh & Downey, 1999), this study treats student and residential mobility as conceptually distinct. I have focused particularly on student mobility for two reasons. First, the incidence of student mobility in the United States has been on the increase (Plank et al, 1993) in spite of decreasing rates of residential mobility (Hansen, 1995; U.S. Census Bureau, 2004).[23] Second, student mobility (unlike residential mobility) occurs in the public realm, so that its potentially negative effects seem more amenable to policy solutions.

If mobility were not so commonplace, it might not warrant the attention of educators and policymakers. A growing body of research, however, shows that student mobility is widespread in the United States (Rumberger, 2003). A majority of children in the United States make a school change without being promoted from one grade level to the next, and many make such changes frequently (GAO, 1994; NCES, 1995a; Rumberger et al., 1999). One national study revealed that more than 40 percent of all third-graders had changed schools at least once since first grade and 17 percent had changed schools two or more times (GAO, 1994). Another national longitudinal survey of 1988 eighth-graders found that 31 percent made two or more non-promotional school changes between the first and eighth grades and 10 percent made two or more non-promotional school changes between the eighth and twelfth grades (Hudis & Rathnam, 1994).

The incidence of mobility is particularly high within large, predominantly minority, urban school districts with high concentrations of students from low socioeconomic backgrounds. Research also shows that public schools evidence higher student mobility rates than Catholic or other private schools (Rumberger et al., 1999). In many districts, the proportion of students enrolled in a school for less than the entire academic year often exceeds 30 to 40 percent (Ligon & Paredes, 1992; McDonnell & Hill, 1993). In the Los Angeles Unified School District, for example, the high school transiency rate (which is the proportion of students who entered after school started or left before school ended) exceeded 35 percent across the district for the 2001-2002 school year (LAUSD, 2004).

Mobility Among U.S. Latinos

Given the high transience rate in impoverished urban areas and among U.S. immigrants (McDonnell & Hill, 1993), it is not surprising that mobility is especially common among U.S. Latinos. Both student and residential mobility among Latinos occur at rates that highlight the relative stability of non-Latino Whites (U.S. Census Bureau, 2000c;

2004). The 1994 General Accounting Office (GAO) study found that among U.S. third-graders, Latinos were twice as mobile as non-Latino White students. Another study found that a greater proportion of Latinos than Whites made two or more non-promotional school changes between the first and eighth grades (NCES, 1995b). Data from the 1998 National Assessment of Educational Progress (NAEP) show that 41 percent of Latino fourth grade students changed schools in the previous two years, compared with 33 percent of Asian-American students and 27 percent of Whites in the same grade cohort (Rumberger 2003). In terms of residential mobility, between 2002-2003, Latinos changed residences at much higher rates (18 percent) than non-Latino Whites (12.4 percent). In fact, Latinos demonstrate higher rates of residential mobility than any other racial/ethnic group in the United States (U.S. Census Bureau News, January, 2000; U.S. Census Bureau, 2004). Not only are Latinos more mobile than Whites, but they are also much more likely to change high schools for reasons other than moving residences (Rumberger et al., 1997). Although mobility may be especially detrimental for Latinos, it may also be more amenable to mitigation since changing schools is less often the inevitable result of family relocation among Latinos.

The Consequences of Mobility

Not only is mobility widespread, but it can also be detrimental to educational achievement and social capital development. Numerous studies document the negative impact of mobility on student performance in the primary grades (GAO, 1994; Schuler, 1990; Reynolds & Temple, 1997). Mobility among elementary school students can lead to adjustment problems that impact students' academic achievement (Holland et al., 1974; Benson et al., 1979; Ingersoll et al., 1989; Crockett et al., 1989; Jason et al., 1992; Tucker et al., 1998; Heinlein & Shinn, 2000). A well-known analysis of the *National Health Interview Survey* uncovered overwhelming evidence to support this notion, associating frequent moves with behavioral maladjustment and subsequent academic problems, including repeating grades (Wood et al., 1993).

The effect of mobility on secondary school students' achievement patterns remains largely unexamined. Indeed, most achievement-related studies at the secondary level fail to include mobility as a factor. Issues such as tracking (Oakes, 1985; Lee & Bryk, 1988) and school organization (Bryk & Driscoll, 1988) are more commonly acknowledged as achievement-related predictors among adolescents. Of the achievement-related research that does include secondary school mobility, the findings are mixed. One study of 643 ninth-graders found that mobility influences math achievement directly and negatively (Benson & Weigel, 1981). A more recent investigation reports that, despite some negative short-term consequences, the incidence of mobility early in high school does not deter modest gains in mathematics achievement for students who thereafter remain in school through the twelfth grade (Swanson & Schneider, 1999). Whether or not these are completely contradictory findings, further research is necessary to establish the impact of mobility on educational achievement at the secondary school level.

The negative impact of mobility on school completion has been more clearly defined in the research literature (Haveman, Wolfe & Spaulding, 1991; Rumberger & Larson, 1998) which indicates that mobility significantly increases the likelihood that a student will drop out of school (Rumberger, 1995). Other studies report that students who make unscheduled (non-promotional) school changes are much less likely to graduate from high school, even after controlling for various background factors (Astone & McLanahan, 1994; Rumberger 2003). Rumberger et al. (1999) demonstrate, for example, that students who made just one non-promotional school change between the eighth and twelfth grades were less than half as likely to graduate from high school compared to students who did not make a non-promotional school change.

Mobility as such not only affects mobile students, it has an impact on schools as well. For example, according to *NELS:88* data students who attended high schools with overall mobility rates of 40 percent scored significantly lower on tenth grade standardized mathematics tests than students who attended high schools with mobility rates of 10 percent. Apparently mobile students are not the only ones who suffer the consequences of student mobility: students with stable attendance records may be academically impaired if they attend schools with highly mobile student populations (Rumberger et al., 1999, p. 51).

Beyond the negative impact mobility has on achievement and educational attainment, research suggests that both student and residential mobility harm students' social capital accumulation by inhibiting their efforts to make new friends and adjust socially to a new school situation (Jason, et al., 1992; Rumberger et al, 1999; Pribesh & Downey, 1999; Ream, 2003). One study of residential mobility found that transience disrupts the social context in which children interact, inhibiting the establishment of social relationships and creating stress for the families and children who relocate (Munton, 1990). Still other studies suggest the negative impact of mobility on children's identity and self-concept development (Kroger, 1980); and recent interviews with both students and school personnel in the Los Angeles Unified School District suggest that making non-promotional school changes and/or changing residences has a negative impact on (a) students' social relationships, (b) their participation in extracurricular activities, and (c) their overall feelings of well-being (Rumberger et al., 1999). Adding support to these findings, Hagan et al., (1996) find in their longitudinal study of adolescents in Toronto, that family moves tend to destroy established bonds, depriving families and children of a major source of social capital and producing setbacks for children's emotional adjustment and educational achievement.

The Causes of Mobility

While numerous studies address the incidence and consequences of student mobility, few have investigated its causes. Non-promotional student mobility appears to be the result, in part, of increasing opportunities for families to choose among public schooling options (Cookson, 1994; Schneider et al., 1996). Moreover, some scholars anticipate that the number of students attending schools outside their neighborhood attendance zones will continue to increase as a consequence of legislation facilitating the creation of charter schools and other public education alternatives (Manno, Finn, Bierlein & Vanourek, 1998; Rumberger & Larson, 1998).

While increasing options for school choice may contribute to increased student transience, one recent study employs both student- and school-level analyses to uncover various other reasons why students change schools and why some schools have high student mobility rates (Rumberger, et al., 1999). Findings from this particularly thorough investigation show that families, students and the schools each contribute to transience in America's public schools. In many cases, families move, requiring students to change schools. In other circumstances, students and their families become unsatisfied with the education they are receiving at one school, transferring in pursuit of a more suitable education (Ream, 2003). In yet another scenario, schools may force students to leave because of academic or social problems, such as poor attendance or getting into fights.

A family's decision to change residences often catalyzes student mobility. One study found that half of all high school changes are the result of families' changing residence (Rumberger et al., 1999). Interview data from the same study suggest that residential mobility is often prompted by economic considerations, such as changing jobs, and by family disruptions, such as divorce or parental separation. Nevertheless, a large portion of non-promotional school changes are not associated with a change of residence, a point accentuated by U.S. Census Bureau data indicating that nearly two-thirds of residential mobility occurs locally, within the same county (Hansen, 1995), in which case students are often not required to change schools.

Especially as adolescents, students themselves often initiate school changes for reasons unrelated to residential mobility. Analysis of parent surveys from the *NELS:88* data suggests that almost one-half of recent high school changes were initiated by adolescents requesting a change of school (Rumberger et al., 1999). In some cases, students were found to do so in a proactive fashion, in order to take advantage of a specific educational opportunity or to participate in a strong athletic program. More often than not, however, adolescents initiated a school change in reaction to unpleasant school experiences, including problems with teachers, racial tension among students, and in some cases, gang violence (Rumberger, et al., 1999).

Although families and students often initiate non-promotional student mobility, the schools themselves also contribute to this phenomenon. For example, about 30 percent of parents of mobile students in California report that their adolescents changed schools because they were forced to do so (Rumberger et al., 1999). Interview data show that school personnel often transfer students for behavior-related reasons—an occurrence euphemistically referred to as "Opportunity Transfer" or "OT." Although OTs are sometimes initiated in response to problems such as fighting or malfeasance, school officials also transfer students to other schools because of poor grades or insufficient credits (Rumberger et al., 1999; Gotbaum, 2002).

Lastly, while families, students, and school personnel initiate school changes for many of the various reasons noted above, the overall composition of a school may also contribute to student mobility. Analysis of the *NELS High School Effectiveness Study (HSES)* data suggest that more than one-third of the differences in student mobility rates among California high schools can be attributed to school characteristics, such as school resources, policies, and practices—a higher proportion than that which can be attributed to the characteristics of the students themselves (Rumberger et al., 1999).

Summary

Over time, various theories across academic disciplines have been employed to investigate group-level differences in academic performance. From human capital theory to reproduction theory, to theories that attempt to find a link between culture and academic achievement, scholars have explored many angles on the issue. And while Bordieu, Coleman, and Putnam offer crucial paradigms founding and guiding empirical research on social capital, there is much work to be done before we can fully understand the ways in which social interaction across domains facilitates and/or obstructs the conversion of resources into student achievement. Emergent research addressing the importance of adolescents' informal networks among family and friends, as well as their more formal interactions with school personnel and members of the broader community, suggests that working-class minorities fortify social ties in ways that may differ from their more privileged counterparts. If these differences affect the accumulation and transmission of the resources embedded within adolescent social networks, then high rates of transience may be especially problematic for transient working-class Latinos who must constantly re-negotiate relationships that have the potential to be crucial to their academic success. Thus, the theoretical and empirical studies noted throughout this chapter offer us a real starting point for investigating the *mobility/social capital dynamic* and its implications for Mexican American underachievement.

---

[16] Steele also notes that, "Those who are less domain identified in the stereotype-threatened group may also underperform on standardized tests. Because they care less about the domain it represents, they may be undermotivated or they may withdraw effort in the face of frustration" (Steele, 1997, p. 622).

[17] Economist Glen Loury's (1977) research addressing the way social connections facilitate differential access to opportunities for minority and non-minority youth, and Mark Granovetter's (1985) critique of a pure market approach to economic action and his conceptions of the "embeddedness" of economic behavior should also be mentioned as catalysts for the work of Bourdieu, Coleman, and Putnam.

[18] Indeed, Putnam footnotes Coleman's contribution to his own understanding of social capital, stating, "James Coleman deserves primary credit for developing the 'social capital' theoretical framework" (Putnam, 1995, p. 78).

[19] Nevertheless, research suggests that the social de-capitalization characteristic of children from single-parent homes may be mitigated, in part, by school environments where the overall level of family social capital is strong (Pong, 1998).

[20] For example, research shows that some peer groups advocate a value system that does not support school involvement and participation (Eckert, 1989; Gibson et al., 2004). Relationships of this nature, in turn, may actually inhibit educational success in a social scenario reflecting the "downside of social capital" (Portes & Landolt, 1996).

[21] Over the three years that Valenzuela collected and analyzed data among Mexican American high school students, she came to locate the "problem" of achievement squarely in school-based relationships and organizational structures and policies designed to erase students' culture. She refers to this as "subtractive education" (Valenzuela, 1999, p. 10).

[22] Coleman goes to great lengths emphasizing trust as a critical element of social capital, whether in his explanations of the rotating credit associations found in Southeast Asia or the trust necessary to sustain a marital relationship (Coleman, 1990, p. 306-307).

[23] For example, the overall drop in annual U.S. residential mobility since the 1960s has been about 4 percentage points, from approximately 20 percent in 1960 to 16 percent in 1998 (U.S. Census Bureau, 2000c).

CHAPTER 3

Mixed-Methods Research Design

You know my method. It is founded upon the observation of trifles.

— Arthur Conan Doyle, *Sherlock Holmes: The Boscombe Valley Mystery*

Over the years, education researchers have employed various techniques to investigate what goes on in the sealed world of the classroom—including strictly controlled experiments, longitudinal studies, surveys, and meta-analyses summarizing effects found across numerous studies. Additionally, in-depth interviews, classroom observations, and micro-analyses of classroom discourse have become common research approaches. Educational research is not wanting for methodological diversity, but still the rigor of methods synthesis—where quantitative and qualitative research techniques are used simultaneously, coherently, and logically[24]—remains less commonly employed by education researchers than it perhaps should be.[25]

The Current Study

This study employs a pragmatist approach to mixed-methods research (Rossman & Wilson, 1985; Bryk, Lee & Holland, 1993) reflected in its iterative data collection and analysis procedures.[26] More specifically, I conducted initial fieldwork, followed by a survey wave (Ream & Rumberger, 1998) and a subsequent study (Rumberger et al., 1999) that built in part on my own previous research. Results from that previous research suggest that mobility, while depending in part on the reasons students change schools, negatively impacts social capital accumulation. To investigate this finding further, I developed composite measures of social capital and introduced them as latent variables in structural models employing national survey data. Using field analyses to explore the reasons students change schools and residences, I concentrated on a purposive sample of adolescents to gain a better understanding of the *mobility/social capital dynamic*.

My quantitative study employed national survey data to examine the incidence, consequences and causes of mobility as well as the domain-specific manifestations of social capital among adolescents. I then studied both mobility and social capital for their direct and indirect impacts on twelfth grade test score performance. The qualitative study, on the other hand, explores the unique educational and social experiences of mobile students, who answered "how-and-why" questions in a situated context. In addition, it draws on interviews conducted with school personnel and others with whom they interact. Neither entirely deductive, nor entirely inductive, this study's iterative process of data collection and analysis informed and enabled the construction of the conceptual framework that follows.

Conceptual Framework

The conceptual framework shown in Figure 3.1 suggests that student and residential mobility, as well as family and academic background, have a direct impact on student achievement in the twelfth grade. More specifically, it suggests that domain-specific forms of social capital, its quality (i.e., the strength and utility of relationships), and the quantity in which it is available, may mediate the impact of student mobility. The *mobility/social capital dynamic*, which is depicted by the dashed-arrows in Figure 3.1 for its potential contribution to differential achievement between Mexican American and non-Latino White adolescents, remains the critical focus of this study.

What is it about mobility and social capital that might contribute to differential outcomes between these groups? That Latinos are more mobile than non-Latino Whites is only a partial answer. Research also suggests that social capital has the potential to mediate or exacerbate the impact of mobility, depending on the form of social capital and its availability (Hagan et al., 1996; Pong, 1998; Tucker et al., 1998; Pribesch & Downey, 1999). It is a largely accepted notion that some groups have greater resources embedded in their social networks than others; but what has rarely been investigated is whether different forms of social capital, like different kinds of currency, give evidence of differential exchange value (Fuller & Hanum, 2002; Ream, 2003). The framework has also been designed to facilitate investigation of this question, painting with broad brush-strokes the ways that mobility and social capital are herein employed.[27]

Figure 3.1. Conceptual Framework

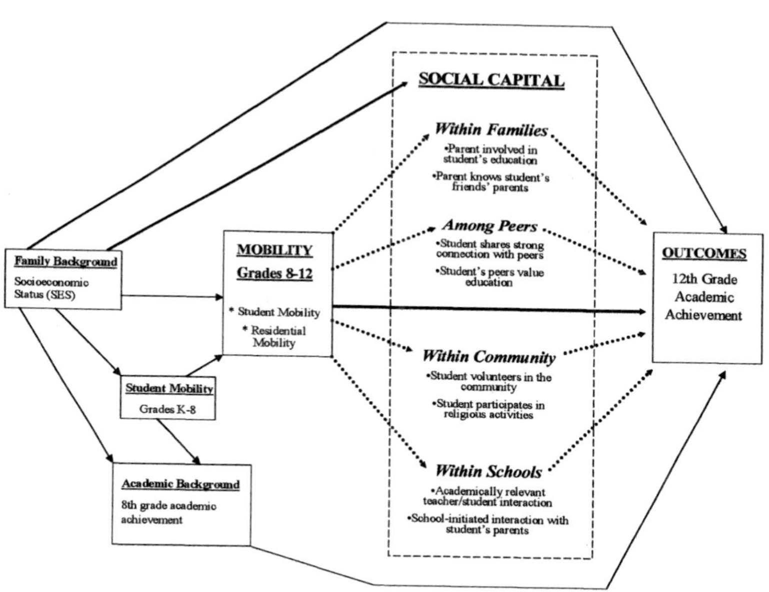

Research Design, Data Collection and Interpretation

The pragmatist approach to research and analysis benefited this study in at least two fundamental ways. First, there is the issue of data access, since this study was designed under the assumption that neither quantitative nor qualitative research methods alone are adequate for investigating the mobility issue, let alone its implications for social capital development and Mexican American underachievement. Second, there is the issue of data analysis. Mixed-methods research has facilitated a nuanced analysis of the various kinds of data collected *via* multiple research methods.

Quantitative Study

Data source and subjects. Base-year (1988) and second year follow-up (1992) data from the *National Education Longitudinal Study of 1988 (NELS:88),* a national longitudinal panel study of a cohort of approximately 25,000 eighth-graders (Carroll, 1996) are employed in this study.[28] The *NELS:88* data are especially suited for this investigation because they contain extensive information on family background, mobility, student socialization (i.e., social capital), and educational achievement among Mexican American (N= 1,952) and non-Latino White (N= 16,317) secondary school students in the United States.

NELS:88 base-year data were collected in 1988, and follow-up data were collected in 1990, 1992 and 1994 on a subset of base-year respondents. The descriptive analyses include weighted values for all the valid responses for each variable, and the predictive analyses are based on data drawn from the panel of base-year students who were re-surveyed in 1990 and 1992 (N=16,489), excluding students who dropped out of school.

The final sample employed in the predictive analyses includes 1,141 Mexican Americans and 10,907 non-Latino Whites.[29] Although the predictive sample is missing at least some important follow-up (twelfth grade) information on a considerable portion of students,[30] I have not excluded these subjects from my analyses, instead retaining them through imputation techniques in order to keep the sample larger and more plausibly representative of disadvantaged students who did not answer all of the questions in the survey.[31] Minority students were over-sampled in the *NELS:88* data in order to increase their respective sample sizes and facilitate comparative analysis of different groups. Sampling weights were also used to compensate for unequal selection probabilities. Moreover, design effect adjustments, compensating for *NELS:88* non-random sampling techniques, were used to compute more appropriate standard errors.

Dependent variable. In order to ascertain the impact of mobility and social capital on student achievement, this study considers a composite measure of mathematics (*f22xmirr*), reading (*f22xrirr*), science (*f22xsirr*), and history (*f22xhirr*) performance, based on cognitive tests given to students who participated in the *NELS:88* second year follow-up survey when most were enrolled in twelfth grade. Students were tested in each year of the *NELS:88* survey, enabling subsequent study of changes in achievement over time, with all scores being re-scaled to the same metric (the IRT-estimated number right). In addition, item response theory (IRT) has made it possible for researchers to estimate students' test scores even when they have not all taken the same version of the test.

Independent measures of mobility and control variables. Based on the work of Swanson & Schneider (1999), distinct measures of student mobility and residential mobility are employed in the survey analysis.[32] Student mobility was measured in 1988 and then again in 1992 in the *NELS:88* data. In the eighth grade survey (1988), parents were asked to identify how many times their children changed schools between first and eighth grade, excluding changes resulting from promotion from one school to another (*byp40*). In the twelfth grade survey (1992), students and dropouts were asked how many times they had changed schools non-promotionally over the previous four years (*f2s103*).[33] Although the *NELS:88* data lack a measure of K-8 residential mobility, the 1992 second year follow-up survey did ask students to identify the number of residential changes they made since eighth grade, and this measure (*f2s102*) is also included in my analysis.

I have also included control variables reflecting students' family background and academic background in the structural models, in an attempt to account for important influences that have been established in other research studies. The family background measure is defined through socioeconomic status—a composite measure reflecting parental education, income, and occupational status (*byses*); whereas academic background reflects a composite measure of eighth grade mathematics (*by2xmirr*), reading (*by2xrirr*), science (*by2xsirr*), and history (*by2xhirr*) achievement test scores.

Intervening variables: refining social capital in the models. As is generally true of scientific constructs, social capital is not a straightforward empirical concept, but rather a postulate; there is no consensus on a single conception of social capital (Woolcock, 1998; Astone et al., 1999). The *NELS:88* data, however, offer numerous specific items that contribute to the empirical estimation of the postulate. For example, *NELS:88* items measured when most students were in twelfth grade were identified as potential contributors to composite measures of social capital across domains (see Appendix A for the extensive list of *NELS:88* variables given initial consideration).[34]

The final social capital composites actually employed in the survey analyses (see Table 3.1) were developed in stages. Every effort was made to identify items that reflect direct person-to-person interaction, since as a fundamental premise of social capital, resources are made available *via* direct social exchange (Coleman, 1988). So if the family social capital composites contain items reflecting direct parent/student interaction and parent-initiated interactions with school personnel, these items enable social capital to be measured in terms of quantity (i.e., the existence of a relationship) *and* quality (i.e., the nature of that relationship). It remains difficult, however, to cross-validate items of this nature since they reflect a respondent's attitudes about a particular relationship. Consider only the obvious case of an abusive father who remains a "caring" dad in the adolescent's eyes. Clearly, in a case like this, the parent/student relationship is less-than-fully reflected in the student's response to a relevant survey question. Even if we could put aside the possibility of such subjective distortions, attitudes regarding social interaction are not static and remain subject to change over time.[35]

Table 3.1. Operationalizing Social Capital

	DOMAINS			
	Family	**Peer**	**Community**	**School**
Forms of Social Capital	*Parent Involved in Student's Education*	*Student Shares Strong Connection with Peers*	*Student Volunteers in the Community*	*Academically Relevant Teacher/Student Interaction*
	Parent Knows Student's Friends' Parents	*Student's Peers Value Education*	*Student Participates in Religious Activities*	*School-Initiated Interaction with Student's Parents*

Taking account of such qualifications, I have developed the composite measures of social capital shown in Table 3.2 by employing factor analysis techniques and the comparison of fit indices across various measurement model configurations. For example, the three composite measures of peer social capital include an omnibus composite and two sub-composites reflecting qualitative differences in the density and range of peer relationships. Specifically, the two sub-composites distinguish more intimate and trusting peer relationships from broader notions of educationally oriented peer networks.[36]

Regardless of the care with which the measures of social capital were developed, neither the *NELS:88* survey instruments nor the scientists employing them were grounded in social capital theory or any other single basic research agenda, so that the methodological inadequacies in the survey data must inhibit what might otherwise have been a more precise examination of different forms of social capital.

Statistical modeling and analysis. I have performed numerous analyses with the *NELS:88* survey data. For instance, in subsequent chapters cross-tabulations compare residential and student mobility demonstrating that a residential change is not always accompanied by a school change, and vice versa. In addition, t-tests reveal significant mean differences in mobility rates, social capital accumulation, and academic achievement levels between the two groups under investigation. Lastly, the social capital constructs in Table 3.2 get introduced as intervening latent variables in structural models in derivations of the formal equation:

$$\text{Outcome12}_i = \beta_0 + \beta_1\text{Mobility}_{8\text{-}12i} + \beta_2\text{Socap}_{12i} + \beta_3\text{Background}_{8i} + \beta_4\text{Outcome8}_i + e_i$$

Here Outcome12_i represents twelfth grade test-score performance for student *i*; Mobility represents school changes or residential changes between the eighth and twelfth grades; Socap represents twelfth grade measures of social capital at the family, peer, school and community level; Background represents student and family background in the form of socioeconomic status and K-8 student mobility; and Outcome8_i represents eighth grade test-score performance for student *i*.

Table 3.2. Social Capital Composites: Construct Validity

Composite Variable Description (Name) - *NELS:88* Questionnaire Items		**Mexican Americans** (N=1,141)		**Non-Latino Whites** (N=10,907)	
	Variable Names	Factor Loading	C's Alpha	Factor Loading	C's Alpha
Family Social Capital, 12th Grade					
Omnibus Family Social Capital (FSC)			.69		.63
***Parents Involved in Student's Education* (FSC1)**			.80		.72
- parent talks with student about selecting school courses	F2P49A	.85		.82	
- parent discusses school activities with student	F2P49B	.88		.80	
- parent talks with student about things studied in class	F2P49C	.81		.79	
***Parent Knows Student's Friends' Parents* (FSC2)**			.65		.50
- parent knows parent of teen's first friend	F2P54B1	.76		.67	
- parent knows parent of teen's second friend	F2P54B2	.81		.74	
- parent knows parent of teen's third friend	F2P54B3	.73		.71	
Peer Social Capital, 12th Grade					
Omnibus Peer Social Capital (PSC)			.70		.73
***Student Shares Strong Connection with Peers* (PSC1)**			.49		.47
- important for student to have strong friendships	F2S40D	.71		.72	
- important to get together among student's close friends	F2S68L	.69		.66	
- chances student will have good friends to count on in the future	F2S67J	.73		.74	
***Student's Peers Value Education* (PSC2)**			.85		.84
- student's close friends think it is important to attend class regularly	F2S68A	.85		.83	
- important to study	F2S68B	.87		.85	
- important to get good grades	F2S68D	.86		.85	
- important to continue education past high school	F2S68H	.75		.76	

Community Social Capital, 12th Grade					
Omnibus Community Social Capital (CSC)			.62		.64
***Student Volunteers in the Community* (CSC1)**	F2S37				
***Student Participates in Religious Activities* (CSC2)**			.70		.72
- student attends religious activities	F2S33C	.87		.89	
- student volunteers with religious group	F2S39D	.81		.76	
- student attends religious services	F2S106	.86		.89	
School Social Capital, 12th Grade					
Omnibus School Social Capital (SSC)			.55		.52
***Academically Relevant Teacher/Student Interaction* (SSC1)**			.38		.42
- teachers demonstrate interested in students	F2S7D	.51		.47	
- teachers important in student's math course-taking	F2S22BA	.75		.77	
- guidance counselor important in student's math course-taking	F2S22BB	.60		.67	
- teachers help student with homework	F2S26A	.55		.50	
***School-Initiated Interaction with Student's Parents* (SSC2)**			.75		.77
- school contacted parent about student's academic program	F2P43B	.69		.72	
- school contacted parent about student's plans after high school	F2P43C	.89		.89	
- school contacted parent about college preparatory course selection	F2P43D	.86		.88	

NOTES: Unlike the other forms of social capital in Table 3.2, *Student Volunteers in the Community* (CSC1) represents a single *NELS:88* item (F2S37). Other relevant items such as "Student volunteers in youth organization" (F2S39A), and "Student volunteers in service organization" (F2S39B) would have been included in the measure of volunteering behavior were it not for the limited spread of scores reflected in the student responses to these items (see Appendix A for complete list of *NELS:88* items considered for inclusion in the social capital constructs). Statistics weighted (*f2pnlwt*/mean *f2pnlwt*).

The chi-square statistic, Tucker-Lewis index (TLI), comparative-fit index (CFI), and root-mean-square-error-of-approximation (RMSEA) test the fit of these structural models. Chi-square is the statistical procedure testing for differences in the observed and estimated matrices.[37] Both TLI and CFI are practical indices of fit designed to address sample size issues (Marsh, Balla & Hau, 1996). For TLI and CFI, values of .9 and above indicate a strong fit of the proposed model (Schumacker & Lomax, 1996). The RMSEA index takes into account the error of approximation in the population[38] and since it is sensitive to the number of estimated parameters in the model, it acts as an indicator of model parsimony. Values for RMSEA that indicate reasonable fit are .08 or less (Byrne, 1998).

Structural equation models. There are many reasons for using structural equation models to conduct the survey analyses. First, SEM can confirm measurement models where multiple *NELS:88* variables are hypothesized to define theoretical constructs of peer social capital, as SEM allows for estimating the relationships between latent constructs free of measurement error. Moreover, SEM improves upon the predictive capacity of multiple regression by allowing for true multivariate estimation, including the estimation of direct and indirect effects. SEM is also able to take advantage of the longitudinal nature of the *NELS:88* data by facilitating path analysis to examine variables in the *mobility/social capital dynamic* over time. Specifically, it enables these variables to be viewed in a manner that is relational (causal) as opposed to additive.

Equality constraints and critical ratios analyses. As I noted above, few have studied whether different groups of students rely on different forms of social capital in the learning process. To get at this question, critical ratios analyses facilitate between-group comparisons of each parameter estimate in the structural models revealing, for example, whether the impact of *Academically Relevant Teacher/Student Interaction* (SSC1) on twelfth grade test scores among Mexican Americans differs significantly from the impact of the same parameter for non-Latino Whites.[39]

Limitations in the quantitative study. There are some limitations in the design of the quantitative investigation. First, since it is difficult to track mobile students *via* surveys, some of the most mobile students may not be included in the *NELS:88* longitudinal data. Second, in the base-year cohort, some Limited English Proficient (LEP) students were included in the sample, but others, generally those most severely limited in their English language proficiency, were excluded (although most of these students were brought back into the *NELS:88* study in

1990).[40] To the extent that mobility rates among LEP students were higher than for other students, the results probably underreport base-year student mobility, particularly among Mexican origin youth. In short, the issue of missing data poses certain limitations regarding the internal and external validity of the survey analysis, since data may be missing at random or for more systematic reasons (Maxim, 1999).

Qualitative Study

The qualitative study examines the incidence, consequences, and causes of student and residential mobility. I investigate the actual process of mobility (i.e., acclimation to the new school environment, school registration), and the relational implications of transience (i.e., its impact on social capital development) largely through semi-structured interviews and observational techniques.

Data collection and samples. Sampling for the qualitative study was both purposive and convenient. In terms of purpose, urban school sites, with highly transient student populations and demographic profiles that include Mexican Americans and non-Latino Whites, were ideally suited for the field study component of this investigation.[41] Prior to the initiation of this study, I had already collected mobility-related qualitative data at three urban high schools in the Los Angeles area. These same high schools were included in this study, along with two additional schools that also fit the parameters of the research project. As a result, what characterized my interaction with the schools as slightly unusual was the level of access less easily achieved, for example, in large urban school districts. Already-established relationships with school personnel proved to be an asset. Assistance from school counselors with whom I'd developed relationships through previous research (an example of my own accrued social capital) helped secure a steady stream of adolescent interviewees. One counselor even offered the use of his front office as an on-campus meeting room, then provided me with an extensive list of high school enrollees (by gender, race/ethnicity and grade) and students' weekly course schedules, so that any student in attendance could be found on campus at any time during the regular school day. What's more, this counselor's bilingual student interns (mostly seniors at the school) provided interviewees with hall passes, and summoned them to my makeshift office. When the potential interviewees arrived, I introduced myself and then explained the study so that we could assess their potential eligibility (considering, for example, whether the student had changed schools non-promotionally at least once between grades eight and twelve). Although not every one of these students proved to be eligible for and interested in the study, this process initiated by the school counselor (coupled with the fact that participants were offered $20 per interview) made the identification of mobile students considerably less problematic than it otherwise would have been.

Sixteen middle to low-income Mexican Americans and sixteen non-Latino Whites (including immigrants, second, and third+ generation participants) were included in the interviews. An equal number of boys and girls participated as interviewees. Most of the students' parents/guardians were also interviewed, bringing the total to 57 interviews.[42] Demographic characteristics of the adolescent interviewees are shown here in Table 3.3.

Interview questions addressed (a) family background, (b) social capital within each domain noted above, (c) reasons for school change, and (d) the impact of mobility on students and their families. I had tested parent and student interview protocols in both English and Spanish prior to the initiation of this study (see Appendix C for interview protocols). The protocols were designed to mirror the survey data, addressing the incidence, consequences, and causes of mobility as well as students' social capital development.

Since preliminary research identified school counselors' important role in helping mobile students make the transition to a new school, I interviewed five high school counselors regarding student placement procedures and the various implications of mobility for transient students. Additionally, interviews with three school administrators and eight classroom teachers addressed curriculum coordination between high schools with highly transient populations, the transfer of mobile student records, and textbook losses. I also probed accountability issues, such as who has jurisdictional authority over mobile students. Demographic characteristics of the five schools from which students and school personnel were interviewed are included in Table 3.4.

Table 3.3. Characteristics of Student Interview Sample

Race/ Ethnicity	Name	Grade	Generation Status	School Changes (grades 8-12)
Mexican American Girls				
	Massiel	9th	Immigrant	1
	Melissa	9th	Immigrant	1
	Marlén	11th	Second Generation	1
	Christina	11th	Second Generation	2
	Patricia	12th	Second Generation	1
	Marta	11th	Second Generation	3
	Margarita	10th	Second Generation	2
	Olivia	11th	Second Generation	1
Mexican American Boys				
	Fernando	9th	Immigrant	1
	Samuel	11th	Second Generation	1
	Roberto	12th	Second Generation	1
	Ricardo	10th	Second Generation	1
	Iván	12th	Second Generation	3
	Carlos	10th	Second Generation	1
	Roiter	10th	Second Generation	1
	Julio	12th	Third+ Generation	1
Non-Latino White Girls				
	Natasha	10th	Immigrant (Russia)	1
	Larissa	11th	Immigrant (Russia)	1
	Becky	12th	Immigrant (Israel)	4
	Lorraine	12th	Second Generation	1
	Dawn	12th	Third+ Generation	1
	Barbara	12th	Third+ Generation	1
	Kary	12th	Third+ Generation	3
	Anne	10th	Third+ Generation	5
Non-Latino White Boys				
	Russ	11th	Immigrant (England)	1
	Richard	12th	Second Generation	5
	Jason	12th	Third+ Generation	5
	Doug	12th	Third+ Generation	3
	Todd	12th	Third+ Generation	1
	Michael	11th	Third+ Generation	2
	Jon	11th	Third+ Generation	3
	Paul	12th	Third+ Generation	5

Table 3.4. School Characteristics

	Senior High Schools				
	1	**2**	**3**	**4**	**5**
Location					
Urban	X	X	X	X	X
Size					
2,000-3,000				X	
3,000-4,000	X	X			X
4,000-5,000			X		
Ethnicity (%)					
Non-Latino White	.1	1	.2	22	52
Latino	79	74	99	68	25
African American	20	14	.3	5	9
Asian	.2	10	.4	2	12
Other	.7	1	.1	3	2
Free/Reduced Lunch (%)	78	83	86	84	13
English Language Learners (%)	38	36	36	38	10

Interview team. Recognizing that race, ethnicity or gender are interviewer characteristics that may exert a biasing effect, I hired graduate students to assist in conducting interviews with mobile adolescents. These interviewers were matched with students of the same gender, race/ethnicity, and language preference, whereas I myself interviewed non-Latino White boys and their parents/guardians.[43] To facilitate contact between the interview team and adolescent interviewees, the names and phone numbers of mobile high school students were forwarded, *via* e-mail, to the graduate students on the interview team. The interviewers then contacted the high school students directly and arranged to interview them, conducting separate interviews with the students' parents/guardians. Generally, interviews were conducted at the student's place of residence and were audio-recorded and later transcribed by the interviewer. Each interview lasted approximately one hour. To familiarize the interview team with the scope of this investigation, I hosted an initial group discussion, providing background information including (1) an introduction to the student and parent interview protocols, (2) basic logistical information regarding, for example, payment of participants (see Appendix D),

(3) student/parent permission forms in English and Spanish (see Appendix E), and (4) the student and parent interview protocols. Although the protocols had been tested in a previous study (Rumberger et al., 1999), I asked the interview team to evaluate the instruments for construct validity and other potential inadequacies. I remained in constant (almost weekly) contact with the interview team for nearly six months during data collection, soliciting input on various aspects of qualitative data analysis. Since each of the four interviewers brought to the table a unique set of skills (i.e., biliteracy, teaching experience in K-12 classrooms, and graduate experience in sociology and education), potential issues regarding inter-interviewer reliability were considered less problematic in light of the offsetting benefits of this teamwork approach to data collection in the field.

Data analysis. One of the difficult tasks in qualitative analysis is mastering a vast amount of data (in this case, scores of interviews and hundreds of pages of transcript data) in a systematic manner. For that reason, I gave particular attention to formalized and comparable data collection and analysis techniques. Systematic data coding and reduction was guided by (1) deductive criteria based on social capital theory with a focus on the hypothesized relationship between mobility, social capital, and differential outcomes between Mexican Americans and non-Latino Whites, and (2) inductive analysis of emergent themes that were anticipated, but not specifically foreseen, in the original conceptualization of this study.

As part of the deductive analytic process, I categorized interview transcript data conceptually and also color-coded the information to reflect the incidence, consequences, and causes of student mobility as well as the various manifestations of social capital development among mobile student interviewees. After the transcripts had been coded, I separated data from Mexican Americans and data from non-Latino Whites and charted my findings with columns reflecting conceptual categories. Coded data were displayed in matrices (see, for example, Table 4.5), providing a visual for the conclusions drawn from the qualitative analysis (Miles & Huberman, 1984).

By analyzing the data inductively for themes or consistent patterns—some of which were related to the theoretical and conceptual underpinnings of this study, and some of which were not—I found, for example, that one emergent theme proved helpful in understanding the causes of student mobility. To whit, sometimes high school students themselves initiated school changes and, depending on the circumstances, such changes could often be categorized as either reactive or strategic in nature. Reactive student-initiated school changes reflect instances when students make their own decisions to change schools in reaction to some phenomenon outside the scope of their control (a reaction to school violence, for example). Strategic student-initiated school changes, on the other hand, reflect circumstances in which, for example, students decide to change schools because they desire to participate in inter-scholastic sports at another school with a particularly strong athletic program.

Limitations in the qualitative study. There are substantial limits in the generalizability of the inferences drawn from the interview data. More specifically, non-random sampling techniques (including convenience and "snowball" sampling) accompany relatively small sample sizes for both the students and school personnel interviewed. Perhaps as a result, mobility rates among interviewees do not reflect the national trend where Mexican Americans change school more frequently than non-Latino Whites. Although non-random sampling techniques and small sample sizes limit the scope of the inferences drawn from the qualitative data (findings from the field are not resultant of the kind of participant observation that might otherwise facilitate "thick description" of the *mobility/social capital dynamic*), themes that emerge from the interviews nevertheless contribute to both the design of the survey analysis and the interpretation of quantitative findings.

Summary

Over the course of my research, survey analyses and the field investigation have been carefully interwoven to address the incidence, consequences, and causes of mobility. Both methods also reveal the availability of various forms of social capital, its variable convertibility into student performance, and the importance of social capital in the adaptation of mobile students. Accordingly, this study proceeds with confidence in the notion that the simultaneous application of survey and field research techniques can illuminate the *mobility/social capital dynamic*, especially as pertains to its impact on group-level educational inequality and the low average level of educational achievement disadvantaging Mexican origin youth in the United States.

---

[24] Quantitative investigation emphasizes research design and principles of analysis derived from the hard sciences, prioritizing experimental design and statistical analysis of multiple cases (Louis, 1982). Qualitative research, arguably less rule bound, narrows the gap between investigator and the subjects under study, answering "how" and "why" questions that are revealed within the context surrounding phenomena under study (Lancy, 1993).

[25] Indeed, the value of multiple investigative methods in education research has at times been overshadowed by a manichaean debate pitting quantitative and qualitative research approaches against one another (Burrell & Morgan, 1979; Lincoln & Guba, 1985; Smith & Heshusius, 1986).

[26] The pragmatist research approach systematically integrates both quantitative and qualitative methods on at least two levels. First, methodological pragmatists stagger data collection, often beginning with (a) an initial field study followed by (b) a survey wave and (c) a confirmatory field study. Then, a re-analysis of the survey data is likely to include additional variables emerging from the field study. Second, field study "variables" are keyed to survey variables to determine the precise degree of overlap and corroboration between the two. Tighter pre-structuring and homogeneity of instruments across methods is a way to focus the data collection process so as to reduce problems with data overload that are common to mixed-methods studies (Huberman & Crandall, 1982).

[27] There were many stages in developing the conceptual framework and subsequent structural models. The initial framework, for example, included eighth *and* twelfth grade social capital composites to look at social capital across time. However, individual items contributing to these composites could not always be matched (i.e., many of the original base-year questions were not included in the *NELS:88* second-year follow up survey). For that reason, eighth grade social capital was removed from the models.

[28] For further information on *NELS:88*, see *http://nces.ed.gov/surveys/nels88.*

[29] Although most Mexican American students in the sample spoke Spanish before entering school, by the eighth grade nearly all report understanding

English at least "pretty well." The *NELS:88* base-year cohort excludes about 5 percent of the eighth grade population who were deemed ineligible to participate due to insufficient English language proficiency.

[30] Illustratively, 21 percent and 19 percent of Mexican Americans and non-Latino Whites, respectively, are missing twelfth grade math and/or reading test scores, while 28 percent and 12 percent of each respective group are missing information regarding student mobility during grades 8-12.

[31] The software employed in the predictive analyses confronts missing data with *estimation* by full information maximum-likelihood (FIML) instead of relying on ad-hoc methods like listwise or pairwise deletion, or mean imputation (Arbuckle & Wothke, 1999). Unlike many other imputation methods, FIML estimation uses *all* the information from the observed data, estimating a coefficient for the relationship between variables (the missing data are built directly into the estimation method), as opposed to imputing a value for an otherwise observed variable (Arbuckle, 1996).

[32] See Appendix B for descriptions and mean characteristics of the variables employed in this study.

[33] The *NELS:88* data also include parent reports of non-promotional student mobility between grades 8 and 12. Since prior research suggests that parents may under-report adolescent student mobility (Rumberger et al., 1999), this study relies on student reports of mobility between the eighth and twelfth grades.

[34] Consistent with the research of Keith et al., (1998), parent *and* student responses to *NELS:88* survey questions are included in composite measures approximating social capital.

[35] Perhaps for purposes of cross-validation, Coleman himself often resorted to various proxy measures (including two-parent family structure—and mobility) when modeling social capital, and more recent scholarship follows suit (Putnam, 2000). This study also reflects that trend. More specifically, where direct measures of social interaction could not be found, indirect *behavioral* measures were employed in the development of social capital constructs. For example, items reflecting community volunteering and

attendance at religious services were considered as variables that might contribute to community social capital. While items of this nature do not reflect quality relationships, per se, they are advantaged over attitudinal measures in that they remain subject to external verification.

[36] The sub-composite *Student Shares Strong Connection with Peers* includes variables that describe students' relationships with their peers, including whether they (a) think it is important to have strong friendships, (b) have close friends who value spending time together, and (c) expect to have good friends in the future. *Student's Peers Value Education* includes variables that describe whether students' friends think it is important to (a) attend class regularly, (b) study, (c) get good grades, and (d) continue education past high school. The omnibus composite incorporates the *NELS:88* items in *Peer Connectedness* and *Student's Peers Value Education* into an aggregate measure of peer social capital.

[37] Since the chi-square statistic is reported to be particularly "sensitive" to large sample sizes, it has a tendency to indicate a significant probability level and hence lead to a rejection of the null hypothesis that the model fits the data well (Browne & Cudeck, 1993; Schumacker & Lomax, 1996).

[38] The discrepancy between the parameter values in the estimated model and the population covariance matrix, as measured by RMSEA, is represented per degrees of freedom.

[39] The critical ratio statistic can be compared to a table of the standard normal distribution to test whether two parameters are virtually equal ($C.R. < 1.96$) in the population.

[40] In the *NELS:88* follow-up rounds, a sample of the originally excluded students were re-assessed for survey eligibility. Seventy-one percent of the sample of LEPs who were excluded in the base year sample were reclassified as eligible and folded into the sample in subsequent years. Students initially excluded from the *NELS:88* sample are not included in this study, however.

[41] To ensure cooperation from informants, full confidentiality was promised. The names used to identify people and schools are pseudonyms.

[42] Most of the student interviews are coupled with a parent/guardian interview. However, initial data analyses revealed few differences in student and parent responses to interview questions. As a result, only twenty-five parent/guardian interviews were conducted.

[43] According to Briggs (1986), "The farther we move away from home, culturally and linguistically, the greater the problem [with the interview]. This hiatus between the communicative norms of the interviewee and researcher can greatly hinder research, and the problems it engenders have sometimes abruptly terminated the investigation. If the fieldworker does not take this gap into account, he or she will fail to see how native communicative patterns have shaped responses..." (p. 3).

CHAPTER 4

Test-Score Performance and Rates of Mobility by Socioeconomic and Nativity Status

Good description of important events is better than bad explanation of anything.

— Gary King, Robert Keohane and Sidney Verba, *Designing Social Inquiry*

Before considering the impact of the *mobility/social capital dynamic* on student achievement and group-level educational inequality, it is important to more fully examine the twelfth grade test score gap, while paying special attention to the incidence and causes of student mobility. NAEP data clearly highlight the magnitude of the test score gap and suggest its persistence over time, but the *NELS:88* data also reveal a test-score disparity between Mexican Americans and non-Latino Whites that remains intact even when the comparison groups are considered according to their socioeconomic and nativity status. Descriptive findings based on the *NELS:88* survey data underscore the many disadvantages precluding Mexican origin youth from meeting their full academic potential. My particular focus here, however, is on student transience, since even the most stable generation of Mexican American students changes schools at significantly higher rates than the most mobile generation of Whites. Through the juxtaposition of both survey and field data, I explore the incidence and causes of student mobility in great detail over the course of the present chapter.

The Twelfth Grade Test Score Gap

Analyses of the *NELS:88* data show that Mexican Americans face significant disadvantages in access to resources, and indeed socioeconomic status (SES) levels lend support to this observation, since the average SES among Mexican Americans in the *NELS:88* sample is more than a standard deviation below mean-level SES among their White counterparts (see Appendix B). Such a discrepancy may be partly attributable to schooling- and employment-related challenges faced by immigrant parents (Trejo 1997), who constitute roughly one-third of the Mexican American parents answering survey questions upon which the composite SES measure was based. Differences in socioeconomic status and nativity status clearly distinguish the two groups (fewer than one-half of the Mexican American students in the *NELS:88* sample hail from families with U.S. born heads-of-household),[44] and this most certainly contributes to the persistent gap in twelfth grade test score performance shown in Figure 4.1, according to which Mexican Americans score significantly below their non-Latino White counterparts on test performance measures, including mathematics, reading, science, and history.

Figure 4.1. Average Twelfth Grade Test Score Performance

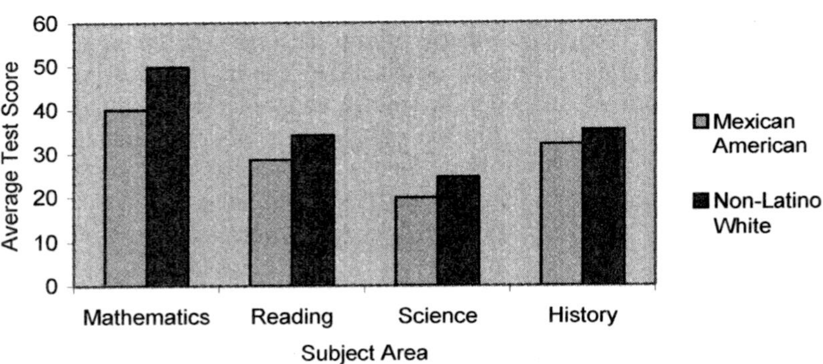

NOTE: Categorized mean differences in test score performance distinguishing Mexican Americans and non-Latino Whites are statistically significant, $p<.01$. SOURCE: *National Education Longitudinal Study of 1988*, panel of 1988 eighth-grade students resurveyed in 1990 and 1992, excluding dropouts. Statistics weighted (*f2pnlwt/mean f2pnlwt*).

Mexican Americans in the sample score on average nearly ten points (.75 SD) lower than Whites in math (40.1 vs. 49.8, respectively); and nearly six points lower (.66 SD) in reading. Although the difference in Mexican-White test scores is fairly consistent across advantaged and disadvantaged SES groups, the gap narrows somewhat across generations. Notice in Table 4.1 that the average gap between third+ generation Mexican Americans and third+ generation Whites is similar to the gap in the entire sample, which has commingled adolescents of similar ages from multiple generations.

Table 4.1. Average Twelfth Grade Test Score Performance by Demographic Characteristics

	Mathematics Test Scores		Reading Test Scores		Science Test Scores		History Test Scores	
	M.A.	W.	M.A.	W.	M.A.	W.	M.A.	W.
Entire Sample (see Figure 4.1)	40.1	49.8	28.5	34.2	19.9	24.4	32.0	35.3
Socioeconomic Status								
Below the mean	38.9	44.4	27.8	31.0	19.5	22.4	31.7	33.5
Above the mean	46.1	53.9	31.6	36.6	22.3	25.8	33.3	36.7
Nativity Status								
Immigrant	40.5	53.8	27.2	36.7	19.8	25.5	31.7	36.8
Second Generation	40.3	53.1	28.9	35.6	20.0	24.9	32.3	36.4
Third+ Generation	40.7	49.7	29.5	34.1	20.5	24.3	32.2	35.2

NOTES: Categorized mean differences in test score performance distinguishing Mexican Americans (M.A.) and non-Latino Whites (W.) are statistically significant, $p<.01$. SOURCE: *National Education Longitudinal Study of 1988*, panel of 1988 eighth-grade students resurveyed in 1990 and 1992, excluding dropouts. Statistics weighted (*f2pnlwt/mean f2pnlwt*).

That the gap in test scores narrows across generations is reason for optimism, but nevertheless the persistence of significant test score differences—even among third+ generation youth—is disconcerting, perhaps all the more so because this finding is not entirely consistent with new research suggesting that cohorts of Mexican immigrants to the United States advance educationally, from one generation to the next, just as quickly as European immigrants have historically done so (Smith, 2003).[45] Indeed, the especially large test score gap separating immigrant youth of Mexican origin from immigrant youth of European descent remains salient among the second-generation children of immigrants, and even among third+ generation youth whose parents were born in the U.S. In short, when it comes to twelfth grade test score performance, group-level differences stubbornly persist, even when comparison groups are matched according to nativity status (e.g., when Mexican immigrants are compared to White immigrants). In addition, it should be noted that the test-score gap is probably understated, since *NELS:88* dropouts—a disproportionate number of whom are Mexican American—are excluded from the sample.

The Incidence of Mobility

While both groups show similar rates of student mobility during the primary (first through eighth grade) school years, the gap with regard to student and residential mobility becomes more pronounced at the secondary level, per Table 4.2.

If we exclude dropouts, 30 percent of Mexican American adolescents in the *NELS:88* sample made at least one non-promotional school change between eighth and twelfth grade, compared to 21 percent of Whites. What's more, the mobility rate for highly mobile students (those with two or more non-promotional school changes between eighth and twelfth grade) is nearly twice as high for Mexican Americans. With regard to residential mobility, 37 percent of Mexican Americans moved at least once between eighth and twelfth grade compared to 31 percent of their White counterparts.

Overall, the data in Table 4.2 support a growing body of research demonstrating that U.S. school children in general are highly transient (Rumberger, 2003), as the large majority of Mexican Americans and most non-Latino Whites make at least one non-promotional school change during their elementary and secondary school careers. It is at the secondary level in particular that Mexican Americans demonstrate comparably high rates of both student and residential mobility.

Table 4.2. Average School and Residential Mobility Rates among Mexican Americans and non-Latino Whites by Grade Level

	Student Mobility			Residential Mobility		
	Zero School Changes (%)	One School Change (%)	Two + School Changes (%)	Zero Residence Changes (%)	One Residence Change (%)	Two + Residence Changes (%)
Grades 1-8						
Mexican Americans	48	21	31			
Non-Latino Whites	48	23	29			
Grades 8-12						
Mexican Americans	70**	19**	11**	63**	20	17**
Non-Latino Whites	79**	15*	6**	69**	19	12**
Grades 1-12						
Mexican Americans	39**	25	36*			
Non-Latino Whites	45**	23	32*			

NOTES: Mexican American and non-Latino White mobility rates differ significantly, *$p<.05$ and **$p<.01$. Student mobility from grades one through eight based on data from eighth grade parent questionnaire. Student mobility from grades eight through twelve based on data from twelfth grade student questionnaire. Student mobility excludes school changes due to promotion from elementary to middle school and from middle school to high school. Data on K-8 residential mobility not available in the *NELS:88* survey. SOURCE: *National Education Longitudinal Study of 1988*, panel of 1988 eighth-grade students resurveyed in 1990 and 1992, excluding dropouts. Statistics weighted (*f2pnlwt/mean f2pnlwt*).

Mobility by SES and immigrant status. In Table 4.3, mobility rates are depicted across socioeconomic and immigrant status groups. For Mexican Americans whose family SES is below the mean of all eighth graders in the entire *NELS:88* sample, rates of student mobility are considerably higher between grades eight and twelve than they are for their more affluent Mexican American peers whose SES is above the sample mean (32 percent compared to 22 percent, respectively).[46] For Whites, the incidence of student mobility remains consistent across lower and upper SES groups at approximately 22 percent. Thus, we can deduce a negative association between SES and student mobility among youth of Mexican descent; whereas SES and student mobility do not reveal associational patterns among non-Latino Whites.

If Mexican immigrants are particularly mobile—with 32 percent making at least one non-promotional school change between grades 8 and 12, compared to 29 percent of second generation and 24 percent of third+ generation Mexican origin youth—the trend moves in the opposite direction among Whites who become slightly more mobile with acculturation. Fourteen percent of non-Latino White immigrants made a non-promotional secondary school change, compared to 17 percent and 21 percent of second and third+ generation White adolescents. Yet even the most stable generation of Mexican American students changes schools at higher rates than the most mobile generation of Whites.

Table 4.3. Student Mobility by Demographic Characteristics among Mexican Americans and non-Latino Whites, Grades Eight through Twelve

	Zero Non-Promotional School Changes (%)		**One Non-Promotional School Change (%)**		**Two or More Non-Promotional School Changes (%)**	
	M.A.	W.	M.A.	W.	M.A.	W.
Socioeconomic Status						
Below the mean	68**	79**	20**	15**	12**	6**
Above the mean	78	78	10	15	12*	7*
Nativity Status						
Immigrant	68**	86**	25**	5**	7	9
Second Generation	71**	83**	19	15	10**	2**
Third+ Generation	76	79	15	15	9	6

NOTES: Mexican American (M.A.) and non-Latino White (W.) mobility rates differ significantly, $**p<.01$, $*p<.05$. Student mobility from grades 8-12 based on data from twelfth grade student questionnaire. Student mobility excludes school changes due to promotion from elementary to middle school and from middle school to high school. SOURCE: *National Education Longitudinal Study of 1988*, panel of 1988 eighth-grade students resurveyed in 1990 and 1992, excluding dropouts. Statistics weighted (*f2pnlwt/mean f2pnlwt*).

Disentangling student and residential mobility. Many people believe the main reason students change schools is because their families move, and in fact residential mobility is often associated with a school change. But changing residences does not always result in changing schools. Some families change residences only to remain in the same school attendance area. Some states, such as California, now have policies enabling students to remain in their initial school placement even if their family moves into the attendance area for another school (Rumberger et al., 1999). Table 4.4 illustrates the distinction between residential and student mobility. So, between the eighth and twelfth grade, for example, 45 percent of residential moves made by Mexican American families did not lead to students' changing schools. Among non-Latino Whites, the figure is even higher, at 51 percent.

Table 4.4. Residential and School Changes between Grades Eight and Twelve (percent distribution)

Mobility Patterns	Mexican Americans (%)	Non-Latino Whites (%)
Moved Residence	**37**	**31**
Moved residence and changed schools	55	49
Moved residence but did not change schools	45	51
Did Not Move Residence	**63**	**69**
Did not move residence but changed schools	15	9
Did not move residence and did not change schools	85	91
Total	**100**	**100**
Percent of school changes not associated with a change of residence	30	27

NOTES: Student and residential mobility from grades 8-12 based on data from twelfth grade student questionnaire. Student mobility excludes school changes due to promotion from elementary to middle school and from middle school to high school. SOURCE: *National Education Longitudinal Study of 1988*, panel of 1988 eighth-grade students resurveyed in 1990 and 1992, excluding dropouts. Statistics weighted (*f2pnlwt/mean f2pnlwt*).

Conversely, just as students may move without changing schools, some students change schools without moving. Indeed, 30 percent of all school changes among Mexican origin youth were not associated with a change of residence (the figure among non-Latino Whites is 27 percent). Not only do these numbers distinguish residential from student mobility, but they also suggest that Mexican American students are less likely to make a residential change without changing schools and are more likely to change schools without changing residences than their non-Latino White peers.

The Causes of Student Mobility

In a study investigating the mitigative influence of family social capital among the residentially mobile, Hagan et al. (1996) conclude by calling for empirical research to investigate the extent to which mobility might be the product of aspiration and opportunity, rather than desperation and decline. In the section that follows, the interview data shed some light on the people who initiate student mobility and their reasons for doing so. It is an unfortunate reality that adolescents often change schools suddenly and *reactively*—perhaps when parents split up and a custodial parent leaves town, or because gang rivalries flare up and affiliated kids opt out of dangerous school settings. Under the best of circumstances there is genuine strategy underlying a planned school change, with students and parents acting as informed consumers in the educational "marketplace." Frequently, however, students change schools for reasons that are neither entirely beyond their control, nor entirely the result of strategic forethought.

Parents, students, and school personnel all make decisions contributing to high rates of student mobility (see Table 4.5.)[47] *Family-initiated* student mobility is commonly reported among Mexican American interviewees, although less so among Whites. In many cases, high school students make independent decisions to change schools, but *student-initiated* mobility of this nature, though commonly reported among non-Latino White interviewees, is less frequently cited among Mexican origin youth. Particularly at the secondary level, school personnel have their say in these matters, and thus we find also a fair amount of school-initiated student mobility.

Family-initiated student mobility. Many of the Mexican Americans who were interviewed for this study attest to the fact that family-initiated student mobility was reactive in nature. For example, Massiel Fernandez reported that when she was an infant, her parents made a deliberate and difficult decision to live apart—her mother in Tijuana and her father across the border in *El Norte*—with the goal of ultimately reuniting the family under improved financial circumstances. A few years later, when the family's economic stability had improved, Massiel and her mother immigrated to the San Diego area, temporarily reuniting the family. Shortly thereafter, however, they fell again on hard times. "There weren't enough jobs and we did not have enough money to pay for the house," her mother said. At the mercy of the marketplace, her father set out for employment in Los Angeles, while Massiel and her mother remained in San Diego. This second separation was not less difficult for having followed upon their prior experience. Then after another five years spent as a "commuter family," a second reunion caused Massiel to make a mid-freshman-year school change to Los Angeles. "The children were growing up living without their father around," Sra. Fernandez explained. "My husband asked me to move here to Los Angeles so we could live together. The move was very difficult, but now the children are adapting (more or less) to the new school."

Table 4.5. The Causes of Student Mobility

	Family-Initiated Student Mobility			**Student-Initiated Student Mobility**			**School-Initiated "Opportunity Transfer"**
	Strategic	**Reactive**	**Both**	**Strategic**	**Reactive**	**Both**	**Reactive**
Mexican Americans	***	******	***	**	***	*	***
Non-Latino Whites	****	**	*****	*****	********* *	****	************

NOTE: Each asterisk represents one of the 63 non-promotional school changes reported by students in the interview sample.

Whereas Massiel made just one non-promotional school change as a result of her father's job search, Iván was whip-sawed from school-to-school as a result of his father's demanding work-related responsibilities. "I do maintenance and I used to work for Z-Property Management," his immigrant father explained, "and so the company forced me to move to different cities." Each time the family moved residences, Iván was forced to change schools, often in the middle of the school year.

Family-initiated student mobility may also be the result of the psycho-social stresses that adolescents must adapt to, overcome, or somehow attempt to avoid. Reflecting on a bad situation that got worse at the private Jewish high school Michael attended his freshman year, his father explained what he perceived as a necessity for Michael's changing schools. "The move was not voluntary—it was mandated by crisis," he said. "Halfway through the school year, Michael pretty much just fell apart. It was a combination of academic and social and emotional factors. He just shut down completely. So then we reacted by putting him into a public school."

Much family-initiated mobility is reactive in nature, but sometimes parents/guardians initiate moves strategically on behalf of their children. Paul's father even went so far as to relocate his family so that they would be within the geographic boundaries of what he perceived to be a good school. "I wanted Paul to graduate from El Sueño—that's the whole reason I moved here. I changed residences to get him into this school district," his father recalled. It was perhaps a last-gasp effort. Unfortunately, engagement in school was a mere afterthought for Paul himself, whose behavior problems and truancy bore a direct relation to his frequent school changes and poor performance in school. "There was no way he was going to a Catholic school or a private school with his grades the way they were...I looked for the best school that I could find," his dad said.

The first time Michael's parents initiated a school change on his behalf, it was clearly a reaction to his emotional difficulties. The second time, however, they did so for combined reactive and strategic reasons—as a reaction to his poor school performance and drug abuse, and as a strategy to get him into a performing arts school. "My parents never liked Ridgemont. I got into heavy drugs there.... My mom is a teacher, so she was always looking around for me. She liked the play that I was in and she was looking for a performing arts school. She found Lockport High."

Michael's father reflected on his wife's efforts to get their son into a school environment that could meet Michael's needs:

> My wife just thought that a change was needed. Michael had some interest in theatre, so she checked it out and the only

> place that had any availability was Lockport High. We had the hope that he would go there, involve himself in the theater program, and be involved in magnet quality classes.

Although in Iván's case his parents initiated a slew of reactive school changes in response to his father's demanding maintenance job, on one occasion they too did what Paul's father did, moving residences for the explicit purpose of helping their son escape an especially poor school and enroll in a markedly better one. "When we moved to San Roque, Iván suffered a lot because that technical school there is one of the worst high schools. That's why I quit my last job. We moved right away, this time because of the schools. And here at Cesar Chavez High School it's five times better."

Student-initiated student mobility. Given the increased autonomy that coincides with adolescent development, it is not surprising that high school students sometimes make independent decisions to change schools. In fact, a large percentage of student mobility at the secondary level—nearly 50 percent in the state of California—is the result of student-initiated requests to change schools (Rumberger, et al., 1999).[48] Most of the student-initiated mobility reported in the field study can be categorized as reactive in nature, often the result of social or academic problems and even a consequence of threats and intimidation among conflicting peer groups.

As a sixteen-year-old living under the guardianship of her grandmother, Anne changed schools halfway through her freshman year in reaction to a sort of social Darwinism that made it difficult to engage in her predominantly White, middle-class school environment. "I started at Freeport and in the middle of the ninth grade year I left to go to El Sueño because there was a lot of drama at Freeport and like, stuff happened and we fought with people—and the rumors." Four school changes later, Anne was still searching for a school with holding power.

While the perceived social cruelties and rumor-mongering of her peer group took their toll on Anne, for Carlos the pressure was more explicit. A second-generation youth whose parents were born in the Mexican state of *Oaxaca*, Carlos decided to change schools in response to direct forms of intimidation. "All these students were racist and all this. They were calling me 'dumb-ass Mexican' and insulting me. I didn't like that."

During the precarious time of adolescence, the line between social pressure and psychological perceptions can sometimes be fine. Accordingly, the causes of alienation and subsequent transience are not always so obviously measurable. Intimidation or overt racism may cause some kids to change schools, but still others are motivated by loneliness, finding themselves bereft of a committed peer group, or feeling trapped in the kinds of uncaring school environments that can cause despairing adolescents to look elsewhere for a sense of belonging. Kary ran away from home during her freshman year, perhaps reacting to her sense of not belonging or her feelings of abandonment. Her mother, a drug addict, was long out of the picture by that time. Were it not for her grandparents, she may well have ended up in a foster home. "She was trying to find a man on a white horse," Kary's grandmother recounted ruefully, "but she didn't." A few months later Kary moved back home, but her school was not willing to reinstate her. "I didn't want to leave the magnet school I attended in ninth grade and I wanted to get back into it when I came back from Kansas—but I couldn't get back in," she lamented.

Among transient interviewees who made their own decision to change high schools, reactive mobility proves to be the norm, but adolescents may also make strategic school changes. At the end of his sophomore year, Roberto, a second generation Mexican American, changed schools because he wanted to "hang with old friends" from junior high and win a starting position on the football team. "My friends at Naperville High told me their football team was less, so I decided if I was going to change schools, I'd go there...first, my friends were there. Second, the football team was less, so I had a better chance of playing." In this case—at least from Robert's perspective—less really seemed like more, enough so to inspire a non-promotional school change.

Strategic mobility can sometimes even be transnational, part of the immigrant's leap-of-faith that there will be better opportunities elsewhere. Fernando, for example, initiated a particularly bold school change by emigrating from Mexico to the U.S where his mother was already living. "First, I went to a place that's set up for immigrants where they asked for my vaccination records and my birth certificate," he recalled. "Later they gave me a physical examination and then I had to take a test to see how much I already know. Finally they sent me to Vasconcellos High School." The red tape of immigration failed to discourage Fernando from pursuing his American dream, and high school was among the first steps he would take to achieve it.

School-initiated student mobility. Finally, besides family- and student-initiated types of mobility, there is the growing phenomenon of mobility as precipitated by the schools themselves (Gotbaum, 2002)—what can most accurately be categorized as a reactive kind of student mobility, known euphemistically as an "Opportunity Transfer" or "OT." Interviews with school personnel were particularly informative regarding OTs. Many teachers readily criticized the practice as counterproductive. "Opportunity Transfers—that's just a revolving door, another euphemism," said one rather indignant teacher. "What it means basically is if a student's in trouble, the principal will kick them out." Another teacher seized the opportunity of our interview to dissent from the prevailing practice of the OT as disciplinary action and affirm his own autonomous practices: "I do my own discipline because I don't want kids thrown into that structure that does nothing but shuffle the cards."

The fact is that, although OTs are sometimes employed to address problems such as fighting in school, often the "cards" are "shuffled" for less egregious reasons, such as students' poor attendance or flagging grades—particularly in the context of policy changes that simultaneously demand greater school-level accountability and higher graduation standards for students (e.g., the New York State Regents exam). Julio was forced to change high schools in the middle of his senior year because of accumulating absences from class. "My grades were fine when I left and everyone was wondering, 'Why did you leave?'" he recalled. His tardiness and truancy were not entirely his fault; his family changed residences the summer before his senior year, making the high school commute far more difficult and time-consuming than it had been before. Nevertheless, the school's attendance guidelines were to be enforced. "Warrenville—it's very strict on seniors. You can't make up hours and you can't make up attendance when you miss school."[49] Julio was subjected to an OT for problems with attendance, whereas Becky, who was born in Israel and immigrated to the U.S. as a young child, was kicked out of high school midway through her sophomore year at least partly because of faltering grades. "What sucks is how they kick you out for little things! I mean, they coulda' let me stay," she lamented. "They would give me all these reasons, try to catch me on stuff..."

Clearly, one of the principles involved in conducting these interviews in the field is to gather students' perspectives on their situation and the educational choices they did or did not exercise. It may be the case, however, that the reasons students themselves give for changing schools may not be fully adequate explanations—some may rationalize their own misfortune and interpret disciplinary problems as arbitrarily imposed punishments. Still we do not have to take just these students' word for it that school officials frequently deploy the OT irresponsibly. Case studies of urban high schools as well as analyses of New York City Department of Education data (Gotbaum, 2002) document that school officials do actively try to "get rid of troublemakers" by telling them they must leave (Bowditch, 1993; Fine, 1991; Rumberger & Larson, 1998). Moreover, to the extent that emergent federal and state accountability schemes are putting increasing pressure on schools to demonstrate standardized test-score improvement (as opposed, say, to increased student retention rates), the OT option seems likely to become an even more attractive "tool" not just for removing troublemakers, but for shuffling under-performing students, such as Becky, elsewhere so as not to tarnish schools' educational performance statistics (Gotbaum, 2002; Lewin & Medina, 2003; Medina & Lewin, 2003; Lewin, 2004).

Summary

In this chapter, then, I have accounted for the gap in twelfth grade test score performance in light of the striking Mexican American socioeconomic disadvantage and the marked increase in the population of working-age Mexican immigrants whose children (second-generation Mexican Americans) have swelled the ranks of the U.S. school population (Hayes-Bautista, Schink & Chapa, 1988; Portes & Rumbaut, 2001). Even when we account for these factors, however, the achievement gap persists. Thus, I have attempted to elaborate in greater detail the incidence and causes of student mobility, through simultaneous analysis of survey and field data. By employing the survey data in terms under which findings may be generalized to the population at large, and incorporating the interview analyses to describe some of the causes of student mobility, we find that the vast majority of Mexican American and most non-Latino White adolescents change schools non-promotionally over the course of their primary and secondary school careers. At the secondary level, however, Mexican Americans are prone to especially high rates of student mobility and are over-represented among the highly mobile. This is not an altogether surprising finding in light of the fact that mobility is especially pronounced among low SES urban school districts with predominantly minority and immigrant students (McDonnell & Hill 1993; Rumberger, 2003; LAUSD, 2004). As I have emphasized, even the most stable generation of Mexican American adolescents change schools non-promotionally at higher rates than the most mobile generation of non-Latino Whites, and these are conservative estimates, since the disproportionately mobile group of *NELS:88* dropouts (many of whom are Mexican American) have been excluded from the sample.

Why, then, do students make non-promotional school changes? Mobility among elementary school students is obviously the result of decisions made by parents, but families also initiate school changes that affect adolescent youth as well. These changes are often quite sudden, coming in the wake of a divorce or job relocation, further intensifying the economic pressures parents already face. Then too adolescents also make their own decisions to change schools, and in these cases moves are, again, often quite sudden, occurring mid-school year as opposed to, say, during summer break. A great portion of student mobility at the secondary level appears to be reactive in nature, arrived at far less often than we might wish through strategic forethought. Finally, school-initiated student mobility—what is euphemistically, even perhaps cynically called the "Opportunity Transfer" option—plays a significant role in perpetuating the reactive dimension of student mobility among transient adolescent youth. Although thoughtful strategies sometimes underlie deliberate school changes—and this is the kind of flexibility that would present the positive face of mobility within what is becoming an increasingly choice-based education system—we cannot afford to think only of best-case scenarios that do not appear to be the predominant ones. The increasingly intense focus on accountability for test scores and graduation rates at the school level may inadvertently encourage administrators and other institutional agents to cast a blind eye to the needs of highly mobile student populations. If schools cannot, and are not encouraged to exemplify the sort of institutional staying power that helps keep students from changing schools, we may continue, instead, to exacerbate the card-shuffling process to the detriment of those adolescents in our secondary schools who face the most explicit educational challenges.

---

[44] These group-level differences in nativity status are corroborated by other research showing that immigrants constitute a rapidly growing portion of U.S. Latinos (Hayes-Bautista et al., 1988; Portes & Rumbaut, 2001). By the mid-nineties, nearly 70 percent of all working-age Latino adults were immigrants, and Latino children were overwhelmingly the children of immigrants (Stanton-Salazar, 2001).

[45] Smith's (2003) findings, recently published in *The American Economic Review,* are particularly compelling, however, in that he tracked educational attainment among Latinos of Mexican descent over successive generations rather than taking a single snapshot of Latinos in any one year.

[46] It should be noted, however, that the vast majority of Mexican Americans in *NELS:88* evidence socioeconomic status levels below the mean SES level of the entire sample.

[47] Snowball sampling techniques may have led to a bias in the interview data, since high mobility rates among White interviewees are largely due to the highly mobile White males included in the interview sample. For this reason, the survey data and the interview data are interpreted in different ways, with the former addressing nationally representative generalizable trends and the latter offering more nuanced description of the *mobility/social capital dynamic*.

[48] That non-Latino White interviewees appear to be somewhat more likely than their Mexican American counterparts to initiate a school change on their own, however, runs contrary to the findings of a national study of multi-ethnic eighth to twelfth graders which found that Latino youth are much more likely to make academic decisions alone (61 percent) compared to 33 percent of Whites (Catsambis & Garland, 1997).

---

[49] Some teachers contend that the children of working-class Latinos are particularly vulnerable to being transferred to another school. "My experience as a teacher—and I have a lot of it—is that schools transfer Hispanic kids because the parents will not protest," said a teacher in a high school with a large Mexican American population. "Hispanic parents are more fearful and more respectful…The middle-class White parents would say, 'You're not transferring my kid!'"

CHAPTER 5

Group-Level Differences in the *Availability* of Social Capital by Socioeconomic and Nativity Status

> *Man is a knot, a web, a mesh into which relationships are tied. Only those relationships matter.*
>
> — Antoine de Saint-Exupéry, *The Little Prince*

While socioeconomic disadvantage, high rates of reactive mobility, and low test scores constitute some of the pressing challenges faced by Mexican origin youth, research also suggests that close-knit personal social networks embodied, for example, in Mexican familism (Valenzuela, 1990; Valenzuela & Dornbusch, 1994), or students' more public relations with school personnel (Stanton-Salazar, 2001) can act to mitigate the burdens of transience (Hagan et al., 1996) as well as other challenges associated with minority status in the United States (Vélez-Ibañez & Greenberg, 1992; Zhou & Bankston, 1998). The premise here—specifically that mitigative stocks of certain forms of social capital vary by race/ethnicity—has largely escaped the attention of social scientists (Brehm & Rahn, 1997; Fuller & Hannum, 2002). This lacunae in the research literature is partly the consequence of complex measurement issues, since social capital, unlike material capital (i.e., income and assets), is a communal postulate resisting simple quantification. Due to its opacity, inequitable distribution of social capital may perpetuate inequality in ways that merit closer scrutiny (Loury, 1977; Granovetter, 1985; Portes, 1998).

As any accountant knows, some resources are more readily quantifiable than others. Even ordinary monetary capital can sometimes be difficult to measure. I'm no accountant, however, so I place a call to mine, asking him whether there's a continuum of difficulty in that profession for assessing various kinds of economic resources and related transactions. After initial greetings, the conversation (abridged version) goes something like this:

> Author: I've got a sort of funny question for you, related to that book I'm writing.
> Accountant: Fire away.
> Author: Can you give me an example of a kind of resource an accountant would find easily quantifiable in preparing someone's tax return, and an alternative example of something of taxable value that is actually quite difficult to quantify?
> Accountant: Well, the W-2s and 1099s are simple. For me, that's the boring part of the tax return. But various types of financial transactions, such as the exchange of real estate properties or various types of business transactions... these are much more complex, partly because so many people operate their financial lives based on their trust of other people, including their attorneys and business partners. They simply don't document their transactions. So five different accountants take a look at the same tax return and offer five different answers because so much of this work is interpretation. It's like a piece of art, you know, make a little tweak here and a little tweak there and—voilà.

While I went to him searching for a better sense of the kinds of *economic* resources an accountant might find difficult to quantify, he instead emphasizes "trust" as a sort of invisible asset (social capital) not readily measured for value and subsequent taxability. Not the answer I was seeking, perhaps, but one that nevertheless brings me closer to my point: quantifying available stocks of social capital—those resources embedded in social networks that can be released *via* social exchange—is a complex process. In this chapter I offer no direct answer to the question of actually how much social capital is available to Mexican Americans and non-Latino Whites. But by exploring group-level comparisons of the social capital inhering in the informal personal social networks constitutive of family and peer relationships and also operative in public social networks (such as the formal relationships that adolescents foster in neighborhoods and in schools), we can begin to answer questions about the availability of social capital in at least relative terms—in other words, in terms of "less" versus "more." Moreover, by referencing the individual items that contribute to the social capital constructs (see Table 3.2) we can make our comparisons slightly more understandable.

Notably, we find that Mexican Americans face comparable disadvantages in terms of social capital accumulation in the family, peer and community domains. Although Mexican Americans report advantages over their White counterparts in terms of available stocks of social capital in the *school* domain, significant gaps in twelfth grade test score performance belie whatever school-based relational advantage the survey analyses reveal. Among Mexican origin youth, poverty, high rates of transience, and what appears to be an overall lack of social capital can overshadow the social buffer school personnel attempt to offer them.

Family Social Capital

Since social exchange between parents and their children harbors the potential to advance student achievement on various fronts, it can be characterized as a form of family social capital (McNeal, 1999; Park & Palardy, 2004). Indeed, when parents are involved, children typically do better in school. Parents can act as advocates beyond the boundaries of the immediate family, initiating contact with school personnel and with other parents to enhance their children's educational experiences. The latter form of family social capital, the practice by which parents form links with the parents of their children's peers, is sometimes referred to as "intergenerational closure" (Coleman, 1988). These networks make it possible for parents to work in unison not only to keep tabs on their children, but also to collaborate for the purpose of influencing school personnel (Stevenson & Baker, 1987; Carbonaro, 1998; Horvat et al., 2003). Beyond the beneficial individual-level effects of parent involvement in the lives of their children, there is the benefit to the schools themselves. One recent study suggests that student achievement improves for students attending schools with elevated levels of parental involvement (Sui-Chu Ho & Willms, 1996).

Given the family-oriented culture described in the extensive literature on Mexican familism (Gilbert, 1978; Buriel, 1984; Keefe, 1984; Valenzuela, 1990; Vélez-Ibañez & Greenberg, 1992; Valenzuela & Dornbusch, 1994), it is perhaps surprising (per Table 5.1) that Mexican Americans average .24 SD below non-Latino Whites in terms of the availability of various forms of family social capital.

Table 5.1. Mean Comparisons of Family Social Capital among Mexican Americans and non-Latino Whites

	Mexican American (N=1,141)		Non-Latino White (N=10,907)		ΔMean
	Mean	SD	Mean	SD	M.A. – W.
Family Social Capital, 12th Grade					
Omnibus Family Social Capital (FSC)	-.16	.68	.08	.56	-.24**
***Parents Involved in Student's Education* (FSC1)**	-.16	.94	.09	.74	-.25**
***Parents Know Student's Friends' Parents* (FSC2)**	-.14	.80	.08	.68	-.22**

NOTES: M.A.: Mexican American; W.: non-Latino White. ΔMean = difference in mean (Mexican Americans - non-Latino Whites). $*p<.05$ $**p<.01$. For mean-level comparisons of social capital, items that contribute to the composites are standardized to a mean of zero and a standard deviation of one, then averaged. Statistics weighted (*f2pnlwt/mean f2pnlwt*). SOURCE: *National Education Longitudinal Study of 1988*, panel of 1988 eighth-grade students resurveyed in 1990 and 1992, excluding dropouts.

It seems likely, however, that these results are at least partly due to the large socioeconomic gap and group-level differences in nativity status that differentiate Mexican origin youth in the *NELS:88* sample from their non-Latino White counterparts (again, see Appendix B).

Family Social Capital by SES and Immigrant Status

The more nuanced analyses of family social capital in the survey data suggest that the unique challenges faced by Mexican Americans—including the struggles of lower socioeconomic status, as well as the special burdens of immigration and of adolescents' rapid acculturation—are not without implication for family social capital accumulation. In fact, students whose socioeconomic status is below the sample mean are particularly disadvantaged (in terms of average levels of family social capital) in comparison to those who benefit from above average SES. Moreover, stocks of family social capital among Mexican American immigrants pale in comparison to the stocks of social capital available to their second and third+ generation counterparts, as is suggested by Table 5.2.

Table 5.2. Family Social Capital by Demographic Characteristics

	Omnibus family social capital composite (FSC)			***Parent Involved in Student's Education* (FSC1)**			***Parent Knows Student's Friends' Parents* (FSC2)**		
	M.A.	W.	ΔMean	M.A.	W.	ΔMean	M.A.	W.	ΔMean
SES									
Below the mean	-.38	-.12	-.26**	-.41	-.16	-.25**	-.31	-.05	-.26**
Above the mean	.05	.15	-.10*	.12	.19	-.07	-.01	.11	-.12*
Nativity Status									
Immigrant	-.61	-.01	-.60**	-.75	.08	-.83**	-.45	-.08	-.37**
Second	-.29	.06	-.35**	-.32	.09	-.41**	-.23	.04	-.27**
Third+	-.15	.04	-.19**	-.12	.03	-.15**	-.17	.05	-.22**

NOTES: M.A.: Mexican American; W.: non-Latino White. ΔMean = difference in mean (Mexican Americans - non-Latino Whites). $*p<.05$ $**p<.01$. For mean-level comparisons of social capital, items that contribute to the composites are standardized to a mean of zero and a standard deviation of one, then averaged. Statistics weighted *(f2pnlwt/mean f2pnlwt)*. SOURCE: *National Education Longitudinal Study of 1988*, panel of 1988 eighth-grade students resurveyed in 1990 and 1992, excluding dropouts.

Interview Findings. While not a single parent/guardian interviewee failed to express interest in and support for the educational advancement of their children,[50] immigrant parents—who commonly see fulfillment of their ambitions not in their own achievement but in that of their offspring (Portes & Rumbaut, 2001)—consistently report limitations in their *ability* to assist with their adolescents' schooling. What's more, the immigrant parent/child bond may be susceptible to the language and cultural differences exacerbating the "generation gap" between immigrant parents and their U.S.-born children (Buriel, 1984; Buriel & Cardoza, 1988; Suarez-Orozco & Suarez-Orozco, 1995; Valenzuela, 1999).

Margarita Nogales' sophomore year experience reflects these overall findings. Her mother immigrated from Zacatecas with only a third grade education. Today she is unemployed, single, and continues to navigate through her life in the United States as a Spanish-speaker. She reports an ongoing struggle to make ends meet, and communication barriers have frustrated her efforts to intervene on behalf of her daughter's schooling. "I've gone to Margarita's school to tell them that she qualifies for the reduced lunch program," Señora Nogales said. "But they tell me she doesn't qualify. They should help me because sometimes I can't...I go to the school, but since I hardly understand English, they should help me like they're supposed to." It seems that the importance Sra. Nogales places on her daughter's education does not readily translate into a substantive comprehension of what Margarita is going through in school, and what her specific role should be in assisting her daughter through the educational gauntlet.

In addition to her difficulties communicating with school personnel, Sra. Nogales also worries about the sort of disconnect that characterizes her relationship with Margarita. Most poignantly, she says that it hurts when Margarita reproaches her for referring to her daughter as *mi'ja* ("my daughter"):

> She doesn't communicate with me. I don't know what the motive is. I sometimes talk to her and she doesn't like me to say, *mi'ja* – she doesn't like me to ask her too much.

Analyzing immigrant parent-adolescent conflict, Ruben Rumbaut, drawing from the data collected from the Children of Immigrants Longitudinal Study (CILS),[51] finds that teenage daughters are significantly more likely than sons to report conflicts with their immigrant parents (Rumbaut, 1996). In his extensive ethnographic study of Mexican origin youth, Stanton-Salazar (2001) corroborates this finding. Both studies explain this conflict as involving a clash between restrictive behavioral standards imposed by immigrant parents and the girls' increasing desire for a partial attainment of independence from parental control as they make the transition to adulthood. Parents and adolescents often have different sets of expectations and ideas about social conventions (Smetana, 1988; Collins, 1990), and these differences may be exacerbated among the children of immigrants, especially among adolescent girls. In a subsequent study of the immigrant second-generation, Portes & Rumbaut (2001) give a slightly different emphasis to familial relations among Mexican immigrants, finding that despite intergenerational pressures of acculturation, most children of immigrants—and in particular youth of Mexican origin—get along fairly well with their parents and are not likely to report feeling embarrassed by their parents' cultural ways. Unlike Margarita, for example, Marlén enjoys a strong friendship with her immigrant mother. Still her mother also frets about the language barriers that prohibit her from being more involved in Marlén's schooling. "I can't help Marlén with her studies. Sometimes they [school personnel] ask for things in school and I can't help her. And I would like it—well, if there's a possibility that the school can help me, I would appreciate it with all my heart."

According to the interview data and a substantial body of research, Latino immigrant parents experience various challenges inhibiting their ability to communicate with school personnel or sometimes with their own children (Delgado-Gaitan & Trueba, 1991; Fernandez-Kelly & Schauffler, 1996; Valenzuela, 1999; Reese, 2001; Menjivar, 2002). Such difficulties appear to be associated with a lack of education, language barriers, and employment-related demands. The percentage of Mexican American children of immigrants far exceeds second-generation youth of European descent, which not only reflects shifting demographics in the United States, but also helps explain what appears to be a relative lack of family social capital as measured here among Mexican Americans in the *NELS:88* sample. It seems that socioeconomic disadvantage and intergenerational dynamics can contribute to family social de-capitalization and perhaps also to group-level differences in achievement that disadvantage Mexican origin youth.

Peer Social Capital

A child's peers exhibit extraordinary influence on his or her school-related activities, including classroom behavior, school attendance, and time spent on homework (Steinberg et al., 1992), and this is especially true during adolescence (Hymel et al., 1996). In turn, peer social capital has been linked with students' academic development (Mehan et al., 1994) and their overall success in school (Vosk et al., 1982; Dishion, 1990; Pittman, 1991). At the same time, school orientation and its social construction among adolescent peers may also differ across groups of students, in one instance encouraging educational advancement while in another catalyzing school disengagement among disaffected youth who share anti-school attitudes (Eckert, 1989; Ogbu 1992; Flores-González, 2002; Gibson et al., 2004).

The group-level comparisons of social capital in Table 5.3 suggest that Mexican Americans, on the whole, may not only be disadvantaged in terms of family social capital as it is operationalized in this study, but perhaps also in terms of the resources that inhere in relations among peers.

Table 5.3. Mean Comparisons of Peer Social Capital among Mexican Americans and non-Latino Whites

	Mexican American (N=1,141)		Non-Latino White (N=10,907)		ΔMean
	Mean	SD	Mean	SD	M.A. - W.
Peer Social Capital, 12th Grade					
Omnibus Peer Social Capital (PSC)	-.15	.70	.01	.62	-.16**
***Student Shares Strong Connection with Peers* (PSC1)**	-.24	.83	.07	.67	-.31**
***Student's Peers Value Education* (PSC2)**	-.04	.82	-.04	.82	.00

NOTES: M.A.: Mexican American; W.: non-Latino White. ΔMean = difference in mean (Mexican Americans - non-Latino Whites). $*p<.05$ $**p<.01$. For mean-level comparisons of social capital, items that contribute to the composites are standardized to a mean of zero and a standard deviation of one, then averaged. Statistics weighted (*f2pnlwt/mean f2pnlwt*). SOURCE: *National Education Longitudinal Study of 1988*, panel of 1988 eighth-grade students resurveyed in 1990 and 1992, excluding dropouts.

Mexican Americans appear to be particularly disadvantaged—by approximately one-third of a standard deviation—as measured by available stocks of *Peer Connectedness* (PSC1), although the two groups are on par in terms of the degree to which their peers value education (PSC2).

Peer Social Capital by SES and Immigrant Status

Increases in SES and generation status also tend to reduce group-level differences in peer social capital accumulation, per Table 5.4. For example, the gap in the omnibus measure of peer social capital (PSC) as well as the gap in the *Peer Connectedness* composite are less pronounced among the sub-sample of students who enjoy above average socioeconomic status.

Table 5.4. Peer Social Capital by Demographic Characteristics

	Omnibus peer social capital composite (PSC)			***Student Shares Strong Connection with Peers* (PSC1)**			***Student's Peers Value Education* (PSC2)**		
	M.A.	W.	ΔMean	M.A.	W.	ΔMean	M.A.	W.	ΔMean
SES									
Below the mean	-.18	-.07	-.11**	-.29	-.01	-.28**	-.04	-.12	+.08*
Above the mean	.01	.06	-.05	-.02	.13	-.15**	-.01	.01	-.02
Nativity Status									
Immigrant	-.24	.16	-.40**	-.42	.24	-.66**	.01	.07	-.06
Second	-.14	.04	-.18**	-.24	.10	-.34**	-.01	.01	-.02
Third+	-.08	.01	-.09**	-.12	.07	-.19**	-.05	-.04	-.01

NOTES: M.A.: Mexican American; W.: non-Latino White. ΔMean = difference in mean (Mexican Americans - non-Latino Whites). *p<.05 **p<.01. For mean-level comparisons of social capital, items that contribute to the composites are standardized to a mean of zero and a standard deviation of one, then averaged. Statistics weighted (*f2pnlwt/mean f2pnlwt*). SOURCE: *National Education Longitudinal Study of 1988*, panel of 1988 eighth-grade students resurveyed in 1990 and 1992, excluding dropouts.

Interestingly, stocks of peer social capital tend to move in opposite directions when comparing the two groups across nativity status. Among Mexican American adolescents, for example, mean levels of the omnibus measure increase from -.24 SD among immigrant youth until they approximate the mean of the entire *NELS:88* sample among third+ generation youth (-.08 SD). Among Whites, however, mean levels of peer social capital depreciate across nativity status, declining from .16 SD among immigrant youth until they settle, among third+ generation Whites, closer to the mean of the entire sample (.01 SD). It is also significant that average comparisons of the composite *Student's Peers Value Education* suggest parity between the two groups, regardless of nativity status—a finding that contradicts notions about the emergence of oppositional identity in the context of schooling among minority students. So while Mexican origin youth may be, on the whole, slightly disadvantaged in terms of the availability of peer social capital and *Peer Connectedness* in particular, they are roughly on par with White students in terms of the degree to which their friends value education. Incremental SES increases as well as the increases in generation status tend to reduce group-level differences in the availability of various forms of peer social capital.

Interview Findings. Might the intergenerational explanation for group-level differences in family social capital also apply to the apparent lack of *Peer Connectedness* disadvantaging Mexican origin youth? Social and structural boundaries separating immigrant youth and their more acculturated peers have been documented in other studies indicating that immigrant and U.S.-born youth of Mexican descent typically associate with their respective immigrant and U.S.-born counterparts (Valenzuela, 1999). Additionally, immigrant youth tend to subdivide further according to the recency of their arrival. This is not particularly surprising in light of a long line of research showing that most adolescents, regardless of nativity status, demonstrate the homophilic tendency to choose as friends people similar to themselves (Kandel, 1978; Cairns et al., 1988; Hogue & Steinberg, 1995; Tatum-Daniel, 1997).

That being said, the interview data in this study do not bear witness to an obvious social disconnection between immigrant students and their more acculturated peers.[52] In fact, one-third of the non-immigrant Mexican American interviewees report friendships with their immigrant counterparts, and most Mexican Americans reflected on a sort of *je ne sais quoi* that motivates feelings of solidarity across nativity status groups and that harbors the potential for mutual growth and academic advancement. Samuel's friendship with a recent immigrant proved to hold just such possibility, providing him with the help he needed to improve his Spanish skills. "My friend speaks a little bit of English," he said. "When he came to my school, well, I know a little bit of Spanish and he knows a little bit of English, so we were teaching each other. That's how we built our friendship."

Structural or institutionalized aspects of schooling often create barriers to social interaction between same-age youth of different nativity status groups—barriers that immigrants and their more acculturated peers may find difficult to bridge (Matute-Bianchi, 1986; Conchas, 2001). The practice of placing non-English-speaking students in English as a second language (ESL) programs, for example, can interrupt the flow of social possibilities, creating social islands, or linguistically segregated classrooms within schools (Flores-González, 2002). Fernando and his immigrant friends have yet to cross the tacit "border" (Anzaldúa, 1999) into more mainstream youth networks, as he does not hang out with non-immigrant youth.[53]

> When I arrived at the new school, since I didn't have any friends, they put me together with other immigrants. We take English classes together. Since none of us speak English, they put us together," he said. "And from there, we begin to make friends.

So while ESL programs can serve as a space for the development of bonding social capital (Briggs, 1998; Putnam, 2000) among immigrant youth (Valenzuela, 1999), these same programs may also have the inadvertent effect of inhibiting the development of social capital bridging (Barr, 1998; Narayan, 1999; Orr, 1999) among linguistically isolated Mexican immigrants and their more acculturated peers (Romo & Falbo, 1996; Olsen, 1997; Ruiz-de-Velasco, Fix & Clewell, 2000).[54] The problem is not, as some believe, bilingual education *per se*. In fact, over the past decade at least four particularly salient studies (Ramírez et al., 1991; Greene, 1997; Thomas & Collier, 1997; Salazar, 1998) have shown that bilingual education, in general, and two-way and late-exit bilingual programs, in particular, can be effective in promoting the learning environment English language learners require in order to gradually close the gap between themselves and the average student who speaks English at home (Guerrero, 2002). Some scholars have wondered whether there is an inherent tension between meeting the needs of ELLs and integrating students across nativity status groups (Cárdenas, 1975; Zerkel, 1977). Nevertheless, educational research shows that in the collective spirit of the *Brown v. Board* (1954) and *Lau v. Nichols* (1974) Supreme Court decisions, schools can provide quality bilingual education to English language learners in integrated classroom settings while advancing the equality of educational opportunity (Stephan & Feagin, 1980; California State Department of Education, 1983; Valencia et al., 2002).

Given the large body of research documenting the importance of adolescent peer networks and the resources they make available *via* social exchange, the apparent lack of *Peer Connectedness* among Mexican origin youth merits closer attention from scholars studying peer relationships. The descriptive findings in this chapter suggest, however, that the relational challenge among Mexican American immigrants and their non-immigrant counterparts may have less to do with students' individual proclivities toward like peers than with the combined effects of homophilic tendencies, which when coupled with the language and school structured boundaries sometimes have the effect of isolating Mexican immigrants from their more acculturated peers.

Community Social Capital

Having addressed the availability of social capital that stems from informal personal social networks within families and among adolescent peers, I turn now to examine the more formal relationship networks that occur in the public sphere, specifically in neighborhoods and schools. Although few studies have investigated the direct effect of community social capital on student achievement, there is a vast literature touting the benefits that accrue to individuals and to the community when networks of social connection are made manifest *via* political and civic activism (Conway, 1991; Knack, 1992; Gutmann, 1998; McCann, 1998; Skocpol & Fiorina, 1999; Small, 2002), volunteering and altruism (Piliavin & Charng, 1990; Skocpol, 1997; Wilson & Musick, 1997), or religious participation (Roof & McKinney, 1987; Harris, 1994; Wuthnow, 1994).

While the data in Table 5.5 suggest that non-Latino Whites enjoy a comparable advantage in social capital, as reflected in mean comparisons of the omnibus composite measure (CSC), neither group appears to be particularly well-endowed with stocks of community social capital. Although Whites are just above the sample mean in civic and community involvement reflected in *Student Volunteers in the Community* (CSC1), Mexican Americans are nearly .20 SD below the sample mean. Also, neither group demonstrates particularly high rates of involvement in religious activities (CSC2), as each falls below the sample mean.

Table 5.5. Mean Comparisons of Community Social Capital among Mexican Americans and non-Latino Whites

	Mexican American (N=1,141)		Non-Latino White (N=10,907)		ΔMean
	Mean	SD	Mean	SD	M.A. - W.
Community Social Capital, 12th Grade					
Omnibus Community Social Capital (CSC)	-.14	.68	-.07	.76	-.07**
***Student Volunteers in the Community* (CSC1)**	-.19	.96	.02	1.00	-.21**
***Student Participates in Religious Activities* (CSC2)**	-.07	.82	-.06	.88	-.01

NOTES: M.A.: Mexican American; W.: non-Latino White. ΔMean = difference in mean (Mexican Americans - non-Latino Whites). *p<.05 **p<.01. For mean-level comparisons of social capital, items that contribute to the composites are standardized to a mean of zero and a standard deviation of one, then averaged. Statistics weighted (*f2pnlwt/mean f2pnlwt*). SOURCE: *National Education Longitudinal Study of 1988*, panel of 1988 eighth-grade students resurveyed in 1990 and 1992, excluding dropouts.

Community Social Capital by SES and Immigrant Status

The data in Table 5.6 reflect within-group and between-group comparisons of reported levels of community social capital across socioeconomic and nativity status groups. Comparisons between low and high SES groups, for example, suggest that there is a positive relationship between SES and the availability of community social capital for Mexican American and non-Latino White adolescents. According to between group comparisons across nativity status, Mexican Americans report comparably low levels of volunteering, as measured by the item *Student Volunteers in the Community* (CSC1). It seems that immigrants as well as second and third+ generation Mexican Americans, in comparison to their White counterparts of like nativity status, are significantly less likely to report community volunteering. As for religious participation, Mexican Americans and Whites demonstrate similar patterns of involvement, although less affluent Whites who are below the SES sample mean report, on average, less participation in religious activities than their Mexican American counterparts.

Table 5.6. Community Social Capital by Demographic Characteristics

	Omnibus community social capital composite (CSC)			***Student Volunteers in the Community* (CSC1)**			***Student Participates in Religious Activities* (CSC2)**		
	M.A.	W.	ΔMean	M.A.	W.	ΔMean	M.A.	W.	ΔMean
SES									
Below the mean	-.16	-.22	+.06*	-.24	-.19	-.05	-.07	-.19	+.12**
Above the mean	-.06	.04	-.10	.03	.17	-.14	-.05	.03	-.08
Nativity Status									
Immigrant	-.23	-.17	-.06	-.29	.03	-.32**	-.16	-.20	+.04
Second	-.12	.01	-.13**	-.23	.21	-.44**	-.03	-.03	.00
Third+	-.13	-.07	-.06	-.16	.01	-.17**	-.06	-.06	.00

NOTES: M.A.: Mexican American; W.: non-Latino White. ΔMean = difference in mean (Mexican Americans - non-Latino Whites). *$p<.05$ **$p<.01$. For mean-level comparisons of social capital, items that contribute to the composites are standardized to a mean of zero and a standard deviation of one, then averaged. Statistics weighted (*f2pnlwt/mean f2pnlwt*). SOURCE: *National Education Longitudinal Study of 1988*, panel of 1988 eighth-grade students resurveyed in 1990 and 1992, excluding dropouts.

These findings are consistent with other studies suggesting that where socioeconomic advantage exists, advantages in volunteer behavior and other more formal kinds of social capital follow (Granovetter, 1982; Piliavin & Charng, 1990; Loury, 1992; Putnam, 2000). It is not entirely surprising, then, that the stocks of social capital made manifest through community volunteering appear to be less available among Mexican origin youth. The interview data seem less striking for portraying group-level differences in various forms of community social capital than for demonstrating an overwhelming lack of availability for both groups.

Interview Findings. Only one-third of the adolescents who were interviewed report any participation in religious activities, and community participation outside of school is almost non-existent among them. In fact, only one Mexican American and one White student reported any form of organized community involvement outside of school. Parent/guardian interviewees were equally disassociated from religious participation and civic involvement. It would seem, then, that regardless of race/ethnicity, community participation is non-normative among transient lower- and working-class adolescents and their parents/guardians.

One community-level factor emerged from the interview data to distinguish Mexican Americans and Whites, namely, their relations with neighbors. Some studies report that neighborhoods are the place where overlapping social systems most greatly affect family processes and individual development (Bronfenbrenner, 1979; Bronfenbrenner, 1986; Sampson & Morenoff, 1997; Sampson, 1999). If this is so, according to interview data the inner-city neighborhood context can be particularly detrimental to Mexican origin youth. While interviewees across the board report at least knowing their neighbors, how they experience the apparent downside of some neighborly relationships differs markedly. Although Whites reflected sporadically on the overbearing neighbor whose inquisitive nature borders on the intrusive—as Kary, now a senior in high school, recalled with irritation, "They're just into everything,"—some Mexican Americans report a more threatening aspect of the neighborhood downside, including violence and vandalism.

The comments of Iván's father embodied this sentiment. Other than traveling from home to work and back, Iván's parents rarely ventured outside of their own backyard. "We know some of our neighbors—one lady over there and another over here, but we are not close with any of them," said Iván's father. "We don't go out too much, you know? We just stay in the house. It's better to stay in the house than have a *bullet* in your head!"

Julio's family expressed similar concern about community safety and its constraining affect on neighborliness. In fact, they hardly know any of their neighbors, and their interactions with *vecinos* were sometimes spiked with acrimony. "When we moved here our whole wall was tagged, even over the fence," recalled Julio's mother. "I talked to the neighbor and I said, 'You know what? You got to talk to your friends. We *live* here. Don't you understand it's bad enough for us being Chicanos that are discriminated against? You guys are the main ones making the neighborhood look bad,' I told him."

Although research shows that well-established communities of co-ethnics are capable of enforcing external demands and internal constraints (Rumbaut, 1994; Portes, 1995), the interview data corroborate the concern that at least some urban neighborhoods—in their socioeconomic, geographical and segregated manifestations

(Wilson, 1987; Massey & Eggers, 1990)—exacerbate the consequences of poverty, and can even function as "invisible social prisons" for the urban poor (Stanton-Salazar, 2001), where it's not worth "dodging bullets" for a stick of butter.

School Social Capital

Students' and parents' relations with school personnel also constitute a formal and public form of *school* social capital, since the resources that inhere in school-based social networks are convertible into (a) student engagement and expectations for school achievement (Goodenow, 1993; Snyder, Morrison & Smith, 1996; Carbonaro, 1998), (b) young people's perception of the extent to which youth find school a welcoming or alienating place (Valenzuela, 1999; Stanton-Salazar, 2001), and (c) students' social and emotional well-being and subsequent educational success (Bensman, 1994; Ryan et al., 1994; Lee & Smith, 1999; Crosnoe et al., 2004).

In apparent contrast to research suggesting minority students and their parents often find it especially difficult to acquire school social capital because of their lack of "connectedness" with institutional agents (Alexander, Entwisle & Thompson, 1987) and because of their disinclination to seek help from mainstream school personnel (Courtney & Noblit, 1994; Stanton-Salazar & Dornbusch, 1995; Valenzuela, 1999), Mexican American survey respondents appear to be advantaged in terms of *Academically Relevant Teacher/Student Interaction* (SSC1). Mean differences fail to materialize when comparing stocks of *School-Initiated Interaction with Student's Parents* (SSC2), per Table 5.7.

Table 5.7. Mean Comparisons of School Social Capital among Mexican Americans and non-Latino Whites

	Mexican American (N=1,141)		Non-Latino White (N=10,907)		ΔMean
	Mean	SD	Mean	SD	M.A. - W.
School Social Capital, 12th Grade					
Omnibus School Social Capital (SSC)	.00	.64	-.05	.58	+.05*
***Academically Relevant Teacher/Student Interaction* (SSC1)**	.02	.73	-.05	.69	+.07**
***School-Initiated Interaction with Student's Parents* (SSC2)**	-.04	.81	-.03	.80	-.01

NOTES: M.A.: Mexican American; W.: non-Latino White. ΔMean = difference in mean (Mexican Americans - non-Latino Whites). *p<.05 **p<.01. For mean-level comparisons of social capital, items that contribute to the composites are standardized to a mean of zero and a standard deviation of one, then averaged. Statistics weighted (*f2pnlwt/mean f2pnlwt*). SOURCE: *National Education Longitudinal Study of 1988*, panel of 1988 eighth-grade students resurveyed in 1990 and 1992, excluding dropouts.

School Social Capital by SES and Immigrant Status

According to the mean level comparisons of school social capital in Table 5.8, there is an interesting anomaly among youth of Mexican descent. To whit, while greater stocks of family, peer, and community social capital are found among adolescents whose socioeconomic status is above the sample mean, the social interaction shared among school personnel and Mexican origin youth and their parents is reportedly different. This is indicated by a sort of inverse relationship between SES and school social capital accumulation. In fact, Mexican Americans in the higher SES group appear to possess reduced stocks of school social capital in comparison to lower SES youth of Mexican ancestry. It is perhaps surprising, then, that this same pattern is not reflected in comparisons across nativity status, where Mexican Americans report similar stocks of school social capital, regardless of immigrant status. Whites, on the other hand, reflect the expected pattern, clearly benefiting from the school-based social advantage that accompanies individuals' more privileged socioeconomic status.

Table 5.8. School Social Capital by Demographic Characteristics

	Omnibus school social capital composite (SSC)			***Academically Relevant Teacher/Student Interaction* (SSC1)**			***School-Initiated Interaction with Student's Parents* (SSC2)**		
	M.A.	W.	ΔMean	M.A.	W.	ΔMean	M.A.	W.	ΔMean
SES									
Below the mean	-.01	-.15	+.14**	.03	-.10	+.13**	-.04	-.17	+.13**
Above the mean	-.08	.01	-.09*	.01	-.01	+.02	-.14	.05	-.19**
Nativity Status									
Immigrant	-.05	-.06	+.01	.07	-.02	+.09	-.19	-.12	-.07
Second	.01	-.03	+.04	-.09	-.06	-.03	.05	.03	+.02
Third+	-.04	-.06	+.02	.08	-.04	+.12**	-.12	-.05	-.07

NOTES: M.A.: Mexican American; W.: non-Latino White. ΔMean = difference in mean (Mexican Americans - non-Latino Whites). $*p<.05$ $**p<.01$. For mean-level comparisons of social capital, items that contribute to the composites are standardized to a mean of zero and a standard deviation of one, then averaged. Statistics weighted (*f2pnlwt/mean f2pnlwt*). SOURCE: *National Education Longitudinal Study of 1988*, panel of 1988 eighth-grade students resurveyed in 1990 and 1992, excluding dropouts.

Interview Findings. On the whole, Mexican Americans and non-Latino Whites in the field study typically report similar, positive interactions with school personnel, regardless of socioeconomic background or nativity status. Every interviewee recounted that at least some teachers showed interest in the student's schoolwork, and that school officials were generally supportive of further academic endeavors, encouraging them to go on to college.

Roberto, noted earlier in this study for having made a strategic school change in order to increase his chances at getting a starting position on the high school football team, offered an especially poignant example of just how valuable teacher support can be in motivating students toward academic success:

> I kept my grades up because the teachers would really motivate us. They were after us. They would not stop—always trying to tutor us… And they were always on your back about your grades and that really helped a lot, you

> know? When you know someone cares about you, it really means a lot.

One teacher I interviewed went to somewhat incredible lengths to connect with students and their parents. "I try to contact maybe ten parents a night, just to tell them that their child is doing well… sometimes you have to push the issue," she said. Much in line with this claim, Jason, an interviewee who was struggling as a senior to remain on track to graduate in the wake of numerous school changes, reported, "All my counselors pushed me to go to college. They said it would be the best thing I ever did."

In short, according to the interview data there is little difference in the degree to which school personnel provide social support for the two groups under investigation.[55] Interviews do not offer an explanation for why Mexican Americans, and in particular, third+ generation Mexican origin youth, appear to be advantaged over their White peers in terms of the availability of *Academically Relevant Teacher/Student Interaction*. Nor does the field data explain why various forms of school social capital appear to be *less* available among high SES Mexican origin youth. The survey instrument may provide us with a partial explanation, however, since the *NELS:88* items in the *Academically Relevant Teacher/Student Interaction* composite (SSC1) are measures of students' perceived support, which does have a history of being used as a proxy for social capital (Lee & Smith, 1999; Croninger & Lee, 2001), but might be differentiated from actual social capital. In support of this point, high levels of perceived support among *Spanish-dominant* Latinos are not always correlated with actual help-seeking ties to school personnel (Stanton-Salazar, 2001). In other words, the suspect validity of the construct might partly be at work here.

Summary

Although the social capital postulate holds appeal for its potential to mitigate challenges associated with the burdens of immigrant and minority status in the United States, it remains an enigmatic resource that is difficult to measure empirically. Unlike more obvious taxable economic resources, the opacity of social capital allows its conversion to be virtually imperceptible. Thus, the advantageous as well as the potentially problematic aspects of the postulate must be carefully considered. Pairing Glen Loury's breakthrough insights regarding the way social connections facilitate differential access to opportunities for minority and non-minority youth with Mark Granovetter's (1985) criticisms of the pure market approach to economic action, including his assertions about the "embeddedness" of economic behavior, may be informative in this regard. This study, in turn, examines social capital in its various *forms*—in personal social networks within families and among peers, and also in more formal community and school settings—as well as across socioeconomic and immigrant status boundaries.

Although the descriptive findings admittedly fail to answer the question of how much social capital is available to Mexican Americans and non-Latino Whites, the comparative framework suggests that stocks of at least some forms of social capital vary significantly between racial/ethnic groups. Socioeconomic and intergenerational barriers facing immigrant and non-immigrant Chicanos may partly explain these differences, since Mexican immigrant parents face challenges that inhibit their ability to communicate with school personnel and sometimes even with their own children. Moreover, language and spatial boundaries segregating Mexican immigrants from their more acculturated peers—as well as a widespread tendency among immigrants (like the rest of us) to choose friends who are similar to themselves—are factors combining to contribute to the overall lack of *Peer Connectedness* among youth of Mexican descent. In terms of community social capital, depressed levels of volunteer behavior in the Mexican American sample may be attributed to socioeconomic disadvantage. Yet, while Mexican Americans face comparable deprivation in terms of the forms of social capital employed in the family, peer, and community domains in this study, they report comparable social network advantages in and around the school domain.

What is it about students' relations with teachers and school personnel that—contrary to prevailing notions—gives some advantage to Mexican Americans in secondary schools? Since the underlying social organization of everyday life is more complicated than what is herein reflected by the constructs of social capital, the reader may be left with any number of outstanding questions. What seems clear, however, is that more research is required to examine the impact of group-level differences on the availability of social capital. In the meantime, significant gaps in twelfth grade test score performance suggest that socioeconomic disadvantage, differences in nativity status, high rates of transience and what appears to be an overall lack of social capital significantly outweigh the apparent social buffer school personnel offer Mexican origin youth.

---

[50] This finding is corroborated, in part, by the work of Harriet Romo (1986), who compared the perspectives of recent Mexican immigrant parents, legal residents, and parents of Mexican descent whose families had resided in the U.S. for generations. In short, Romo's works suggests that Mexican origin parents, across generations, place great value on the educational advancement of their children.

[51] The CILS is among the largest surveys of teenage second-generation youth in the U.S., representing more than 77 nationalities. The survey includes a total of 5,266 eighth- and ninth-graders in 42 schools in San Diego, California, and South Florida (Miami and Fort Lauderdale).

[52] At least one parent, Iván's father, provides anecdotal evidence of intergeneration tension, however. His comments are in reference to frustrating interactions with school personnel:

> We would go and we would have interviews with the principal and teachers, but the teachers that we met – I didn't like them because they were the old *Cholo* type…I mean, well, we're not accustomed – we're Mexicans, but we don't like *Cholos*. These guys act the old *Cholo* style, let's say like during the 1950s. They don't want to be a Mexican and they don't want to be an American, so they're kinda divided between the Mexicans and the Americans. I mean, for *real* Mexicans, that type of Mexican people – personally, they're kinda renegades. They don't know if they want to be a Mexican or an American. But that's my own thought.

[53] This reference to "border crossing" (Anzaldua, 1999; Lewis-Charp, Yu & Friedlaender, 2004), refers to the adaptation that low-income minority adolescents must undergo in order to cope with incongruities in values, beliefs, expectations and actions (Erickson, 1987) that characterize the

disparate home and school environments—the "multiple worlds" (Phelan, Davidson & Yu, 1998)—they must frequently navigate.

[54] The boundaries separating immigrant and non-immigrant youth go far beyond the school cafeteria and ESL classes, however. In the sprawling Los Angeles Latino metropolis, for example, the new immigrant core clusters around downtown and southcentral, while the more politically enfranchised suburban belt of well-off Chicanos—households earning more than $35,000—live in the San Gabriel Valley (Davis, 2001).

[55] This is not to imply, however, that mobile students are embedded in a consistent and coordinated web of teachers, counselors, and staff. On the contrary, most students recall sporadic support from certain institutional agents under particular circumstances.

CHAPTER 6

Informal Social Networks and the *Mobility/Social Capital Dynamic*

> *Yeah, moving affected most of my friendships. I was moved into those places and I didn't know anybody and so I didn't really want to go and not fit in and feel out of place. I would usually just go home after school.*
>
> — Iván, second generation Mexican American

I have assumed from the outset of this study that social networks influence school performance and that this idea is not a novel one. Nevertheless, the process by which the resources embedded in social networks become available to students so as to benefit academic performance is less well understood than it should be. For instance, with Melissa, an immigrant from Mexico, her close-knit network of friends took the initiative and deployed their know-how to her benefit. Well aware that she was struggling to complete a difficult algebra assignment, her friends reached out almost instinctively. "They're like…'Do you need help?'" she recalled, "and I'm like 'Yeah – can you?' They really helped me a lot!" This freed her from having to undertake a more costly help-seeking effort beyond the bounds of her intimate peer group, and probably contributed to the subsequent improvement of her algebra grades. There are perhaps too few students fortunate enough to have peers who reach out to them in such a proactive fashion; more consistently the challenge is for students to enact more assertive help-seeking behaviors. Much of the field data in this study serve to uncover the processes by which embedded resources are unleashed, especially *via* social exchange, among the personal networks that include the social fabric of families and the influence of adolescent peer groups. One of the most obvious costs of student mobility (the example of Iván cited in my epigraph above is only one such exemplary case) is that it interrupts social networks and sometimes serves to isolate students, impinging on their informal relationship ties and hindering the accumulation of social capital.

Beyond the question of how social capital gets used and the degree to which mobility detracts from its accretion and short-circuits the process of its conversion, there is a question about whether different forms of social capital give evidence of differential exchange value. Having already reviewed social capital in terms of group-level differences with regard to its *availability*, in this chapter and the next I investigate domain-specific forms of social capital with emphasis on its *convertibility* into valued educational outcomes. In addition, I discuss the varied consequences of student and residential mobility on this process.

The *Dynamic* Within Families

The interview data provide numerous examples of how parent advocacy and support can contribute to academic improvement among adolescents. Sometimes family support occurs in the form of parents' direct intervention in their adolescent's schooling experiences. In other cases, the support is of a more affective nature, realized through parent/adolescent interactions and by way of the moral imperatives that parents and other older family members instill in the younger generation.

Barbara's case was an example of the former type, characterized by her mother's intervention in her schooling. By the end of her junior year, Barbara was well on her way to dropping out of high school, and her involvement in a magnet program, which forced her to spend a great deal of time in transit, was not improving things. She was often tired from the long bus rides, and her education suffered. Just when she was on the brink of dropping out, however, her mother intervened forcefully and effectively, helping to get Barbara back on track. After strategically shopping around for alternative school placements, Mrs. McKay and her husband became convinced that North Bay High School had a program that suited their daughter. Mrs. McKay reflected on her meeting at the school:

> Before the magnet deadline, I made an appointment with North Bay's guidance counselor. She really impressed us because the first thing she said to us was, 'I know this is a performing arts magnet and your daughter will be here to sing and dance, but she will also be taking college prep courses

> because every one of my children knows that there is no silver bullet and you have to work for what you want.' It was just such a breath of fresh air after having gone through such hell for three years at Barbara's other school!

Barbara, who does not enjoy an especially close relationship with either of her parents, was reluctant to change schools. Nevertheless, in the end, she did so, very much to her academic benefit.

Other research suggests that middle-class parents, such as Barbara's, often proceed from a distinct sense of entitlement, employing what has been called a strategy of "concerted cultivation." In exercising this strategy, parents aim to facilitate their children's social growth directly through targeted institutional interventions (Lareau, 2002). The result of Barbara's parents' concerted strategy was that she joined a performing arts group and her grades began to improve. "I'm understanding things now and yeah, my grades have picked up… they actually went through the roof 'cause I am finally in classes where there are no gaps in learning," she said.

While direct parental intervention proved to be of considerable value to Barbara, in spite of the fact—or perhaps because of the fact—that it involved a *strategic* school change, Julio, a student mentioned in the previous chapter for his problems with school attendance, benefited from a multi-dimensional and strongly normative family support structure. Both his brother-in-law and his mother are important players in his social world, and these relationships, which were imbued with significant moral weight for Julio, contributed to his perseverance in school. "I look up to my brother-in-law," Julio said. "He's a cool person, in the military....he's been there for me since I was like six years old. My whole life, he is the one I look up to. He has inspired me a lot because he did so much."

Julio's brother-in-law served as a role model and made an important, albeit largely indirect, contribution to Julio's schooling, but his mother offered consistent, concerted, and perhaps "authoritative" parental support.[56] Although neither she nor Julio's father had graduated from high school, she was determined that her son would not follow the same path. Sparing no effort to ensure that he stayed on track, she intervened, at times forcefully, throughout Julio's academic career. When Julio was in elementary school, for example, she sensed he needed special help and so went to a parent conference to speak to one of the teachers. "I need to have my son tested!" she implored. She later recalled her satisfaction at successfully pulling the levers of institutional authority to her son's benefit:

> And the counselor goes, 'You know what? Let's send him down to another counselor and have him tested.' Sure enough, they had him tested.

As it turns out, Julio had a slight learning disorder that might well have gone undetected without his mother's focused advocacy.

Although Julio continued to struggle throughout his elementary and secondary schooling, both his brother-in-law and his mother provided constant inspiration and tangible support along the way. So, while Julio's disability taxed his academic performance significantly, he finally started turning things around during his senior year of high school. His mother's moral authority and her single-minded determination to see her son graduate finally had their effect:

> There came a time when I wanted to give up. It was like, you know, 'I can't do it no more.' And then me and my mom had this talk and she told me how rough it was for her when she grew up and how history is repeating itself with me. And when she told me about my responsibilities and things I need to do in life, it woke me up! And you know what? I said, 'I can do this. I know I can do this.' And that's why I continue in school.

The actions of Julio's mother seem in many ways a model case demonstrating how personal social networks within the family, and parents' concerted efforts on behalf of their children in particular, can be effectively deployed to the educational benefit of students.

In short, the interview data can help us illustrate a few of the ways that the energy, norms, and capabilities that inhere within families can have direct impact on students' efforts and their educational output. Although middle-class families such as Barbara's have the luxury of drawing upon resources extending well beyond what is available to working- and lower-class families, the concerted efforts of Julio's mother remind us that a sense of entitlement can come in many forms, that it need not be seen as the exclusive property of the middle-class, and that it is often crucial to students' academic success. Regardless of family class status, parent-initiated contact with schools can have the effect of encouraging teachers and other school personnel to go to greater lengths to help students.

A Basic Structural Model

According to the survey data in Figure 6.1, parental involvement in students' education, coupled with the resources that can be leveraged when parents work together to help their children succeed in school, can have a direct and positive impact on twelfth grade test score performance. Since the social capital constructs are "latent" variables made up of multiple observed variables, they appear in this figure, according to structural modeling convention, in ovals.[57] Specifically here we note that a standard deviation increase in *Parents Involved in Student's Education* (FSC1) improves twelfth grade test scores by more than one-tenth of a standard deviation for both groups (.13 SD and .14 SD for Whites and Mexican Americans, respectively). In terms of actual test score points, this is not an extremely striking association. Comparatively, a similar increase in FSC1 would improve average twelfth grade math test scores by less than two points for both groups under investigation (Mexican Americans average 41 points and non-Latino Whites average 50 points on the *NELS:88* twelfth grade mathematics test).[58] Indeed, the latent measure of "intergenerational closure," *Parent Knows Student's Friends' Parents* (FSC2), makes an additionally slight contribution to test score improvement among Whites (.04 SD), although the positive coefficient among Mexican origin youth fails to reach the threshold of statistical significance.

Figure 6.1. The Mobility/Family Social Capital Dynamic

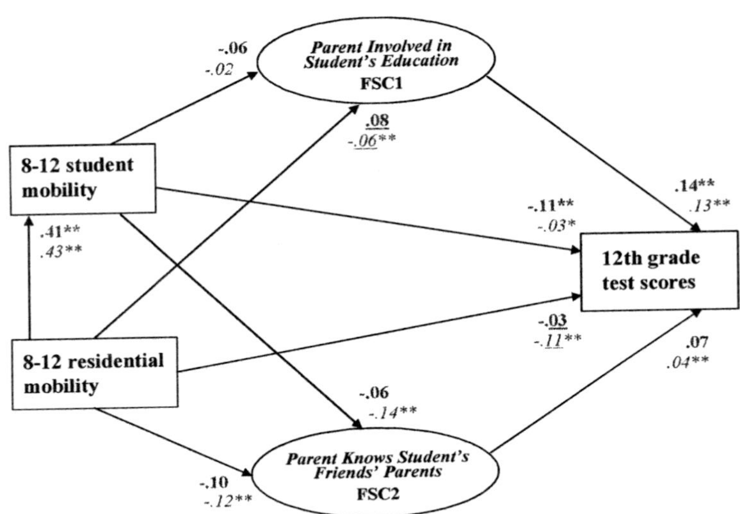

NOTES: $^{**}p<.01$; $^{*}p<.05$. Parameter estimates for Mexican Americans are shown in **bold** just above the *italicized* estimates for non-Latino Whites. The path weights are presented in standard deviation units. Underlined parameters represent statistically significant *between*-group differences in matched paths. Individual items that contribute to the social capital constructs (see Table 3.2), as well as all error terms, are excluded from the figure. I allow the errors to correlate between *Parents Involved in Student's Education* and *Parent Knows Student's Friends' Parents*; the estimate of this error correlation is .23 for Mexican Americans and .30 for non-Latino Whites ($p<.01$). Fit Indices: TLI=.99; CFI=.99; RMSEA=.02.

Both forms of family social capital are associated with slight test score improvement, but mobility encroaches on their accumulation. For example, a standard deviation increase in residential mobility (approximating one additional change of residence) decreases FSC1 and FSC2 by .06 and .12 standard deviations, respectively, among Whites (here the related impacts are not statistically significant for Mexican Americans). While at face value the fact of changing residences seems more likely to impinge on family social capital than would, say, a student's change of schools—a phenomenon which I have established may or may not be associated with a change of residence—student mobility appears also to impede family social capital accumulation. This is especially apparent in the case of intergenerational closure (FSC2) among non-Latino Whites (-.14 SD). For youth of Mexican descent, however, the negative impacts of student mobility on stocks of family social capital are insignificant.

Not only does mobility prove problematic for family social capital, but it also appears to have a direct negative impact on adolescent achievement. An additional residential move reduces twelfth grade test scores by .11 SD among non-Latino Whites, although its impact on Mexican American test score performance (-.03 SD) remains insignificant. And whereas a standard deviation increase in student mobility (approximating one additional non-promotional school change) reduces test scores only slightly for Whites (-.03 SD), its negative impact is more substantial among Mexican origin youth (-.11 SD). So while residential mobility seems to be a notable problem for Whites, the negative effect of student mobility is most egregious among Mexican American adolescents. The reasons for this differential impact, however, are thus far not entirely clear.

Interview Findings. Since mobility seems to be problematic for social capital accumulation and twelfth grade test score performance, one might expect it to detract consistently from academic achievement as measured by school grades. Here the field data begin to tell a surprising story, however, since the proportion of interviewees reporting the negative impact of mobility on school grades is similar to the proportion of students who tout its positive effects, as indicated by matrix Table 6.1.[59] Each cell entry (depicted here as an asterisk) reflects a student's explicit statement in his or her own words. From this table the consequences of student mobility appear to be related to its causes. Many interviewees associate reactive mobility with problematic outcomes—including curricular incoherence—that lead to a drop in grades. Those interviewees who initiated *strategic* school changes, or whose parents did so on their behalf, commonly report improved academic performance.[60]

Table 6.1. The Consequences of Student Mobility as Reported by Students

	School Engagement		School Completion		School Grades		
	Positive	Negative	Positive	Negative	Positive	Neutral	Negative
Mexican American	*	**** **** **** *		**** ****	**** ***	**** *	**** **** **** **
Non-Latino White	*****	**** **** ****		**** **** **** **** **	**** **** *	***	**** **** **

Jon, for example, made three school changes during high school, and each of his transfers was reactive in nature. The first time, his parents divorced, forcing him to change schools since he no longer lived in the school district where he began ninth grade. Subsequent transience followed from two separate expulsions. He recalled his experience with the initial school change, which may have set the pattern of transience in motion:

> Since I started at the middle of the year, I was so lost and I didn't know where anything was. School already started and I got zeros for stuff I missed, so it started off bad. I asked the teacher what I needed to do to catch up and she said, 'You can't – you have to start from right here.'

Like Jon, Marlén lives in her mother's single-parent household. She changed school reactively during the middle of her sophomore year, when economic hardship forced a move to a more affordable apartment. Unfortunately, Marlén was not able to re-enter school right away because her new high school was on a year-round schedule and she'd missed the starting date for the second track. Three months later she finally got back into school, but the "stop-out" hurt her school performance. "If you move when you're in the middle of the semester, then that's bad because you miss a lot," she lamented.[61]

Alternatively, Natasha's school-change, not unlike Barbara's strategic move to a performing arts magnet, speaks to the potential academic benefits of strategic mobility. As an immigrant from the Ukraine who arrived in the United States during her elementary school years, she struggled to learn English and to adapt to her new surroundings. By the time she reached high school, Natasha had begun navigating her life in a remarkably independent fashion, so much so that she took it upon herself to change schools after her freshman year (she recalled not wanting to make a mid-year school change). Like Barbara, she enrolled in a performing arts program that contributed to her academic development.

A More Fully Specified Model

Although the *mobility/social capital dynamic* among families is reflected in the basic structural model, stressful life events that may have occurred prior to the eighth grade remain unaccounted for in Figure 6.1. For example, student mobility during grades K-8 can be particularly problematic for children who live in homes characterized by socioeconomic disadvantage (DuBois et al., 1994). It follows that SES controls may be especially important in mobility-related studies. Moreover, Heinlien & Shinn (2000) have uncovered a spurious correlation between mobility and student achievement once prior achievement is included in predictive models. In light of these concerns, the more fully specified model in Table 6.2 addresses such potential omitted variable bias by including SES, K-8 student mobility, and eighth grade test scores.

Table 6.2. The *Dynamic* Within Families: Standardized Coefficients from the Structural Model

	8th Grade		Grades 8-12								12th Grade	
	Test Scores		Res. Mobility		Student Mobility		FSC1		FSC2		Test Scores	
	M.A.	W.	M.A.	W.	M.A.	W.	M.A.	W.	M.A.	W.	M.A.	W.
Exogenous Variables												
K-8 Student Mobility	.04	-.06**	.27**	.25**	.14**	.13**	.	.	.	.	.	.
SES	.31**	.45**	-.10**	-.14**	-.01	.03**	.27**	.28**	.23**	.16**	.05*	.09**
Endogenous Variables												
8th Grade Test Scores	.	.	.	.	.	.	.	.	.	.	.79**	.80**
8-12 Student Mobility	.	.	.	.	.	.	-.05	-.03*	-.07	-.15**	-.04	-.01*
8-12 Res. Mobility	.	.	.	.	.38**	.40**	.11*	-.03*	-.08	-.10**	-.05*	-.02**
FSC1	.	.	.	.	.	.	.	.	.	.	.04	.01
FSC2	.	.	.	.	.	.	.	.	.	.	-.04	-.01

NOTES: M.A.: Mexican American; W.: non-Latino White; Res.: Residential. FSC1: *Parent Involved in Student's Education*; FSC2: *Parent Knows Student's Friends' Parents*. $^{**}p<.01$; $^{*}p<.05$. Effects marked with a period (.) are not estimated in the models. Underlined coefficients differ significantly from corresponding coefficient for other racial/ethnic group (critical ratios greater than 1.96). The errors are correlated between FSC1 and FSC2; the estimated error correlations are .18 and .27 ($p<.01$), for Mexican Americans and non-Latino Whites, respectively. The model explains 67 percent of the variance in twelfth grade test scores. Fit Indices: TLI=.99, CFI=.99, RMSEA=.03.

What is immediately apparent in this more fully specified model is that eighth grade achievement is far-and-away the most powerful predictor of twelfth grade achievement. Such a finding underscores the importance of including prior achievement in predictive models that employ the *NELS:88* data, but doing this may make it difficult to identify other significant test score predictors. In fact, once one includes background controls in the model, the positive impact of family social capital on twelfth grade achievement washes out; and though student and residential mobility impinge on family social capital accumulation among non-Latino Whites, Mexican Americans appear to be largely impervious to the dynamic, with the surprise exception that residential mobility somehow contributes (.11 SD) to social capital in the form of *Parent Involved in Student's Education* (FSC1). It is also worth noting that a standard deviation increase in SES contributes strongly to stocks of family social capital for both groups—a finding consistent with the descriptive results in the previous chapter, which emphasized that children of middle-class parents have advantages over their working- and lower-class peers when it comes to the availability of resources inherent in family-based social networks. So, whereas residential mobility appears to trump student mobility in terms of its negative impact on twelfth grade test score performance, the effect sizes are quite small, -.05 SD and -.02 SD for Mexican Americans and Whites, respectively.

What are we to make of the fact that, once various background factors are taken into account, the impact of family social capital on twelfth grade test scores appears to be diminished? Some scholars argue that parental influence is efficacious at the grade school level but less so among older, more independent-minded adolescents (Carnegie Council, 1995; Schneider & Stevenson, 1999). As noted in the previous chapter, a "generation gap" between parents and adolescent youth may present notable problems for Margarita and other second-generation children of immigrants, whereas the adolescent "identity crisis" (Erikson, 1968) and notions about "individuation" (Blos, 1967) reflect a social process of experimenting with identity applicable also to students, such as Barbara, whose drive for emotional autonomy is accompanied by the "growing pains" experienced not only by the adolescents themselves, but also by their parents (Steinberg, 2001).

Though the resources that inhere in family social networks do not appear to be robust predictors of twelfth grade test scores according to the more fully specified model, there may be other forms of social capital with greater staying power among adolescents. In her controversial book, *The Nurture Assumption*, Judith Harris (1998) claims that to the extent that adolescent development is influenced by social networks, it is *peers*—and not parents—who have the strongest influence. Although Harris's work has been subjected to sharp criticism (Collins et al., 2000), her underlying premise reflects a central assumption of my own investigation—namely, that different forms of social capital, like different forms of currency, will give evidence of differential exchange value. In the section that follows, then, I explore in greater depth the relative importance of peers in the *mobility/social capital dynamic*.

The *Dynamic* Among Peers

According to the interview data, resources embedded in peer social networks can be made available, *via* social exchange, to benefit students in their educational endeavors. Whether the social capital is manifested in a good friend who is "always willing to listen," or the smart kid in the group who "gets" the tough homework assignments and takes pleasure in showing others how to do it, most interviewees attest to the advantages of pro-school *esprit de corps* among friends. The proactive support of friends and the kinds of support that bridge gaps in learning were the two most commonly observed examples of peer networks functioning as educational resources.

Adolescents in close-knit peer networks often share an implicit understanding of one another's needs, and thus embedded resources may be released *proactively* without having to be asked for. As I mentioned at the top of this chapter, Melissa's friends reached out to her when they intuited that she was struggling to complete a difficult algebra assignment. Similarly, although Jon struggled academically (his inconsistent attendance reflecting an overall lack of engagement throughout his junior year of high school), his friends were constantly pushing him along. "They look out for me," he said. "If I am spacing out or whatever, they will say, 'Hey, get back to work!'"

There may also be gender patterns implicit in the workings of social networks. Patricia, a second generation Mexican American, enjoys a group of friends who share high educational expectations. Pro-school attitudes and college aspirations are among the characteristics that define their group and for which they are known by others.

> All of my friends plan on graduating from high school and going on to college. You know, we talk about it, like, 'Oh yeah, what college are you planning to go to?'

At least some research indicates that girls are especially important sources of peer social capital among Mexican origin youth

(Valenzuela, 1999).[62] My interview data suggests further that cross-gender friendships are included in—and sometimes particularly valuable components of—the peer social capital rubric. During his sophomore year, for example, Roiter, a second generation Mexican American, relied heavily on the educational support that Christina was willing to offer him. One year ahead of Roiter in school, Christina had already successfully navigated many of the educational challenges he was now facing. Her generosity in sharing her experience and conveying some of her know-how to Roiter proved to be of real assistance when it came to challenging homework assignments and other taxing aspects of school. "She's pretty smart and she's just the type of person who is willing to help," he said.

Sometimes friends share support that can bridge learning gaps. For example, the interviews revealed numerous examples in which biliterate students offered an especially important form of *bridging* social capital. "It all depends on your ability to speak English," said Natasha. "The first people I met when I got to the U.S. were Russians and they helped me adapt to school – they helped with everything." But placing non-English-speaking students in ESL and structured English immersion programs can create barriers to social integration by segregating students within schools (Cárdenas, 1975; Valencia et al., 2002) which, in turn, may inhibit the development of bridging support between immigrants and their more acculturated peers (Romo & Falbo 1996; Olsen 1997). Indeed, a growing body of research shows that Latinos and other student groups are increasingly segregated not only among the different schools within the overall educational system (Orfield & Yun, 1999; Orfield, 2001; Frankenberg et al., 2003; Rumberger & Palardy, forthcoming), but within their individual schools due to tracking (Lee & Bryk, 1988; Gamoran & Mare, 1989; Lucas, 1999; Noguera, 2003).

Tied up with both the techniques by which peers bolster academic achievement and the structural barriers inhibiting this process, peer networks are in-and-of-themselves fraught with ambivalences, such that social pressures often conflict with academic demands (Gibson et al., 2004; Kao, 2004). Margarita said that although most of her friends "take school seriously," there are occasions when they think and act differently. "Sometimes," said the second generation youth, "They're like, 'Let's ditch and go to somebody's house.'"

Beyond students' typical ambivalences about school, there are examples of peer groups that actually take an oppositional stance to learning, which often depends on the socio-political environment in which their interactions are embedded (Gibson et al., 2004). A long line of research suggests that for every "leading crowd" there's also a "rebellious crowd" (Coleman, 1961), that where there are "jocks" there are "burnouts" (Eckert, 1989). Almost by definition, perhaps especially in urban school settings, "school-oriented" adolescent peer networks co-exist, however tenuously, alongside their "street-oriented" counterparts (Flores-González, 2002). During his freshman year, Michael joined what he called "a group of kids who are non-achievers." Two years later he and his buddies had fallen considerably behind in school, with Michael's grades plummeting. His attorney father placed the blame squarely on his son's shoulders. "He hung out with a bunch of losers. Instead of having peer pressure to succeed, it was peer pressure to fail!"

Thus, while the exchange of resources embedded in peer social networks can contribute to student achievement, there are also many structural barriers, such as tracking, that potentially isolate groups of students from other students. Moreover, according to the field data, we need to be concerned that while ambivalence expressed about school among certain peer groups may neutralize the otherwise positive impact of peer social networks on specific educational outcomes, at least some disaffected students may have been conditioned to share markedly anti-school attitudes within their peer networks that actively work against academic achievement.

A Basic Structural Model

So far, then, the interview data illustrate an upside and, to a lesser extent, what might be considered a downside to peer relations. According to the standardized parameter estimates in Figure 6.2, close-knit peer networks and the extent to which peers value education are both forms of peer social capital that contribute to student achievement. More specifically, a standard deviation increase in *Peer Connectedness* (PSC1) increases twelfth grade test scores by .14 SD for non-Latino Whites; and *Peer Connectedness* appears to be a fairly strong achievement-related predictor (.23 SD) among youth of Mexican descent (a standard deviation increase in *Peer Connectedness* would increase average twelfth grade *math* test scores from 40 to 43 points).

The degree to which *Student's Peers Value Education* (PSC2) also predicts test score improvement among non-Latino Whites (.12 SD), although the parameter in question is insignificant, even surprisingly negative, for Mexican American adolescents.

Though both forms of peer social capital impact test score performance, mobility appears to detract from peer social capital, especially the latent measure of peers' relative appreciation of education. Even one additional school change reduces *Student's Peers Value Education* among Whites and Mexican Americans by .05 and .08 SD, respectively. For Whites, residential mobility also reduces *Student's Peers Value Education* (-.05 SD), although for Mexican Americans the impact of residential mobility is not significant. Mobility may also impinge on *Peer Connectedness*, although the negative parameter estimates are small and statistically insignificant.

Interview Findings. During the course of this investigation, adolescent interviewees remained intent on reporting the negative impact of mobility on the development and maintenance of their peer relationships. Similarly, school personnel report that student mobility contributes to social de-capitalization among adolescents. One teacher reflected on the importance of social continuity among high school students, stating, "If you stay in one place you develop roots. And if you have those roots, you have a sense of belonging and then you may do better because you belong to that place." Or, as Mr. Humay, a high school counselor and basketball coach, put it, "Mobile students often feel lonely. If they don't have at least one person to bond with, a lot of them don't want to come to school."

Figure 6.2. The Mobility/Peer Social Capital Dynamic

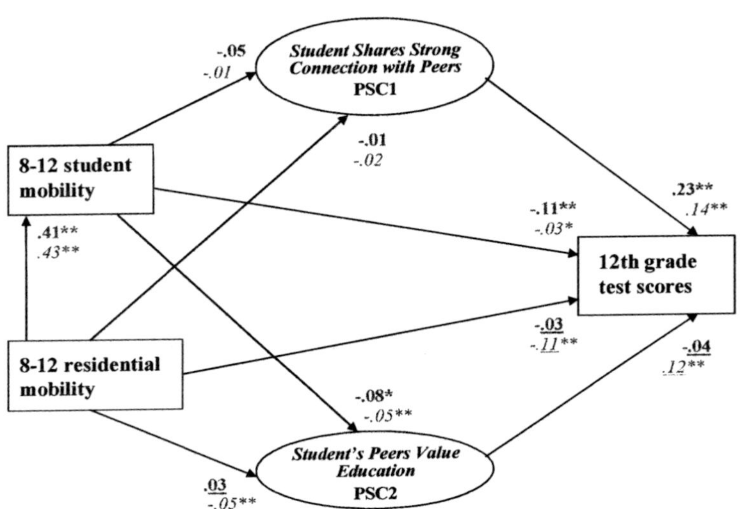

NOTES: $^{**}p<.01$; $^{*}p<.05$. Parameter estimates for Mexican Americans are shown in **bold** just above the *italicized* estimates for non-Latino Whites. The path weights are presented in standard deviation units. Underlined parameters represent statistically significant *between*-group differences in matched paths. Individual items that contribute to the social capital constructs (see Table 3.2), as well as all error terms, are excluded from the figure. I allow the errors to correlate between *Student Shares Strong Connection with Peers* and *Student's Peers Value Education*; the estimate of this error correlation is .29 and .34 ($p<.01$), for Mexican Americans and non-Latino Whites, respectively. Fit Indices: TLI=.99; CFI=.99; RMSEA=.04.

Such was the case for Iván, who attended four different high schools as a result of his father's ever-changing job requirements. Frequent mobility coupled with an admittedly shy personality intensified his social isolation. "It's hard for me to make friends – I don't socialize very much." He paused for a moment and then continued, saying, "Yeah, moving affected most of my friendships. I was moved into those places and I didn't know anybody and so I didn't really want to go and not fit in and feel out of place. I would usually just go home after school." Like Iván, Richard's parents were also born abroad—in Iran—and he, too, changed schools frequently throughout high school. Offering a bluntly negative assessment of the consequences of mobility, Richard said, "I seem to lose all of my friends when I change schools; you lose touch with one another."

Olivia, another second-generation immigrant interviewed in this study, attested that changing high schools had a negative impact on her long-standing friendships. Although she was able to make new friends after changing schools, she openly questioned the depth of those friendships:

> I made some new friends, but it's not going to be the same like the friends I had for five years in San Marino. I feel like I really don't know them the way I knew my other friends. I don't really *trust* them like I used to trust my other friends.

Thus, she was greatly limited in developing the level of trust that Coleman (1988) and others (e.g., Bryk & Schneider, 2002) see as a fundamental building block in social capital development.

A More Fully Specified Model

As I once again modify the model by adding further specification, we notice again that the hypothesized relationships between mobility, social capital, and test score performance are supported by the parameter estimates in the basic structural model. But this working model has been under-specified, insofar as students' background characteristics—including socioeconomic status, K-8 student mobility and prior test scores—remain unaccounted for. With Table 6.3, I offer a more thorough analysis of the *dynamic* among peers. As was also previously noted, prior achievement here accounts for most of the variance in twelfth grade test score performance for both groups. But even though the measurable utility of family social capital washes out of the more fully specified structural model, peer social capital remains a slightly more robust achievement-related predictor.

Table 6.3. The Dynamic Among Peers: Standardized Coefficients from the Structural Model

	8th Grade		Grades 8-12								12th Grade	
	Test Scores		Res. Mobility		Student Mobility		PSC1		PSC2		Test Scores	
	M.A.	W.	M.A.	W.	M.A.	W.	M.A.	W.	M.A.	W.	M.A.	W.
Exogenous Variables												
K-8 Student Mobility	.04	-.06**	.27**	.25**	.14**	.13**	.	.	.	.	.	.
SES	.31**	.45**	-.10**	-.14**	-.01	.03**	.21**	.20**	-.01**	.12**	.05*	.09**
Endogenous Variables												
8th Grade Test Scores	.	.	.	.	.	.	.	.	.	.	.79**	.80**
8-12 Student Mobility	.	.	.	.	.	.	-.05	-.01	-.07	-.05**	-.04	-.01*
8-12 Res. Mobility	.	.	.	.	.38**	.40**	-.02	.01**	.04	-.03**	-.05*	-.02**
PSC1	.	.	.	.	.	.	.	.	.	.	.06*	.02*
PSC2	.	.	.	.	.	.	.	.	.	.	.01	.04**

NOTES: M.A.: Mexican American; W.: non-Latino White; Res.: Residential. PSC1: *Student Shares Strong Connection with Peers*; PSC2: *Student's Peers Value Education*. $^{**}p<.01$; $^{*}p<.05$. Effects marked with a period (.) are not estimated in the models. Underlined coefficients differ significantly from corresponding coefficient for other racial/ethnic group (critical ratios greater than 1.96). The errors are correlated between PSC1 and PSC2; the estimated error correlations are .29 and .32 ($p<.01$), for Mexican Americans and non-Latino Whites, respectively. The model explains 67 percent of the variance in twelfth grade test scores. Fit Indices: TLI=.99, CFI=.99, RMSEA=.04.

Among non-Latino Whites, *Peer Connectedness* and *Student's Peers Value Education* compare favorably as significant, albeit rather slight, predictors of twelfth grade test scores (.02 SD and .04 SD, respectively). Perhaps surprisingly, however, *Peer Connectedness* is a stronger test score predictor (.06 SD) than *Student's Peers Value Education* among Mexican origin youth. The difference in the magnitude of association (.05 SD) hints at the utility of *Peer Connectedness* among Mexican American adolescents. Then too, the between-group difference in matched parameter estimates is statistically significant, suggesting that Mexican American adolescents, in comparison to their White counterparts, may be especially amenable to the beneficial aspects of *Peer Connectedness*.

Studies suggest that close-knit and trusting peer interactions—what some anthropologists and cultural psychologists have termed *confianza en confianza* (Vélez-Ibañez 1997)—may be of particular value to Mexican American adolescents (Valenzuela 1999; Stanton-Salazar 2001). Roughly translatable as "trusting mutual trust," *confianza en confianza* is a construct learned through intimate, often family-based social interactions among U.S. Latinos. As such, it is also a vehicle for self-reference, social esteem, and cultural meaning-making (Montero-Sieburth & Villarruel 2000). Ironically, however, the descriptive data in Chapter 5 show that Mexican Americans are at a significant disadvantage in terms of the availability of *Peer Connectedness* when compared to their White adolescent counterparts. Nevertheless, the direct association of *Peer Connectedness* with twelfth grade test scores eclipses the direct relevance of an entire standard deviation increase in SES, at least among adolescents of Mexican descent.[63] This is somewhat surprising, since research confirms that peer networks can encourage school success [or, in their more problematic manifestations, disengagement from school], but in any event one might reasonably expect *Student's Peers Value Education* to be comparably more powerful as an achievement-related predictor, as is in fact the case for non-Latino Whites. Again, the interview data shed light on this unanticipated, even somewhat implausible finding.

Thus, the multi-dimensionality of Julio's social network makes his case an especially intriguing one in the context of this study, since it illustrates the ways in which social capital can both increase and buffer adolescent challenges, including the seductive attractions of life in the fast lane. Julio's easy smile seems far less casual once his ambivalence about a growing-up-too-fast personal history comes to the surface, once he admits to his ongoing struggle to balance a chaotic urban party life with his goal to secure the high school diploma that previously eluded both his parents. He and his closest friends share a connection that at least sometimes emerges as educational motivation. In a comment, the significance of which is enhanced by the projective identifications implicit in it, Julio says:

> My friend, Martín, is the party type; so we actually get on him by saying, 'Come on, dude, catch up on your grades – you got to pass!' All four of us look out for each other; we are there for each other. We tell each other what we need to know, not what we want to hear.

On the surface, the attitudes of educational orientation among Julio and his friends look more like *Student's Peers Value Education* than *Peer Connectedness*, but closer scrutiny of the interview data suggests that trust and mutual respect are the sort of glue that actually makes their normative exhortations stick. In fact, Julio makes it clear that his fun-loving peers are first-and-foremost "straight-up with each other." They look out for one another. "I see my buddies as close friends. And Arturo – I see him as a brother," Julio said.

Undoubtedly there are still holes remaining in the case being made here for the importance of *Peer Connectedness* among Mexican origin youth, yet the findings of this study effectively bring us closer to an understanding of how close-knit peers often see each other and function as family members, through whom *confianza* and mutual understanding flow as resources that fortify normative expectations (Valenzuela 1999). It should also be clear by now that any potential *effectiveness* in conveying educational norms, especially among Mexican American adolescents, must be rooted in connectedness and expectations for ongoing exchange and mutual trust (Stanton-Salazar 2001). We have to keep in mind, however, that the descriptive data from the preceding chapter offer an ironic interpretive twist on this finding, since Mexican American adolescents appear to be disadvantaged in comparison to Whites in terms of the availability of *Peer Connectedness*. This difference might be partly explainable according to cross-generational barriers that inhibit relationship development between adolescents of different nativity status. What's more, certain school organizational practices, such as tracking, contribute to the social cohesion of certain groups of students vis-à-vis adolescents of Mexican descent. It is simply not plausible, however, to make such causal interpretations from the data in this study, without more fully investigating the social institutions that enable these peer relationships to exist as such.

Summary

Whereas the previous chapter addressed the *availability* of various forms of social capital across socioeconomic and immigrant status groups, in the present chapter I have investigated the convertibility of social capital among adolescents' families and peers. Having also considered the incidence and causes of mobility, in this chapter I have sought to shift our focus to a review of its consequences. Through survey and interview data analyses, we have obtained a better understanding of the *mobility/social capital dynamic*.

In this respect, the hypothesis that mobility impinges on social capital, which, in turn, inhibits student achievement, has been largely supported by the structural models executed without background controls. But for the most part the effects of family social capital wash out in the more fully specified models, and the impact of student and residential mobility is markedly reduced when socioeconomic status, K-8 student mobility, and prior test scores are taken into consideration. We might well ask, then, whether early childhood experiences within the family, as well as other background factors, trump parents' later influence over adolescent educational trajectories? And we also might now wonder whether the impact of mobility on test score performance is indeed largely accounted for in other background factors.

Before rendering a verdict, it should be noted that year-to-year correlations in *NELS:88* test scores are particularly large during high school (eighth grade test scores are far-and-away the most powerful predictor of twelfth grade test scores); so, in those models that include prior achievement, it is difficult to identify any other significant twelfth grade achievement-related predictors in the *NELS:88* data (Phillips, 2000). Further elaborating and also qualifying the survey results, the interview findings suggest that strategic mobility probably limits the degree to which its reactive manifestations can be accounted for by the survey data. So while Harris (1998) may be correct to assert that we have underemphasized the role of socialization agents other than families in shaping adolescents' development, the concerted strategy employed by Barbara's parents as well as the multi-dimensional and authoritative family support system that assisted Julio should leave us with little doubt that families continue to contribute, well beyond the early childhood years, to adolescents' schooling trajectories. Consider also that the awkward transitions inevitably accompanying reactive mid-year school changes (i.e., curricular incoherence, misplaced transcripts, and misdirected classroom placements) are probably less than fully accounted for by survey data commingling reactive and strategic kinds of mobility. So while more carefully specified survey models at least partially ameliorate concern about the *mobility/social capital dynamic*, my findings legitimate what should be a continuing concern among educators and society at large about the potentially problematic influences of mobility, particularly in its more reactive manifestations. At the same time, findings offer room for optimism about the efficacy of family social capital. Additionally, peer social capital remains a robust achievement-related predictor, even according to the more fully specified models. Regardless of the likelihood that the *NELS:88* survey data commingle school-oriented youth like Patricia, street-oriented kids like Michael, and others whose peer networks are fraught with Julio's school-related ambivalence, there remains something about peer social capital that, on the whole, benefits twelfth grade student performance.

It would appear then that different forms of social capital do indeed yield evidence of differential convertibility and suggest the relative importance of those resources that inhere in adolescent peer networks. But do these differences in the convertibility of various forms of social capital vary significantly between Mexican American students and non-Latino Whites? The fact that *Peer Connectedness* stands out for its effect on twelfth test scores among Mexican origin youth suggests that *confianza en confianza* may be particularly important among Mexican Americans with regard to their psychocultural expectations for ongoing exchange, for mutual generosity, and for basic trust in the sphere of intimate relations (Stanton-Salazar 2001). At any rate, further research is required to confirm how the sort of *confianza en confianza* shared by Julio and his buddies is achieved and to assess how or whether it indeed works as a fundamental organizing principle underlying the formation of interpersonal networks and educational advancement among youth of Mexican descent.

[56] Psychologists have carefully documented the positive impact of "authoritative" parenting styles on children's development (Baumrind, 1971; Steinberg et al., 1994), including psychological and social adjustment and students' success in schools (Lamborn, Mounts, Steinberg, & Dornbusch, 1991; Gray & Steinberg, 1999). Authoritative parenting styles are typically characterized as warm and involved, yet consistently firm in clarifying and enforcing guidelines, limits and developmentally appropriate expectations (Steinberg, 2001).

[57] For the sake of clarity, I exclude the observed variables and error terms associated with latent measures of social capital.

[58] The dependent measure of twelfth grade test scores in the structural models is a *standardized* composite of the aggregate of math, reading, science, and history test score performance. For unstandardized subject-specific test score means and standard deviations, refer to Appendix B.

[59] And about one-fifth of the student interviewees expressed ambivalence, citing both positive and negative effects of mobility on school grades.

[60] Another explanation for the varied impact of mobility on student achievement has to do with the curricular diversity offered at each school, the intensity of coursework associated with that diversity, and the expectations and demands of school personnel charged with implementing the curriculum. Put simply, some schools are more academically rigorous than others. When students change from less challenging academic environments to schools that uphold more rigorous standards, their grades sometimes decline. And the reverse is also true. Indeed, sometimes *less* (i.e., less challenging schooling) is *more* (i.e., improved grades based on less competitive standards).

[61] As a rule, mid-year school changes are nearly synonymous with awkwardly reactive transitions for students. Interruptive factors include the lack of curricular continuity from school to school, inefficient administrative procedures (such as missing or misplaced transcripts that lead to inappropriate classroom placement), and the many challenges students face while trying to adjust to a new environment and navigate a school that is still as yet unknown.

[62] "Judging by what I saw among the females in the friendship groups I interviewed, [Mexican-American] girls... are indisputably the chief purveyors of social capital" (Valenzuela, 1999, p. 143).

[63] For non-Latino Whites however, socioeconomic status is a more powerful predictor of twelfth grade test score performance than either form of peer social capital. Note also that a standard deviation increase in SES makes a strong contribution to the accumulation of both forms of peer social capital among non-Latino Whites. And its contribution to *Student's Peers Value Education* is much more pronounced among Whites (.12 SD) than among Mexican origin youth. Between-group differences in the instrumental utility of SES should not be overlooked as yet another potential contributor to low average Mexican American achievement—a proposition that goes beyond the focus of this investigation.

CHAPTER 7

Formal Social Networks: The *Mobility/Social Capital Dynamic* and the "Downside" of Social Capital

> *Sometimes the teacher will say, 'Massiel, what's wrong? You're not doing your work as normal.' And I'll be like, 'I don't know, my head hurts...' And they're like, 'OK, if you want just put your head down and then at home you'll finish it; turn it in to me tomorrow.'*
>
> — Massiel, *Immigrant from Mexico*

Questions about the availability and convertibility of social capital involve more than just its relative opacity or the difficulty of adequately measuring its varied forms. Even when one considers how resources embedded in social networks are distributed and function across various domains, it is next to impossible to define the fundamental essence of social capital, only partly because the domains in which it is located are typically complex and inter-connected. In the previous chapter I examined the *mobility/social capital dynamic* within families and among adolescent peers. As I shift my focus in this chapter to the public realm of communities and schools, it is important to recall that the interpersonal aspects of the dynamic remain even here at the heart of my investigation. For that reason, I do not concentrate on the obviously collective aspects of social capital, such as civic vitality and "generalized reciprocity" (Putnam, 2000), but rather on public expressions shared on a smaller scale, which is to say, between individuals within communities and schools.

In preceding chapters I have highlighted the disadvantages that are often the results of an *absence* of social capital. Such a framework remains operative in this chapter, but a somewhat surprising finding leads me to take a closer look at the negative outcomes surfacing in the presence of a sort of *counterfeit* social capital that does not necessarily present itself as such to its recipients, even though it may ultimately detract from their academic achievement.

It is partly my contention that the inherent properties of social capital at the individual level—say, the trust shared between Julio and his friends—can have a much broader impact. This is so, in part, because relationships foster sturdy norms of obligation and reciprocity that encourage people to behave in socially desirable, or undesirable, ways. At the same time, the communal properties of social capital evident in schools, volunteer groups, and religious organizations intimate a much broader social fabric, in which individual lives are interwoven, reflecting greater and lesser degrees of conformity. Clearly, the costs and benefits of social connections accrue to both individuals and communities alike (Woolcock, 1998; Putnam, 2000). Where long-time neighbors share trust and cooperate with one another, lawns get mowed and mail gets brought in—even when one family is out of town on summer vacation. In this way, neighborhoods often become safer and more aesthetically pleasing, to the benefit of community security and home values. In the language of economists, such "externalities" are bi-directional, moving from individual to community and from community to individual (Putnam, 2000). Even as I continue to give emphasis to the interpersonal aspects of the *dynamic*, I have tried to offer in this chapter a better sense of its public expressions as they occur within the context of communities and schools.

The *Dynamic* Within the Community

Most of the fieldwork in this investigation was carried out among families and peer groups, and within schools. In the absence of other possibly relevant data from the field, I have relied heavily on the existing literature to describe the mechanisms by which broader community social networks influence those behaviors that might, in turn, influence educational outcomes.

Cooperative behavior—say, as inspired by big brother/sister mentorships and non-profit community action programs, or by government-sponsored programs like Head Start (Soss; 1999)—has the potential to improve a community's quality of life and to benefit more particularly, the individuals who live in neighborhoods where such programs flourish (Putnam, 1993; Portes 1998). In fact, volunteer programs often facilitate external demands (through formal requests to local officials for community redevelopment), and enforce internal constraints (through neighborhood watch groups and community-wide standards of moral conduct) that pertain to social capital (Coleman & Hoffer, 1987; Portes & Zhou, 1993; Putnam, 1993; Greeley, 1997).

Participation in religious groups can encourage cooperative behavior and norms of reciprocity that produce externalities affecting individuals as well as the broader community (Coleman, 1988; Portes, 1998; Putnam, 2000). Religious participation has been considered a proxy for community social capital (Putnam, 2000), and church attendance has been deemed to increase the likelihood of school completion (Coleman, 1988). Nevertheless, few studies offer empirical analyses of the direct effects of students' involvement in community and religious social networks on their academic achievement.

A Basic Structural Model

The standardized parameter estimates in Figure 7.1 below chart the prospective educational benefits associated with community volunteering and religious participation among adolescent youth. A standard deviation increase in *Student Volunteers in the Community* (CSC1) improves twelfth grade test scores by .31 SD and .18 SD among White and Mexican origin youth, respectively. The matched parameter estimates are underlined since the effect sizes differ significantly between the two groups, and it appears that volunteerism directed toward the community may be a particularly effective achievement-related predictor among White adolescents.

Figure 7.1. The Mobility/Community Social Capital Dynamic

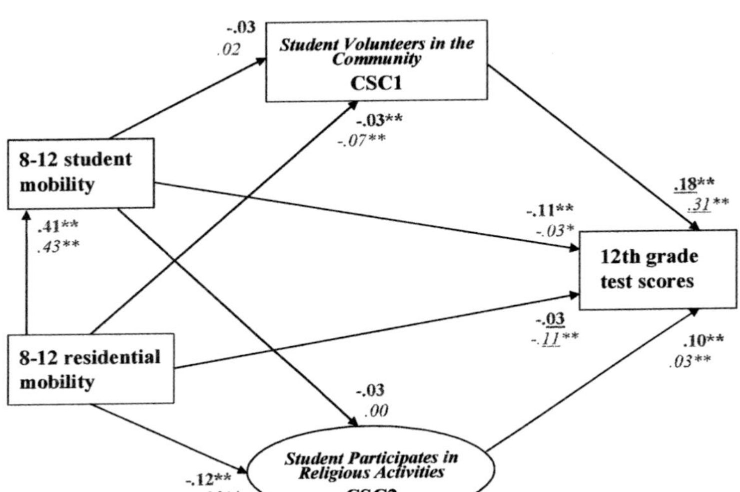

NOTES: $**p<.01$; $**p<.05$. Parameter estimates for Mexican Americans are shown in **bold** just above the *italicized* estimates for non-Latino Whites. The path weights are presented in standard deviation units. Underlined parameters represent statistically significant between-group differences in matched paths. Individual items that contribute to the social capital constructs as well as all error terms, are excluded from the figure. I allow the errors to correlate between CSC1 and CSC2; the estimate of this error correlation is .23 and .32, ($p<.01$) for Mexican Americans and non-Latino Whites, respectively. *Student Volunteers in the Community* (CSC1) represents a single *NELS:88* item (F2S37), so it appears in a rectangle according to structural modeling convention. Fit Indices: TLI=.99; CFI=.99; RMSEA=.03.

If we wished to illustrate this effect *via* extrapolation, a standard deviation increase in CSC1 could be expected to improve average twelfth grade math test score performance by more than four points among Whites, and by approximately two points among Mexican origin youth. *Student Participates in Religious Activities* (CSC2) suggests a directly positive impact on test score performance for both groups (.03 SD and .10 SD for Whites and Mexican Americans, respectively). In this case, the *between*-group difference is not statistically significant.

Increases in both forms of community social capital predict test score improvement, even as mobility, as I have demonstrated previously in this study, detracts from the accumulation of social capital. Here, residential mobility associated with changing neighborhoods—as opposed to student mobility—seems the logical antecedent to social de-capitalization in the community domain (Rumberger et al., 1999; Putnam, 2000; Small, 2002). As it turns out, an additional residential move decreases *Student Volunteers in the Community* by .07 SD for Whites and .03 SD for Mexican American adolescents, and residential mobility also detracts from *Student Participates in Religious Activities* by .12 SD for both groups. Student mobility does not appear to impact either form of community social capital, however.

A More Fully Specified Model

Once again, the hypothesized relationship between mobility, social capital, and test score performance is supported in the basic structural model insofar as it excludes students' background characteristics. Yet when SES, K-8 student mobility, and eighth grade test scores are also taken into consideration, the impact of community social capital on twelfth grade test score performance is reduced (per Table 7.1) to statistical insignificance among Mexican origin youth. That said, *Student Volunteers in the Community* (CSC1) remains a significant test score predictor among non-Latino Whites, and the group-level difference in its impact is statistically significant, per the underlined matched parameters. As such, this finding would corroborate other research suggesting that some groups harness the strength of community resources and social networks to enhance their prospects for upward mobility and educational advancement, while others seem less able to do so (Crane, 1991; Portes & Zhou, 1993; Putnam, 2000; Portes & Rumbaut, 2001).

Table 7.1. The Dynamic Within the Community: Standardized Coefficients from the Structural Model

	8th Grade		Grades 8-12								12th Grade	
	Test Scores		Res. Mobility		Student Mobility		CSC1		CSC2		Test Scores	
	M-A	W	M-A	W	M-A	W	M-A	W	M-A	W	M-A	W
Exogenous Variables												
K-8 Student Mobility	.04	-.06**	.27**	.25**	.14**	.13**	.	.	.	.	.	.
SES	.31**	.45**	-.10**	-.14**	-.01	.03**	.11**	.24**	.07**	.11**	.05*	.09**
Endogenous Variables												
8th Grade Test Scores	.	.	.	.	.	.	.	.	.	.	.79**	.80**
8-12 Student Mobility	.	.	.	.	.	.	-.04	.01	-.03	-.01	-.04	-.01*
8-12 Res. Mobility	.	.	.	.	.38**	.40**	-.01	-.04**	-.12	-.11**	-.05*	-.02**
CSC1	.	.	.	.	.	.	.	.	.	.	.02	.07**
CSC2	.	.	.	.	.	.	.	.	.	.	.05	.01

NOTES: M.A.: Mexican American; W.: non-Latino White; Res.: Residential. CSC1: *Student Volunteers in the Community*; CSC2: *Student Participates in Religious Activities.* ***p*<.01; **p*<.05. Effects marked with a period (.) are not estimated in the models. Underlined coefficients differ significantly from corresponding coefficient for other racial/ethnic group (critical ratios greater than 1.96). The errors are correlated between CSC1 and CSC2; the estimated error correlations are .22 and .31 (*p*<.01), for Mexican Americans and non-Latino Whites, respectively. The model explains 67 percent of the variance in twelfth grade test scores. Fit Indices: TLI=.96, CFI=.98, RMSEA=.04.

Even in the more fully specified model, the finding that residential mobility impinges on community social capital accumulation remains robust, although its impact on *Student Volunteers in the Community* is not significant among Mexican origin youth. In a trenchant analysis of changing patterns of neighborhood participation in local community activities in Villa Victoria, a predominantly Puerto Rican housing project in Boston, Mario Small demonstrates that civic participation is sometimes associated with how members "frame" their community according to shared perceptions of its history (Small, 2002).[64] Small also notes that, among other factors, residential mobility can work against historical framing, communal memory, and the realization of common values in support of social goods by erasing a shared history that might otherwise promote greater community participation. Indeed, those who are recent arrivals in any community are less likely to belong to civic organizations, less likely to vote, and less likely to have supportive networks of friends and neighbors. Moreover, according to Putnam's research (2002), people who expect to move in the next five years are 20 to 25 percent less likely to volunteer or to attend church than people who stay put.

Although my findings in this study are not based on the kind of participatory observation of a neighborhood facilitating Small's "thick description," the data I obtained from adolescent interviewees and their families nevertheless suggest that people who are on the move are susceptible to disassociation from the broader community. Indeed, as I noted in Chapter 5, community participation outside of school is almost non-existent among the interview sample of transient youth. Taken in the context of a broader literature on social organization and neighborhood effects (Shaw & McKay, 1969; Sampson & Groves, 1989; Sampson, 1999), it would appear that residential instability is a likely contributor to social isolation and to patterns of behavior not conducive to upward social mobility.

The School Social Capital *Dynamic*

Given the frequency of adolescents' interaction with school personnel over an extended period of their life, it is perhaps surprising that studies employing the social capital postulate often ignore the impact of in-school relationships between teachers and students (Dika & Singh, 2002). In contrast, two fairly recent studies analyze teacher/student interaction as social capital, arguing that teachers provide students with direct and convertible sources of educational assistance (Stanton-Salazar & Dornbusch, 1995; Croninger & Lee, 2001). Although the effectiveness of outreach by school personnel to parents, or of parental involvement in schools has been frequently studied apart from the social capital rubric (e.g., Fehrmann, Keith, & Reimers, 1987; Stevenson & Baker, 1987; Paulson, 1994; Kao & Tienda, 1998), the results have seemed inconsistent, varying often according to the minority or social status of the students studied

(Madigan, 1994). As a result, researchers have speculated that notions of school outreach and parent involvement might—alternatively and perhaps more adequately—be conceptualized as public forms of social capital (McNeal, 1999; Park & Palardy, 2004).

A Basic Structural Model

In light of some of this previous research, I have attempted to model, here in Figure 7.2, students' relationships with teachers and school-initiated contact with parents as forms of school social capital. Much as Madigan (1994) and McNeal (1999) suggested in their studies of students' minority status, the results here seem inconsistent. So, while *Academically Relevant Teacher/Student Interaction* (SSC1) gives evidence of the expected positive (.14 SD) impact on twelfth grade test score performance among non-Latino Whites, the corollary parameter estimate among adolescent Mexican Americans is large and surprisingly negative (-.44 SD), albeit statistically insignificant. Also the positive impact of *School-Initiated Interaction with Student's Parents* (SSC2) on test score performance is significantly larger (hence the underlined parameters) among non-Latino Whites than it is among Mexican origin youth (.15 SD versus .05 SD). Yet again the convertibility of certain forms of social capital seems conditioned, dependent on the people who possess it and the places where they attempt to exchange it (Stanton-Salazar; 1997; Lin, 2001; Ream, 2003).

Figure 7.2. The Mobility/School Social Capital Dynamic

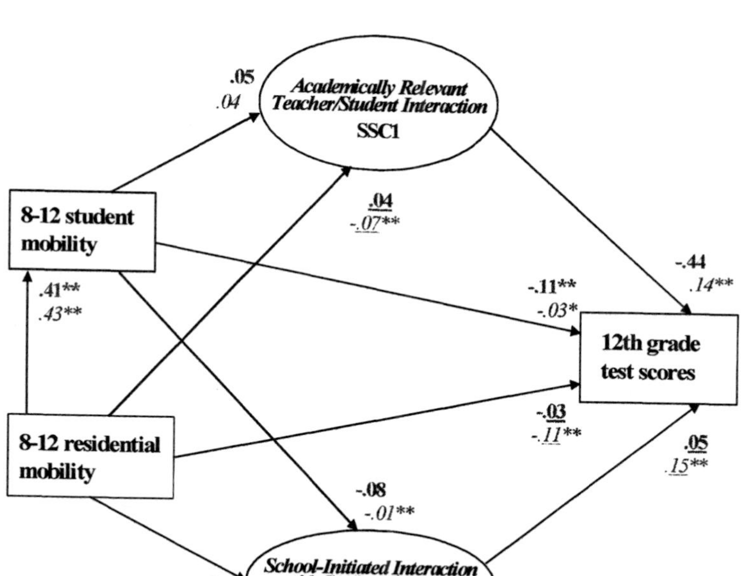

NOTES: **p<.01; **p<.05. Parameter estimates for Mexican Americans are shown in **bold** just above the *italicized* estimates for non-Latino Whites. The path weights are presented in standard deviation units. Underlined parameters represent statistically significant between-group differences in matched paths. Individual items that contribute to the social capital constructs (see Table 7.2), as well as all error terms, are excluded from the figure. I allow the errors to correlate between SSC1 and SSC2; the estimate of this error correlation is .10 and insignificant for Mexican Americans and .24 (p<.01) for non-Latino Whites. Fit Indices: TLI=.98; CFI=.99; RMSEA=.04.

Interview Findings. What is perhaps more surprising is that my survey results suggest that student mobility does not greatly influence the accumulation of school social capital for either group, although residential mobility contributes to social de-capitalization among non-Latino Whites. And yet at the same time school personnel and students consistently report that transience impinges on school-based relationships. One instructor declared with confidence that "the connection to success is the connection children feel to the teacher...," and her view reflects many other teachers' perspectives (Rumberger et al., 1999). As she also observed, reestablishing social roots is a difficult and often time-consuming proposition:

> It takes a while for teachers and students to feel comfortable with one another, to take risks and all those wonderful mysterious factors of learning – student mobility keeps interrupting that process.

Perhaps, then, it should not be surprising that when a student such as Carlos changes schools midway through his freshman year, his new teachers may benignly neglect him, discouraging his motivation and apparently contributing to his complacency about school. "When I changed to Linbloom High, well, mostly they didn't ask for much so I didn't give them that much; so my grades failed."

In schools with highly transient student populations, it seems quite likely that disaffected attitudes of this nature are *learned* behaviors, having much to do with the pragmatic reciprocity expectations (Coleman, 1988; Stanton-Salazar, 2001) through which teachers invest in students' academic development and students react to expectations placed upon them (most concretely, by demonstrating the knowledge imparted to them). Student mobility disables the premise of reciprocity, since teachers know that newly arriving students, especially mid-year school changers, are often here today and gone tomorrow.65 Under such conditions the human capital development of students suffers, since teachers may be less inclined to invest in students (e.g. mobile students) when they seem unlikely to fulfill the implicit reciprocal "contract"—not exactly a behavior consistent with what Dewey (1916) imagined in his conception of the school as family. The comments of one frustrated second-year English instructor tell the teachers' side of the story. "Teachers put effort into teaching and the kids leave," she lamented. "So we don't have that sense of continuity and accomplishment with the transient students—and that affects morale."

Roberto, a second generation Mexican American, enjoyed healthy and motivating relationships with school personnel at his first high school placement, but his school change experience undermined morale:

> I kept my grades up at Topanga because the teachers there, they would really motivate you... And when I transferred to Montalvo, the teachers there didn't care. When nobody is there for you, you just keep on it like a little black hole – and you rarely try to get out of it.

Patricia, whose parents were also born in Mexico, had a similar experience after changing high schools. "I didn't really meet any teachers that actually helped students. And some teachers were harder on me because they didn't know me," she recalled.

The negative impact of mobility on students' relations with teachers is a common theme in the interview data, but exceptions to this pattern do emerge, most commonly, as a consequence of *strategic* student mobility. Barbara's school change experience is only one such exception. Intent on improving her academic performance, her parents cultivated relationships with school personnel at various alternative placements. As a result of their highly interventionist strategy, Barbara was already well known by the counselor to whom her parents had taken such a liking when she re-enrolled. It's not particularly surprising therefore that Barbara, unlike many other interviewees, found herself attending classes where there were "no gaps in learning."

Might the story of Barbara's strategic school change experience partly explain the weak association between student mobility and the two forms of school social capital employed in the survey analyses? As an elaboration and also a qualification of the *NELS:88* survey results, my findings suggest that by commingling reactive and strategic mobility in the survey data we may limit the degree to which its positive and its negative manifestations can be accounted for.

The Downside of Social Capital

Throughout this investigation I have suggested that, at the very least, social relationships can grease the wheels of individuals' academic advancement, yet other critical analyses (Portes & Sensenbrenner, 1993; Stanton-Salazar, 1997; Gutmann, 1998) warn against single-minded depictions of the beneficial dimension of social capital. There is no doubt that social relationships possess a potential not only for positive outcomes (i.e., deliberative democracy and healthy civil society), but also for negative outcomes (e.g., the constriction of individual liberty). In one extreme, they may even contribute to a normative, community-wide regression toward the mean. People's social networks have the power to demand seemingly slavish social conformity, as Putnam's (2000) reference to Nobel Laureate Sinclair Lewis's 1922 infamously typical American, George F. Babbitt, is meant to suggest. The negative externalities of community obligation may even, in some cases, outweigh the benefits of communal life. An entrepreneurial immigrant, for example, may abandon her familiar ethnic enclaves and voluntarily divest herself of bonding social capital in lonely pursuit of the American dream.

My descriptive analyses in Chapter 5 focused largely on the disadvantages that derive from the absence of social capital, yet most of the available literature addressing the downside of social capital has been directed toward negative outcomes generated by its *presence*. Ironically, it was an overdose of fraternity, in its most generic sense, that exposed the dull conformity of Babbitt's life. According to my interview data, it is also possible for social capital to manifest itself in simultaneously beneficial and counterproductive ways, so that Barbara's parents' interventions on her behalf may have enhanced her educational opportunities at the expense of her relationship with them:

> Certain things, particularly emotional and personal problems, I don't bring to my parents, because my parents are too zealous... I had a grade drop from an *A* to a *B* so my father wanted to enroll me into tutoring six days a week. He wanted the teacher to sign a paper every day saying what the homework was and he wanted the teacher to sign an attendance sheet saying I was there every day! My parents go a little too far, and they kind of scared me into talking to them too much. So things that bother me emotionally – I get it out in my writing or tell it to other people.

The interventions of overly involved parents can produce short-term educational gains, but—since parents may also be perceived by young people as meddlesome or controlling—these results may damage elements of trust in parent/adolescent relationships. Not entirely recognizing the extent of the damage, Barbara's mother commented almost sanctimoniously, "We used to bug her to the point of excess. And she used to get into a lot of arguments with her father... We do like to follow up." Their parental activism nevertheless undercut Barbara's individual liberty and further alienated her from them. "My parents are really gung-ho – you know, 'Let's take action and let's get this thing righted,'" she said. "And that was the last thing I really wanted. So I kept them away from it all for the past three years…"

The extent to which social resources may be deployed at cross purposes is also apparent among adolescent peer groups. If the normative function of peer social capital is to encourage educational advancement among school-oriented peers (as was noted above in the case of Patricia), shared norms can just as easily lead to disengagement among disaffected youth who, like Michael, share anti-school attitudes (Birman & Natriello, 1978; Hallinan & Williams, 1990; Gibson et al., 2004).

Furthermore, a lack of social capital at the community level may surface in destructive ways. Iván's parents' fear of the neighborhood—"It's better to stay in the house than have a bullet in hour head!"—and Julio's mother's frustrations with gang-related tagging and violence, speak forcefully about how the perceived absence of community social capital in unsafe neighborhoods may inhibit families' neighborliness and help-seeking inclinations (Cocharan & Riley, 1988; Rumbaut & Cornelius, 1995). So despite many positive manifestations, the relationships that constitute social capital are fraught with subtractive elements. Under optimal conditions, social capital is convertible into socially desirable outcomes. Yet when it gets manifested in the wrong proportion or in unhealthy circumstances, its negative manifestations can be detrimental or even devastating in an increasingly connected, but as often disaffected, world.

A More Fully Specified Model

There may also be need for further qualification, from a scientific standpoint, even of the seemingly beneficial aspects of social capital across domains. Accordingly, in the more fully specified model offered here in Table 7.2, the parameter estimates associating *Academically Relevant Teacher/Student Interaction* (SSC1) and twelfth grade test score outcomes suggest that the very same social mechanisms giving rise to appropriable resources for individual and collective use can constrain action, or even derail the goals toward which it has been applied (Portes & Sensenbrenner, 1993).

Table 7.2. The School Social Capital Dynamic: Standardized Coefficients from the Structural Model

	8th Grade		Grades 8-12								12th Grade	
	Test Scores		Res. Mobility		Student Mobility		SSC1		SSC2		Test Scores	
	M.A.	W.	M.A.	W.	M.A.	W.	M.A.	W.	M.A.	W.	M.A.	W.
Exogenous Variables												
K-8 Student Mobility	.04	-.06**	.27**	.25**	.14**	.13**	.	.	.	.	.	.
SES	.31**	.45**	-.10**	-.14**	-.01	.03**	-.19**	.15**	.02	.25**	.05*	.09**
Endogenous Variables												
8th Gade Test Scores	.	.	.	.	.	.	.	.	.	.	.79**	.80**
8-12 Student Mobility	.	.	.	.	.	.	.02	.04	-.08	-.02	-.04	-.01*
8-12 Resi-dential Mobility	.	.	.	.	.38**	.40**	-.02	-.05**	.06	-.01	-.05*	-.02**
SSC1	.	.	.	.	.	.	.	.	.	.	-.12**	.05**
SSC2	.	.	.	.	.	.	.	.	.	.	.01	.02**

NOTES: M.A.: Mexican American; W.: non-Latino White; Res.: Residential. SSC1: *Academically Relevant Teacher/Student Interaction*; SSC2: *School-Initiated Interaction with Student's Parents*. $**p<.01$; $*p<.05$. Effects marked with a period (.) are not estimated in the models. Underlined coefficients differ significantly from corresponding coefficient for other racial/ethnic group (critical ratios greater than 1.96). The errors are correlated between SSC1 and SSC2; the estimated error correlations are .18 and .21 ($p<.01$), for Mexican Americans and non-Latino Whites, respectively. The model explains 68 percent of the variance in twelfth grade test scores. Fit Indices: TLI=.98, CFI=.99, RMSEA=.03.

For example, while *Academically Relevant Teacher/Student Interaction* is a significant and positive predictor of twelfth grade test scores among White adolescents, it has the opposite effect among Mexican origin youth (-.12, $p<.01$). How is it possible that *Academically Relevant Teacher/Student Interaction* clearly benefits Whites, yet works to the disadvantage of Mexican origin youth? It is tempting to interpret these findings as following from biased tracking practices (Lee & Bryk, 1988; Gamoran & Mare, 1989; Noguera, 2003), but, in fact, the structural models control for powerful tracking predictors, including socioeconomic status and prior academic achievement, so that this ready explanation merits skepticism.

Counterfeit Social Capital. From the interview data, it is possible to offer another explanation for between-group differences in the utility of *Academically Relevant Teacher/Student Interaction.* For in certain circumstances school personnel may offer patronizing forms of social support directed less toward Mexican American academic achievement than toward low-level expediency in the classroom. Massiel, who emigrated from Mexico as a child, recalls her teachers' apparent eagerness to accommodate her request for a reprieve from classroom responsibilities:

> Sometimes the teacher will say, 'Massiel, what's wrong? You're not doing your work as normal.' And I'll be like, 'I don't know, my head hurts…' And they're like, 'OK, if you want just put your head down and then at home you'll finish it; turn it in to me tomorrow.'

That teachers sometimes seek to ameliorate potential classroom conflict by adjusting their expectations and pedagogical rigor to suit disengaged students is a phenomenon that is well documented in the literature on classroom practices (Platt, 1973; Metz, 1978; Owen, 1981; Feinman-Nemser & Floden, 1986; Sedlak et al., 1986; Muncey & McQuillan, 1996). In these cases, teachers may cultivate social relations in the classroom that maintain classroom harmony at the expense of academic content. Such situations are excellent examples of "social traps" (Platt, 1973), wherein teachers acting on immediate interests—making a classroom more orderly and peaceful, perhaps—can severely limit long-term educational objectives (Sedlak et al., 1986).

Some scholars refer to the accommodation strategies exemplified by Massiel's teacher as "defensive teaching." This quasi-pedagogical technique may help maintain classroom tranquility (and it may even partly explain Mexican Americans' reported advantages in the availability of certain forms of school social capital), but it takes a toll on students' academic advancement, especially when it comes to the most challenged students in the classroom (Dusek & Joseph, 1983;

Cusick, 1983; Goodlad, 1984). In other words, the *counterfeit* social capital reflected in a teacher's willingness to go easy on a student such as Massiel will not facilitate her human capital development and may actually preclude it. Defensive and accommodating teaching strategies may be the ironic result of increasing students' *perceptions* of teachers' concern for their well-being (perceptions not readily amenable to validity cross-checks in the *NELS:88* questionnaire), even while they concomitantly short-circuit, for example, the convertibility of school social capital into twelfth grade test score performance among Mexican American adolescents. The interview data alone do not entirely confirm this hypothesis, and the element of subjective perception—the tension between what kinds of help students believe they're getting versus a more genuinely caring pedagogical praxis—may be relevant here. Many interviewees from both groups report that their relationships with school personnel are of great value in terms of motivation, school engagement and academic achievement. Olivia's immigrant mother, for example, reflects appreciatively on the valuable support her daughter received from at least some of her teachers:

> Her science teacher and her math teacher – I notice that they are the ones who help Olivia the most because she is always telling me how her teachers always encourage her to do well and not miss school.

Nevertheless, Massiel's classroom experience highlights the disconcerting although not particularly surprising fact that not all social relationships shared between students and school personnel have beneficial outcomes. Assenting to school authority involves a basic trust on the part of students that the authority will be exercised fairly and appropriately, but students' interests may not always be served by compliance with the exercise of teacher authority. Sociability, in its formal components, can be a double-edged sword. At the very least, more directed investigations of the factors inhibiting the conversion of school social capital into minority student achievement demand our further consideration.[66]

My survey analyses may offer further insight into this phenomenon. Consider again the pronounced group-level differences when it comes to the impact of socioeconomic status on both forms of school social capital. Although socioeconomic status is a comparably powerful and positive predictor among Whites, it negatively impacts teacher/student interaction (SSC1) and is in fact insignificantly associated with school outreach to students' parents (SSC2) among Mexican American adolescents. Could it be that lower SES youth of Mexican descent have garnered only a patronizing form of *counterfeit* social capital even while their higher SES counterparts are cloaked by relative invisibility? Or are lower SES Mexican Americans simply more likely to report positive interactions with school personnel in comparison to their wealthier, perhaps more acculturated Mexican American counterparts (Portes & Rumbaut, 2001)? These are both questions that could sustain important subsequent lines of inquiry.

Summary

Again in this chapter as in the previous one, it appears that the *mobility/social capital dynamic* in the community and school domains acts largely in expected ways—as mobility detracts from social capital accumulation, while social capital nevertheless remains a resilient and mostly positive twelfth grade test score predictor. By controlling for prior test scores and other background factors, however, I showed that the impact of community social capital for the most part washes out of the models, with the exception of community volunteering among non-Latino Whites. So while descriptive findings in Chapter 5 pointed to its overall lack of availability for both groups under consideration, the findings of this chapter reveal an apparent limit to the utility of community social capital when considered for its impact at the individual level and particularly among youth of Mexican descent.

The more surprising finding appears to occur in the school domain, where available stocks of social capital are more or less equally distributed between both groups, per Chapter 5. Nevertheless, while *Academically Relevant Teacher/Student Interaction* benefits Whites, it appears to detract from Mexican American test score performance. So whereas most of the data in this study points us to beneficial—or, at worse, neutral—aspects of social capital across domains, we must keep in mind that the same social mechanisms giving rise to appropriable resources for individual and collective use can sometimes constrain or even derail the goals such resources are supposed to serve (Portes & Sensenbrenner, 1993). By and large, the convertibility of certain forms of social capital appears to be conditioned by the people who possess it as well as the places where they attempt to use or exchange it (Stanton-Salazar; 1997; Lin, 2001; Ream, 2003).

There may yet be alternative explanations for this anomalous finding. Mexican Americans and non-Latino Whites may have different teachers who have differential access to resources that benefit students. This study has considered the *mobility/social capital dynamic* without taking the school context fully into account,[67] yet there is little doubt that Latinos and other minorities are increasingly isolated, even segregated at particular schools within the system (Orfield & Yun, 1999; Rumberger & Palardy, forthcoming; Valencia et al., 2002) and even, as a result of tracking, within the individual schools they attend (Lee & Bryk, 1988; Gamoran & Mare, 1989; Noguera, 2003). Moreover, schools serving a clientele characterized by high-poverty rates and high numbers of minorities have fewer resources and poorer learning environments than low-poverty and low-minority schools (National Research Council and the Institute of Medicine, 2004). Research has also shown that students in lower track classes, even within the same schools, tend to have teachers with lower qualifications (Lucas, 1999; Mickelson, 2001). Although the more fully specified structural models attempted to control for powerful tracking predictors, such as prior achievement and socioeconomic status, minorities are still far more likely to be tracked into less challenging classes (even when we control for relevant background factors). Thus, explanations for group-level differences with regard to the impact of *Academically Relevant Teacher/Student Interaction* (SSC1) on student achievement may have less to do with the same teachers doling out differential treatment across groups, and more to do with the fact that there are *different* teachers interacting with Mexican American and White adolescents across segregated schools and classrooms.

If indeed it can be demonstrated that counterfeit forms of teacher/student interaction are a widespread byproduct of segregation and school-level differences in resource availability and workforce preparation, it may be necessary to call for immediate policy action. But since policy solutions are most wisely undertaken in the context of a cumulative body of findings rather than in response to the results of any single study (McDonnell, 2000), we have first to consider further research designed to illuminate the incidence and causes of the social capital downside and its counterfeit manifestations. In the meantime, in keeping with the tenets of "standards based" reform, my research results might serve as a reminder that school personnel should avoid falling into old patterns of benign neglect and to counterfeit modes of niceness that may be particularly, if unintentionally, detrimental to minority youth (Ream, 2003).

---

[64] Small (2002) employs the concept of the "frame" in reference to the cultural categories through which residents perceive and interpret their neighborhood. Thus, a frame is an interpretive schema that simplifies and condenses the "world out there" to affect community participation by selectively punctuating and encoding one's present or past environment (see Goffman, 1974; Morris & Mueller, 1992).

[65] Many teachers seem to be aware of the fact that mobility begets mobility. In California, for example, one out of every eight students is chronically mobile, experiencing high mobility through their elementary and secondary years (Rumberger et al., 1999).

[66] For example, underestimates of Latino student ability on the part of mainstream teachers may render Latinos susceptible to disingenuously patronizing kinds of teacher-student interactions. Since Rosenthal and Jacobsen published *Pygmalion in the Classroom*, in 1968, social psychologists have shown that teachers can develop differential expectations for their students (Dusek & Joseph, 1983), and act on those expectations by treating students unequally. Moreover, children sometimes confirm teachers' expectations of them in a sort of self-fulfilling prophesy (Jussim & Eccles, 1992). One recent study found that teacher expectations tend to favor non-stigmatized student groups and penalize groups about whom negative stereotypes exist, which may in turn exacerbate group-level differences in academic achievement (McKown & Weinstein, 2002).

[67] Researchers have long recognized that both the individual background characteristics of students as well as the compositional characteristics of their school's student body can affect individual student achievement (Coleman, Campbell, Hobson, McPartland, Mood, Weinfield & York, 1966; Jencks & Mayer, 1990; Gamoran, 1992). For example, children from single-parent homes are known to benefit from school environments where the *overall* level of students' family social capital is high (Pong, 1998).

CHAPTER 8

Summary of Findings and Recommendations

> *There is a portion of the community who do not attach sufficient value to the system [of education] to do the things necessary to its healthful and energetic working. They may say excellent things about it, they may have a conviction of its general utility; but they do not understand, that the wisest conversation not embodied in action, that convictions too gentle and quiet to coerce performance, are little better than worthless...So children, without some favoring influences to woo out and cheer their faculties, may remain mere inanimate forms, while surrounded by the paradise of knowledge.*
>
> — Horace Mann, *The Republic and the School*

I opened this book by remarking upon the stubborn persistence of the achievement gap and its growing importance in the face of a tectonic demographic shift throughout the United States. Indeed, no ethnic group will do more to change the nation's schools in the next quarter century than Latinos, whose numbers, according to current demographic momentum, will surge to nearly 60 million—one-quarter of the entire U.S. population—by the year 2025 (U.S. Census Bureau, 2000a; Tienda, 2001). The possibility that a significant portion of the eligible U.S. voting and working population will be comprised of individuals drawn from groups whose academic achievement and educational attainment is significantly below the rest of the nation presents a serious moral, civic, and economic challenge. What manner of democratic people are we, and what sort of progressive republic can we possibly envision, if a persistent gap in educational performance continues to differentiate such a large group of people from mainstream society and its benefits? Whether we can muster the collective will to do what it takes to eliminate the gap—including low average educational achievement and attainment among Mexican origin youth—may become one of the most significant measures in the early part of the twenty-first century of our commitment to a truly democratic culture.

In a landmark study of Congressional agenda-setting, John Kingdon (1995) suggests that three factors must converge in order for an issue, such as the underachievement of Mexican origin youth, to be placed front-and-center on the policy agenda. First, the issue—in this case, the gap itself—must be broadly recognized as a problem with clear social implications. Second, the political winds must blow in a direction giving elected officials practical reasons to believe the issue may be relevant to concerns about their own career viability before it will get incorporated as an important item in her/his political platform. Third, there must be policy solutions available to address the problem. In this closing chapter, then, I review and reexamine my findings to consider what might be fairly concluded and what might subsequently be done about the problem of Mexican American underachievement, offering pragmatic ideas based on what we can learn from the *mobility/social capital dynamic*.

Recapping the findings. Throughout this book I have attempted to weave apparently disparate factors influencing education, such as student transience or the various networks informing adolescents' social lives, into our predominant conceptions of educational praxis. By linking research on social capital to mobility, I have suggested that Mexican Americans learn less in school than their non-Latino White counterparts, in part because they have less access to social capital, which follows at least in part from the fact that they are more mobile during their school careers. Of course, as I have already shown, the story proves to be a complicated one, and some of my mixed-methods results effectively qualify our concern about the *dynamic*. It's not exactly the "smoking gun" I'd hoped to find, but then again academic researchers rarely discover such transparent evidence or terribly simple answers to the questions they pose. Alas, the road to a firm research consensus is extraordinarily arduous (Kuhn, 1962). Despite various qualifications, the results of this study do give cause for some concern about mobility, especially with regard to mid-year reactive school changes. My findings also yield a better understanding of the potential for social capital to reproduce or interfere with the reproduction of Mexican American underachievement. Let me review some of the evidence that has led to this more tempered conclusion about what was initially presumed to be the *problem* of mobility, the *utility* of social capital, and the anticipated tension between the two.

What does this study reveal about the incidence, consequences and causes of student mobility?

Incidence. In one respect, the findings of this study pertaining to the incidence of mobility are unequivocal: America's youth are a transient bunch. The vast majority of school children make at least one non-promotional school change, and some, as shown in the interview sample, transfer multiple times during their school careers. Mexican origin youth, however, are particularly mobile—especially at the secondary level where the mobility rate among highly transient Mexican Americans is nearly twice that of Whites.

The incidence of student mobility is clearly associated with socioeconomic disadvantage among youth of Mexican descent. Findings in Chapter 4 show that Mexican Americans from challenged SES backgrounds are more mobile than the much smaller numbers of affluent Chicanos commingled in the *NELS:88* sample. Socioeconomic status and student mobility do not reveal associational patterns among non-Latino Whites, but nativity status is significant insofar as Mexican immigrants seem particularly transient in comparison to their more acculturated peers. Non-Latino White immigrants in the *NELS:88* sample, however, demonstrate relative stability in comparison to non-immigrants who are White, and also when compared to Mexican origin youth across nativity status groupings. Even the most stable generation of Mexican American youth change schools at higher rates than the most mobile generation of Whites. On the whole, these findings support other studies that suggest mobility is commonplace, especially among low SES inner-city Latinos (McDonnell & Hill 1993; Rumberger, 2003; U.S. Census Bureau, 2004), the vast majority of whom are economically challenged immigrants and children of immigrants (Hayes-Bautista et al., 1988; Portes & Rumbaut, 2001).

Consequences. While there is little doubt that transience is commonplace among adolescents in general and particularly among Mexican origin youth, the overall consequences of mobility are less clear. According to the basic structural models depicting the *mobility/social capital dynamic* in Chapters 6 and 7, the original premise of this investigation is sustained: mobility disrupts social networks and tends to be detrimental to adolescents' academic achievement. In the more fully specified models, however, the negative impact of mobility on various forms of social capital seems not only less pronounced, but more often than not, statistically insignificant. What's more, the direct effect of student mobility on twelfth grade achievement is similarly insignificant, and residential mobility hardly reduces twelfth grade test scores for either group.

So what can be made of these findings? Is mobility a spurious correlate of social capital development and test-score performance? Is it a dead-end issue better left alone in deference to other potentially more fruitful policy options designed to mitigate low average levels of academic achievement among Mexican origin youth? Before jumping to conclusions, let's consider some reasons why mobility should not be written off as a contributor to adolescent educational trajectories.

First, the high incidence of mobility is if anything under-reported in the *NELS:88* data, since mobile students are particularly difficult to track in longitudinal surveys spanning a number of years. Second, dropouts (a disproportionate number of whom are of Mexican descent) are not included in the investigation, and if accounted, these student might significantly alter the available data on these issues. So if the educational achievement of non-dropouts reflected in twelfth grade test scores does not seem hugely effected by transience, the sample here involves relatively successful students and not any of those who have abandoned their education perhaps because the system partly failed them. A growing body of research underscores the negative impact of mobility on school completion and educational *attainment*, even when background factors are controlled for (Astone & McLanahan 1994; Rumberger & Larson 1998; Rumberger, 2003). It has also been stated that the impact of student mobility may have a collective impact, above and beyond its individual-level effects, at the school level – yet another reason that its consequences are likely understated in this study.[68] A more definitive answer then may depend on closer scrutiny of the aggregate impact of student and residential mobility at the individual and the collective or systemic level.

Finally, the interview findings indicate that the impact of student mobility may have much to do with its timing, which is frequently associated with the reasons students change schools. So while reactive mobility appears to be a catalyst for social *de*-capitalization and academic under-performance, strategic mobility may just as well facilitate social *re*-capitalization and test score improvement. Thus, closer scrutiny of the reasons adolescents change residences and schools, and also where they end up, should lead to more comprehensive and robust findings regarding the impact of mobility on social capital development (Tienda, 1991; Pettit & McLanahan, 2003) and educational achievement (Pribesh & Downey, 1999; Ream, 2003).

Causes. Most of the reasons given for student transience at the secondary level, as reported in the field study of Chapter 4, can be categorized as reactive in nature, often the result of mid-year school changes. Iván's seemingly incessant journey from school to school, and Massiel's move from San Diego to Los Angeles halfway through her freshman year are poignant examples of reactive moves. Sometimes changing schools functions as an escape mechanism when social pressures get to be too much for adolescents. Anne's struggle against the "rumor-mill" and Carlos's ugly encounter with blatant racism are revealing in this regard; and then there is Becky, who was strongly encouraged by school administrators to make an "Opportunity Transfer" because of her less than stellar grades. According to the interview data, mid-year school changes are nearly synonymous with awkwardly reactive transitions during which students may be mistakenly transplanted into classes they've already taken, or placed in classrooms where they are ill prepared to succeed, due in part to curricular incoherence between the sending and receiving schools.

Under the best circumstances, however, a thoughtful strategy underlies a planned school change. In the case I cited in Chapter 6, Barbara's parents carefully surveyed the market for schools before finally coming to the conclusion that the performing arts program at North Bay High School best suited their daughter's needs, and Paul's father went so far as to strategically purchase a new home in order to get his son into a better school district. Since the survey data commingle reactive and strategic mobility, it is likely that social and educational consequences have been diluted, which leaves open the possibility that the underlying mechanism by which mobility impacts social capital development and/or academic achievement has much to do with the reasons for transience, exercising a greater influence perhaps than does the frequency of its occurrence.

What can be done about reactive student mobility?

Although adolescents frequently change schools when their families change residences, survey results from Chapter 4 show that a large share of student mobility in middle schools and high schools does *not* follow inevitably from family relocation. This would suggest that reactive forms of student transience may be amenable to thoughtful policy solutions. Since the survey findings also suggest that Mexican origin youth are more apt to change schools without changing residences than are their non-Latino White counterparts, they may have more to gain from strategies designed to reduce unnecessary student mobility.

Reducing unnecessary student mobility. Is it possible to diminish high rates of student mobility? Case studies have shown that schools undertaking substantial and meaningful reforms can in fact do so (Rumberger, 2003). In a three-year period from 1987 to 1990, Hollibrook Accelerated School in Houston, Texas reduced its student mobility rate from 104 percent to 47 percent. Programs that target "high-risk" students have also been shown to reduce student mobility dramatically. For instance, a successful dropout prevention program in Southern California reduced student turnover by one-half among the most at-risk Latino students in a Los Angeles area middle school (Rumberger, 1995).

In today's accountability-oriented environment, however, there may be an inherent disincentive for schools to work toward the retention of otherwise transient youth. More specifically, the reauthorization of the Elementary and Secondary Education Act, No Child Left Behind, requires states to assess the "Adequate Yearly Progress" (AYP) of each school each year. One way to demonstrate improvement with regard to school-level test score performance and dropout rates is to enroll higher performing students while encouraging academically challenged students to head elsewhere, a disturbing phenomenon that has been thoroughly reported in a recent series of articles in *The New York Times* (Lewin, 2003a, 2003b, 2004; Lewin & Medina, 2003; Medina & Lewin, 2003). In the emergent education reform environment, schools must grapple honestly and self-critically with accountability incentives that implicitly encourage the removal of under-performing students, as was noted in the case of Becky in Chapter 4. Moreover, working-class Latinos—depending in part on whether immigrant parents can bridge language and cultural barriers to intervene effectively on behalf of their children—may be particularly vulnerable to the "card shuffling" that results when school administrators push underperforming students out their doors, often by employing Opportunity Transfers to be rid of the so-called "trouble-makers" (Bowditch, 1993; Fine, 1991; Rumberger & Larson, 1998; Gotbaum, 2002).

Report cohort mobility rates. What are the alternative means of support and accountability policies that might be established so as to encourage secondary schools to undertake efforts to reduce student mobility? Perhaps districts and/or schools should be provided with extra funding to document cohort graduation rates (the proportion of students who graduate from a specific entering class or cohort of students). Measuring mobility and graduation rates in this way would at least provide a partial reflection of the "holding power" of schools—by which I mean schools' capacity to engage students in the educational process so as to assure more stable student populations. As the U.S. Department of Education points out, cohort graduation rates provide a much better picture of how many students from each grade cohort complete or drop out of school over time. Knowing this information would also enable researchers, educators, and policymakers to calculate the number of students from each cohort who left before completion—the cohort mobility rate (Rumberger et al., 1999). Schools required to report base-year cohort mobility rates could be evaluated over set periods to measure increase or decrease in overall rates of student transience in comparison to base year figures. In short, districts and schools with intrepid student populations, particularly those in the inner-city, face a set of special challenges that merit support that is commensurate to those challenges. Those schools that succeed in reducing the incidence of reactive mobility across time should be rewarded for promoting a more stable educational environment precisely because it is likely to have direct bearing on the standards of educational achievement for all students who participate in the system.[69] As things stand now, however, no one in the public sector is directly or adequately accountable for the educational performance of mobile adolescents.

If we are sensitive to the tension between current accountability schemes and the responsibility of doing the right thing for highly mobile students, it should be apparent that we need to frame the problem of accountability as a systemic one. Beyond examining aggregate test scores of individual schools in isolation (a method that might reward schools for using OT's to distribute their responsibilities elsewhere), we should also measure accountability more broadly, at the school district level. Indeed, student mobility is best understood as an intra-district phenomenon that occurs within a localized geographic area (Hansen, 1995; Kerbow, 1996; Rumberger & Larson, 1998; Offenberg, forthcoming).[70] If AYP was redefined in such a way that it could function as both a district and a school performance standard, such a policy would encourage effective district-level strategies and a greater degree of between-school coordination and collaboration. Thus, high rates of non-promotional student transience could be seen for what they really are, and schools would see themselves as part of the solution to the wider problems within a district. In sum, mobility-related accountability mechanisms should be adjusted to draw district-level and school-level distinctions regarding student mobility in order to allow for more thoughtful, systemic educational reform efforts (Offenberg, forthcoming).

What does this study reveal about the availability of social capital and its convertibility into valued educational outcomes?

At this point in time little is known about the relative importance of social capital across domains and between racial/ethnic groups. A central argument put forth in this book is that some forms of social capital may be more instrumental to the educational performance of adolescent youth than others, depending on and conditioned by the people who possess the social capital and the places where they attempt its exchange. To investigate this premise, I have evaluated various forms of social capital with regard to its availability (Chapter 5) and also its convertibility into twelfth grade test score performance (Chapters 6 and 7). The results suggest that in many instances Mexican Americans are disadvantaged on both fronts. Again, it is worth emphasizing that these findings are partly the consequence of the unique challenges faced by Mexican Americans, including the difficulties accompanying lower socioeconomic status and the special burdens faced by the immigrant second generation, some of the very same factors contributing to high rates of mobility among Mexican origin youth. For example, the descriptive statistics in Chapter 5 suggest that greater stocks of family, peer, and community social capital are available among adolescents whose SES is above the sample mean, and these findings support the notion that the children of middle-class parents share advantages, in terms of the availability of resources that inhere in their social networks, over their working- and lower-class peers (McNeal, 1999; Horvat et al., 2003).

Exceptions to the patterns of contextualized Mexican American network disadvantage do also emerge from the *NELS:88* data. For instance, although adolescents of Mexican descent report a comparable shortage in the accumulation of many forms of social capital measured in this study, they still note higher levels of social capital than Whites when it comes to the *school* domain, particularly with regard to *Academically Relevant Teacher/Student Interaction*. As pertains to the utility of social capital, *Peer Connectedness* within more personal social networks emerges, per the structural models in Chapter 6, as an especially strong twelfth grade achievement predictor among Mexican origin youth. A troubling irony accompanies these findings, however. To whit, although Mexican origin youth may be advantaged in reported stocks of *Academically Relevant Teacher/Student Interaction*, this form of social capital apparently exercises a significantly *negative* influence on their twelfth grade test score performance, whereas, according to the same outcome measure, Whites appear to benefit from its positive impact. Also while *Peer Connectedness* emerges as a robust and especially salient test score predictor among adolescent Mexican Americans, Whites are advantaged in terms of its availability.

In at least some circumstances where Chicanos seem to have the advantage in terms of available stocks of social capital, they are already disadvantaged in terms of its instrumental utility. Even where social capital acts to lubricate the wheels of Mexican American educational advancement, there may not be enough of it to go around. Although these findings do not in-and-of-themselves confirm the *counterfeit* social capital hypothesis, Massiel's classroom experience in Chapter 7 illustrates a disconcerting, albeit not entirely surprising, social reality—which is simply that not all relationships are convertible into beneficial outcomes. Even as my findings arc toward the notion that close-knit peers, such as Julio and Arturo, benefit from shared *confianza* and mutual understanding as resources fortifying normative expectations (Chapter 6), I have cited, and my findings partly support, other research underscoring impediments to the formation of adolescents' interpersonal networks—e.g., socioeconomic disadvantage and nativity status barriers—that seem particularly problematic for Mexican origin youth (Valenzuela, 1999; Stanton-Salazar, 2001). It follows that more directed investigations of factors inhibiting the availability of social capital and its convertibility into minority achievement merit further consideration.

On the whole, then, this study offers mixed reviews regarding the educational utility of social capital across domains. Within the family, involved parents, who are consistently firm in clarifying and enforcing guidelines, enact authoritative support that can jumpstart kids like Julio into realizing, "I can do this." Even though most parents typically express interest in and support for their children's schooling, this study mirrors other studies showing that economic hardship and language barriers often impinge on immigrant parents' ability to influence school personnel on behalf of their children. With regard to social capital among peers, students such as Melissa and Patricia, whose friends share pro-school attitudes, appear to benefit from the *proactive* nature of unsolicited friendship support (Chapter 6). And again, *Peer Connectedness* is a robust twelfth grade test score predictor. Nevertheless, it is also the case that adolescents who orient themselves toward schooling coexist precariously, particularly in the inner-city schools, alongside their more "street-oriented" counterparts.

Social capital at the community level can also produce beneficial outcomes, and the structural models show that test scores improve as a result of community volunteering, at least among non-Latino Whites. Interview findings suggest, however, that dangerous inner-city neighborhoods sometimes cause residents to "stay in the house," choosing relative isolation over the perceived risks of neighborliness, as Iván's father so forcefully articulated in Chapter 5. Lastly, successful interactions with caring school personnel can improve students' motivation and their educational expectations, and indeed such exemplarily trusting relationships may encourage students like Jason to persevere toward higher educational goals. The findings of Chapter 7 sound a cautionary note, however, suggesting that Mexican origin youth in possession of apparently valued forms of social currency may sometimes be the unwitting recipients of a form of *counterfeit* social capital which actually impinges on their educational success (Ream, 2003). As if counterbalancing the many positive manifestations of social capital I have described, we are reminded that relationships are also fraught with subtractive elements. Under optimal conditions, social capital is convertible into socially desirable outcomes, but when deployed in the wrong proportion or in unhealthy or disingenuous circumstances, it can be counterproductive.

Schools as the fulcrum for social capital development

Given the sort of multi-directionality of the ways in which interpersonal relationships manifest themselves, we may wonder how the resources inherent in social networks might be harnessed to the explicit educational *benefit* of adolescents, and, in particular, working-class youth of Mexican descent. As the most obviously public social network serving children, our public schools offer a good place to start looking for and providing answers.

I would hardly be alone in re-asserting the Jeffersonian proposition that schools remain to this day the most powerful American institution for the advancement of republican ideals and social good. But the achievement gap offers *prima facie* evidence that contradicts our faith in the beneficent power of schools to act as "the great leveler" of social hierarchy (McMurrer & Sawhill, 1998) or, as the 19th century educator and philosopher Horace Mann once stated so optimistically, as the "balance wheel of the social machinery" (Cremin, 1957). American public schools are still a work-in progress, and thus the social networks they either do or do not foster are amenable to policy manipulation and better accountability schemes. Existing at the intersection between family and community, public schools constitute a crucial public space for augmenting beneficial forms of family, peer, community and, of course, school social capital—all under the same roof.

But, specifically, what sort of actions might schools take to *capital-ize* the social networks available to working-class, frequently transient, and minority adolescents, and how can thoughtful policy facilitate appropriate educational action? Can secondary schools be better designed to act as the fulcrum for social capital development among working-class minority youth across family, peer, community, and school domains? The nationwide movement designed to create a new generation of smaller and more personalized public high schools might offer at least a partial answer. Borne, in part, of public-private partnerships with the Bill & Melinda Gates Foundation and the Carnegie Corporation of New York, many of these new small high schools are structured in collaboration with community partners outside the education bureaucracy, including social service organizations, museums, and higher education institutions (Hendrie, 2004), in order to bolster forms of community social capital that can improve students' school performance.

Other more programmatic approaches target test score performance as well as the below average rate of both high school completion and college attendance among Latinos who demonstrate varied levels of achievement upon entering secondary schools. One such effort, the ALAS program—*Achievement for Latinos through Academic Success*—is a dropout prevention program targeting high-risk middle-school Latino youth who live in impoverished urban neighborhoods. The program's four components include: (1) the *family* component, whereby school personnel encourage parents to become more involved in their children's education; (2) the *adolescent* component, focused on locating students in supportive peer groups to enhance their social problem solving skills, reinforce achievement-oriented behaviors, and encourage engagement in school; (3) the *community* component, focused on enhancing collaboration between the school and family service agencies, community mental health organizations, gang intervention projects, and recreation and sports programs; and (4) the *school* component, whereby ALAS counselors work with middle school teachers to initiate more regular feedback to students and parents regarding students' educational progress and needs (Gándara et al., 1998). One study evaluating ALAS concluded that the program had a substantial, practical impact on students directly affected by its interventions, reducing student turnover by one half among the most at-risk Latino students in a Los Angeles area middle school (Rumberger, 1995).

Another such program, the Puente Project, targets Latino students across a wide achievement spectrum and within the first two years of high school, offering to help them graduate and go on to college. Explicitly designed to bridge the high school/college divide, there are three major components of the Puente Project intervention. The *instructional* component includes a two-year-long class during the ninth and tenth grades in which a Puente cohort of 30 students maintain their own writing portfolios covering the regular English curriculum as well as a Latino literature component. Student cohorts prepare for college eligibility *via* classroom processes that include collective deliberation, engaging cultural discussions, classroom presentations, and shared knowledge about what it takes to attain a college education and subsequent career success. The *counseling* component is largely designed to ensure that Puente students are placed in college preparatory classes and offered the information necessary to prepare themselves for college eligibility. Counselors supervise college visits, initiate meetings between parents and Puente personnel, and even oversee the extramural Puente Club through which students socialize in structured extracurricular environments. Lastly, a community mentor liaison is responsible for the Puente Project's *mentoring* component, which is fashioned so as to harness the power of community social capital by identifying, training, and then matching Latino community mentors with ninth graders. By this process, the mentoring component facilitates capital-rich and mutually rewarding relationships between students and community volunteers. The Chicano/Latino Policy Project, a research program affiliated with the Institute for the Study of Social Change at UC Berkeley, offers a thorough overview of ALAS and the Puente Project, including cost-benefit analyses (Gándara et al., 1998). The authors also review a third program known by its acronym, AVID (*Advancement Via Individual Determination*), that seems to me outstanding for its particular sensitivity to the notion that underachieving ethnic or linguistic minority students from low-income families might benefit from the thoughtful re-organization of social life in and beyond the school.

AVID. Perhaps awkwardly described as an "untracking" program,[71] AVID aims to counter current education trends whereby student groups are increasingly segregated within schools as a result of tracking practices (Lucas, 1999; Noguera, 2003). More specifically, AVID identifies students of mid-range abilities in the eighth grade who demonstrate the potential to go on to college, enrolling them in college-preparatory classes while also offering a system of social scaffolding (Vygotsky, 1978) to help ensure their academic success. There are at least two fairly recent studies that suggest AVID students are enrolling in college more frequently than their early high school records would predict (Mehan, et al., 1996; Guthrie & Guthrie, 2000).

One way AVID taps the resources that inhere in social networks is by targeting the potentially valuable school/home connection, recognizing that the role of minority parents in their children's education is not fixed (Chrispeels & Rivero, 2001; Epstein, 1992), but can be altered *via* formal programs encouraging parental involvement (Bryk & Schneider, 2002) and through the development of trusting and reciprocal school/parent relations. Parents who agree to support their children's academic engagement sign contracts to have their children participate in AVID in middle school and high school. Parent advisory boards, family study skills gatherings (the "AVID Family Study Skills" series and "Destined for College" series are available in both English and Spanish), and college awareness meetings are among the AVID activities facilitating parent involvement in schools. Family Night Dinners are another way that AVID bridges the family-school gap. For example, the AVID program at Hayfield Secondary in Alexandria, Virginia, hosts bi-monthly dinners where the entire AVID Site Team plans and prepares a meal, while the AVID students make invitations, set tables, and report on AVID academic goings-on. Family Night Dinners routinely occur at AVID sites throughout the country.[72]

Peer social networks are also the focus of thoughtful development in the AVID program, challenging the typically individualized emphasis of the current educational experience by helping students become part of a trusting, school-oriented network of peers that share common educational goals. By bringing mid-performing adolescents together in collaborative learning environments—study groups, reader-writer workshops, and a special elective class that meets for one academic period a day, 180 days a year, for three or four years—AVID reframes achievement as a group experience rather than as an individual one (Mehan et al., 1996; Gándara et al., 1998; Stanton-Salazar et al., 2000). If peer social capital in the form of *Peer Connectedness* is indeed the achievement-related predictor this study suggests, then programs such as AVID, endeavoring to connect students across generation, language, cultural, and grade-level barriers merit further study and policy consideration for their potential to mitigate Mexican American underachievement.

AVID, not unlike ALAS and the Puente Project, also stands by the notion that the broader community must be woven into the fabric of the school experience, and the program even expects colleges and universities, as well as area businesses, to share in the task of preparing and motivating underserved students who are willing to work hard to get into college. For example, area college students (often AVID program graduates), including those who embody "bridging skills" such as bi-literacy and cross-cultural sensitivity, are recruited into AVID programs as tutors and role models on a 1:7 tutor-student ratio. AVID also invites college counselors to answer questions, to assist adolescents with college and scholarship applications, and to acquaint them with the colleges and universities they might attend. AVID also promotes "service learning" whereby adolescents are encouraged to do community service. Thus, the program acts on the "two-way street" notion that healthy community elements should be directed into the school ethos and that, at the same time, adolescents should be directed outward toward the broader community (Gándara & Gibson, 2004).

Lastly, AVID reconceptualizes teaching by discouraging the idea of the teacher as an imparter of knowledge or information and imagining the role of teacher as a kind of "academic parent," learning facilitator, and co-participant in the learning process. As a result, teacher-centered classrooms give way to classrooms managed by a lead teacher who not only shares in the development of students' knowledge, but also charges college tutors with the responsibility for appropriate, individualized instruction of students. Benefiting from the reciprocal nature of the relationships developed in classrooms and structured under the notion that learning is a cooperative endeavor, school personnel may be less inclined to fall into patterns of benign neglect and counterfeit niceness that are so detrimental to minority youth. If it is indeed the case, as this study suggests, that the question of how social capital influences specific groups of students depends on how valued their development is by school personnel and by other adults in key institutional roles, then the AVID program appears to be headed in the right direction.

The roots of each of the three programs noted above—ALAS, the Puente Project, and AVID—tap into the notion that successfully implementing effective school programs must be predicated on a social paradigm, one in which it is understood that relationships, and the funds of knowledge that inhere within them (Delpit, 1995; Stanton-Salazar, 1997), are dramatically important to the success of all students, and perhaps to low-status students in particular. Although findings on *counterfeit* social capital suggest that key participants in the school-based social networks of adolescent youth sometimes contribute to the reproduction of inequality, the importance of high school counselors and their ability to interfere with reproductive processes should never be underestimated, particularly in schools with high rates of student transience.

Bolster school guidance counseling. School personnel, and perhaps school counselors in particular, are in a unique position to act as important bridges between the world of children and the world of adults, especially during adolescence, when this process of transition becomes explicit (Lombana, 1985; Zeldin & Price, 1995; Stanton-

Salazar, 2001). Yet guidance counseling in many urban high schools is woefully inadequate, with overwhelming counselor/student ratios—1:740 in four of the ten largest U.S. cities in 1990. Counselors offer even less advising in California, where the counselor-to-student ratio is a pathetic 1:979. Even the most optimistic estimate of the current national average of one guidance counselor to 561 students paints a less than rosy picture of what appears quite literally to be a lonely profession (McClafferty, McDonough & Nuñez, 2002). As a result, it is not uncommon for new students—particularly those who arrive in the middle of the school year—to be misplaced in classrooms for which they are either over-prepared or under-prepared. Consequently, student mobility is often a prelude to subsequent classroom-to-classroom transfers in the wake of a non-promotional school change, before students are finally settled into a more stabilized routine (Rumberger et al., 1999). Since school counselors are largely responsible for guiding mobile students on both the departure and arrival ends of the school transfer process, bolstering the bilingual and bicultural counseling staffs at schools serving an especially transient immigrant second generation would undoubtedly help mitigate the potential negative impacts of student mobility.

Let me offer two caveats before closing with recommendations for bolstering social capital in the service of Latino youth—and, in particular, Mexican origin youth. First, education reform, programmatic intervention, and school personnel considerations are most wisely undertaken in the context of a cumulative body of research and evaluation findings (McDonnell, 2000). Moreover, since policy recommendations as well as program and personnel adaptations are not one-size-fits-all propositions that can be readily applied across diverse contexts, they aught to be acted upon only after careful analyses of local data and needs have been undertaken, and subsequently tailored to the local circumstances in which they are to be applied.

Conclusion

Fifty years ago, on May 17, 1954, Chief Justice Earl Warren gave legal expression to a changing America when the Supreme Court disavowed the doctrine permitting "separate but equal" schools. The Court's unanimous decision in *Brown vs. Board of Education of Topeka, Kansas* marked a winning battle that ended *dejure* segregation in a continuing war on the *defacto* elements of racial inequality. Twelve years later, in spite of the optimism that followed the *Brown* decision, the *Coleman Report* described in great detail the persistence of racial/ethnic differences in school performance. And today, the achievement gap stubbornly persists in a society that prides itself on meritocracy and the equality of educational opportunity. While the equal opportunity premise merits skepticism, particularly in light of the troubling re-segregating of America's schools (Orfield, 2001; Frankenberg et al., 2003; Rumberger & Palardy, forthcoming), the undeniable existence of group-level achievement differences demonstrates that regardless of opportunity distribution—or perhaps because of a lack thereof—educational outcomes remain stratified along racial/ethnic lines.

This study suggests that while the *mobility/social capital dynamic* may contribute to the persistence of that problem, there are also many other paths, both individual and collective, by which group-level achievement differences and the low average level of Mexican American student performance are perpetuated. An exclusive focus on the *dynamic* and the social underpinnings of educational inequality will not alone solve the problem. A fair reading of this study not only calls for reducing unnecessary student mobility and increasing stocks of beneficial forms of social capital, but also affirms the importance of ongoing efforts to explore ways in which other kinds of economic, human and cultural capital can also contribute to or detract from the educational advancement of school children in the U.S. In simplest terms, money matters, information and knowledge matter, and genuinely beneficent social relationships, when given structured support, can also help minority children overcome huge resource gaps to meet their true potential. Since a nation cannot long remain under-educated and free, it is imperative that we harness the full weight of our individual and collectively convertible resources—material, human, cultural, and social forms of capital—to erase the achievement gap and the particular causes of Mexican American underachievement from America's educational landscape.

[68] Even stable students who attended California high schools with high mobility rates (where 40 percent of tenth graders left high school by the twelfth grade) score 1.5 points lower on the *NELS:88* standardized tenth grade math test than otherwise similar students who attended high schools with mobility rates of 10 percent (Rumberger et al., 1999).

[69] As with all measures of school effectiveness, however, other demographic characteristics that can contribute to the overall rate of student mobility (i.e., school-level measures of socioeconomic status) should be considered in any policy formula of this nature.

[70] Rumberger & Larson (1998) found that 80 percent of non-promotional school changes for a cohort of urban Los Angeles area Latino students were within the same district.

[71] Untracking is different from detracking. Whereas untracking places low-track students in high-track classes as a way to incrementally atrophy the tracking system, the intent of detracking is to dismantle the entire tracking system at once (Gándara et al., 1998).

[72] It should be noted, however, that while AVID's expressed policy emphasizes parent involvement in school, and school outreach to parents, Mehan et al., (1996) identify instances where there is a "downside" to the program-parent relationship—at least as it played out in their ethnographic analysis of the AVID program in eight San Diego Unified School District high schools. More specifically, the authors report that AVID sometimes acts on behalf of parents to such an extent that parents are not as involved in their adolescent's education as they might otherwise be.

REFERENCES

Aguirre, A. and R. Martinez. 1993. *Chicanos in higher education: Issues and dilemmas for the 21st century*. Washington, D.C.: George Washington University, School of Education and Human Development.

Ainsworth-Darnell, J. and D. Downey. 1998. Assessing the oppositional culture explanation for racial/ethnic differences in school performance. *American Sociological Review* 63: 536-53.

Alexander, K., D. Entwisle, and M. Thompson. 1987. School performance, status relations, and the structure of sentiment: Bringing the teacher back in. *American Sociological Review* 52: 665-82.

Alexander, K., D. Entwisle, and S. Dauber. 1996. Children in motion: School transfers and elementary school performance. *The Journal of Educational Research* 90 (September-October): 3-12

Amato, P. 1987. Family processes in one-parent, step-parent, and intact families: The child's point of view. *Journal of Marriage and the Family* 49: 327-37.

Anderson, J. and D. Gerbing. 1988. Structural equation modeling in practice: A review and recommended two-step approach. *Psychological Bulletin* 103: 411-23.

Anzaldúa, G. 1999. *Borderlands la frontera: The new Mestiza.* 2d ed. San Francisco: Aunt Lute Books.

Appiah, K. 1992. *In my father's house: Africa in the philosophy of culture.* Oxford: Oxford University Press.

Arbuckle, J. 1996. Full information estimation in the presence of incomplete data. In *Advanced structural equation modeling: Issues and techniques*, edited by G. Marcoulides and R. Schumacker. Mahwah, New Jersey: Lawrence Erlbaum Associates.

Arbuckle, J. and W. Wothke. 1999. *Amos 4 user's guide.* Chicago: SmallWaters Corporation.

Arvizu, S. 1996. Family, community and school collaboration. In *Handbook of research on teacher education.* 2d ed. New York: Simon & Schuster Macmillan.

Astone N. and S. McLanahan. 1991. Family structure, parental practices and high school completion. *American Sociological Review* 51: 403-12.

———. 1994. Family structure, residential mobility, and school dropout: A research note. *Demography* 31: 575-84.

Astone, N., C. Nathanson, R. Schoen, and Y. Kim. 1999. Family demography, Social theory, and investment in social capital. *Population and Development Review* 25 (1): 1-31.

Au, K. and J. Mason. 1981. Social organizational factors in learning to read: the balance of rights hypothesis. *Reading Research Quarterly* 17 (1): 115-52.

Baratz, J. and S. Baratz. 1970. Early childhood intervention: The social scientific basis of institutionalized racism. *Harvard Educational Review* 39: 29-50.

Barr, A. 1998. *Enterprise performance and the functional diversity of social capital.* Working paper series 98-1. Oxford: University of Oxford, Institute of Economics and Statistics.

Baumol, W., S. Blackman, and E. Wolff. 1989. *Productivity and American leadership: The long view*. Cambridge: MIT Press.

Baumrind, D. 1971. Current patterns of parental authority. *Developmental Psychology Monographs*, Part 2, 4 (1): 1-103.

Bean, F. and M. Tienda. 1987. *The Hispanic population of the United States*. New York: Russell Sage Foundation.

Becerra, R. 1988. The Mexican-American family. In *Ethnic families in America: Patterns and variations*, edited by C. Mindel, R. Gabenstein and R. Wright. New York: Elsevier.

Becker, G. 1964. *Human capital*. New York: National Bureau of Economic Research.

Becker, G. and N. Tomes. 1986. Human capital and the rise and fall of families. *Journal of Labor Economics* 4: S1-S39.

Bellah, R., R. Madsen, W. Sullivan, A. Swidler, and S. Tipton. 1986. *Habits of the heart: Individualism and commitment in American life*. New York: Harper & Row.

Bensman, D. 1994. *Lives of the Graduates of Central Park East Elementary School: Where Have They Gone? What Did They Really Learn?* New York: Columbia University, Teachers College, National Center for Restructuring Education, Schools and Teaching.

Benson, C. and D. Weigel. 1981. Ninth-grade adjustments and achievement as related to mobility. *Educational Research Quarterly* 5 (4): 15-19.

Benson, T., J. Haycraft, J. Steyaert, and D. Weigel. 1979. Mobility in sixth graders as related to achievement, adjustment, and socioeconomic status. *Psychology in the Schools* 16: 444-47.

Bereiter, C. and S. Englemann. 1966. *Teaching disadvantaged children in preschool*. Englewood Cliffs, New Jersey: Prentice-Hall.

Berndt, T. and G. Ladd, eds. 1989. *Peer relationships in child development.* New York: Wiley.

Birman, B. and G. Natriello. 1978. Perspectives in absenteeism in high school. *Journal of Research and Development in Education* 11 (summer): 29-38.

Blos, P. 1967. The second individuation process of adolescence. *Psychoanalytic Study of the Child* 1: 183-98.

Boisjoly, J., G. Duncan, and S. Hofferth. 1995. Access to social capital. *Journal of Family Issues* 16: 609-31.

Bourdieu, P. 1973. Cultural reproduction and social reproduction. In *Knowledge, education, and cultural change*, edited by R. Brown. London: Tavistock.

———. 1977. Cultural reproduction and social reproduction. In *Power and ideology in education*, edited by J. Karabel & A.H. Halsey. New York: Oxford University Press.

———. 1979. *Outline of a theory of practice.* Cambridge: Cambridge University Press.

———. 1984. *Distinction: A social critique of the judgment of taste.* Cambridge: Harvard University Press.

———. 1986. The forms of capital. In *Handbook of Theory and Research on the Sociology of Education*, edited by J. Richardson. New York: Greenwood Press.

———. 1990. *Reproduction in education, society and culture.* London: Sage Publications.

Bourdieu, P. and J. Passerson. 1977. *Reproduction in education, society and culture.* Translated by R. Nice. Beverly Hills, CA: Sage Publications.

Bourdieu, P. and L. Wacquant. 1992. *An Invitation to Reflexive Sociology.* Chicago: University of Chicago Press

Bowditch, C. 1993. Getting rid of troublemakers: High school disciplinary procedures and the production of dropouts. *Social Problems* 40: 493-509.

Bowles, S. 1971. Unequal Education and the Reproduction of the Social Division of Labor. In *Schooling in a Corporate Society*, edited by M. Carnoy. New York: David McKay.

Bowles, S. and H. Gintis. 1972. I.Q. in the U.S. class structure. *Social Policy* 3: 65-96.

———. 1976. *Schooling in capitalist America: Educational reform and the contradictions of economic life.* New York: Basic Books.

Brantlinger, E. 1993. *The politics of social class in secondary school: Views of affluent and impoverished youth.* New York: Teachers College Press.

Brehm, J. and W. Rahn. 1997. Individual-level evidence for the causes and consequences of social capital. *American Journal of Political Science* 41: 999-1023.

Briggs, C. 1986. *Learning how to ask: A sociolinguistic appraisal of the role of the interview in social science research.* Cambridge: Cambridge University Press.

Briggs, X. 1998. Brown kids in White suburbs: Housing mobility and the multiple faces of social capital. *Housing Policy Debate* 9 (1): 177-221. Washington, D.C.: Fannie Mae Foundation.

Brittain, C. 1963. Adolescent choices and parent-peer cross pressures. *American Sociological Review* 28: 385-91.

Bronfenbrenner, U. 1979. *The ecology of human development.* Cambridge: Harvard University Press.

———. 1986. Ecology of the family as a context for human development. *Developmental Psychology* 22: 723-42.

Brooks-Gunn, J. and G. Duncan. 1997. The effects of poverty on children. *The Future of Children* 7 (2): 55-71.

Browne, M. and R. Cudeck. 1993. Alternative ways of assessing model fit. In *Testing structural equation models*, edited by K. Bollen and J. Long. Newbury Park, CA: Sage Publications.

Bryk, A. and B. Schneider. 2002. *Trust in schools: A core resource for improvement.* New York: Russell Sage Foundation.

Bryk, A. and M. Driscoll. 1988. *The school as community: Theoretical foundations, contextual influences, and consequences for students and teachers.* Madison: University of Wisconsin, National Center of Effective Secondary Schools.

Bryk, A., V. Lee, and P. Holland. 1993. *Catholic schools and the common good.* Cambridge: Harvard University Press.

Bumpass, L. 1984. Children and marital disruption: A replication and update. *Demography* 21: 71-82.

Buriel, R. 1984. Integration with traditional Mexican-American culture and sociocultural adjustment. In *Chicano/a Psychology*. 2d ed. Edited by J. Martinez Jr. and R. Mendoza. Orlando, Florida: Academic Press.

Buriel, R. and D. Cardoza. 1988. Sociocultural correlates of achievement among three generations of Mexican American high school seniors. *American Educational Research Journal* 25: 177-92.

Burrell, G. and G. Morgan. 1979. *Sociological paradigms and organizational analysis.* London: Heinemann.

Byrne, B. 1998. *Structural equation modeling with LISREL, PRELIS, and SIMPLIS: Basic concepts, application, and programming.* Hillside, New Jersey: Lawrence Erlbaum Associates.

Cairns, R., B. Cairns, H. Neckerman, S. Gest, and J. Gariepy. 1988. Social networks and aggressive behavior: Peer support or peer rejection? *Developmental Psychology* 24: 815-23.

California State Department of Education. 1983. *Desegregation and bilingual education: Partners in quality education.* Conference Proceedings. Sacramento, CA: California State Department of Education.

Carbonaro, W. 1998. A little help from my friend's parents: Intergenerational closure and educational outcomes. *Sociology of Education* 71: 295-313.

Cárdenas, J. 1975. Bilingual education, desegregation and a third alternative. *Inequality in Education* 19 (February): 19-22.

Carnegie Council on Adolescent Development. 1995. *Great transitions, preparing adolescents for a new century.* New York: Carnegie Corporation.

Carnoy, M. 1974. *Education as cultural imperialism.* New York: David McKay.

Carnoy, M., R. Elmore, and L. Sisken, eds. 2003. *The new accountability: High schools and high-stakes testing.* New York: RoutledgeFalmer.

Carroll, D. 1996. *National Education Longitudinal Study (NELS:88/94): Methodology Report.* Washington, DC: U.S. Government Printing Office.

Catsambis, S. and J. Garland. 1997. *Parental involvement in students' education during middle school and high school.* Report No. 18. New York: Center for Research on the Education of Students Placed at Risk.

Chapa, J. and R. Valencia. 1993. Latino population growth, demographic characteristics, and educational stagnation: An examination of recent trends. *Hispanic Journal of Behavioral Sciences* 15: 165-87.

Chrispeels, J. and E. Rivero. 2001. Engaging Latino families for student success: How parent education can reshape parents' sense of place in the education of their children. *Peabody Journal of Education* 76: 119-69.

Chrispeels, J., S. Castillo, and J. Brown. 2000. School leadership teams: A process model of team development. *School Effectiveness and School Improvement* 11 (1): 20-56.

Claes, M. 1992. Friendship and personal adjustment during adolescence. *Journal of Adolescence* 15: 39-55.

Cochran, M. and D. Riley. 1988. Mother reports of children's personal networks: Antecedents, concomitants, and consequences. In *Social networks of children, adolescents and college students*, edited by S.

Salzinger, J. Antrobus and M. Hammer. Hillsdale, New Jersey: Lawrence Erlbaum Associates.

Coleman, J. 1961. *The adolescent society*. New York: Free Press of Glencoe.

———. 1971. *Resources for social change: Race in the United States*. New York: Wiley.

———. 1988. Social capital in the creation of human capital. *American Journal of Sociology* 94: S95-S120.

———. 1990. *Foundations of social theory*. Cambridge: Harvard University Press.

Coleman, J., E. Campbell, C. Hobson, J. McPartland, A. Mood, F. Weinfield, and R. York. 1966. *Equality of educational opportunity*. Washington, D.C.: U.S. Government Printing Office.

Coleman, J. and T. Hoffer. 1987. *Public and private high schools: The impact of communities. New* York: Basic Books.

Coleman, J., T. Hoffer, and S. Kilgore. 1982. *High school achievement*. New York: Basic Books.

College Entrance Examination Board. 1999. *Reaching the top: A report of the national task force of minority high achievement.* New York: The College Board.

Collins, R. 1971. Functional and conflict theories of educational stratification. *American Sociological Review* 36: 1002-19.

Collins, W. 1990. Parent-child relationships and the transition to adolescence: Continuity and change in interaction, affect and cognition. In *From Childhood to Adolescence: A Transitional Period? Advances in Adolescent Development*. Vol. 2. Edited by R. Montemayor and G. Adams. Newbury Park, California: Sage Publications, 1990.

Collins, W., E. Maccoby, L. Steinberg, E. Hetherington, and M. Bornstein. 2000. Contemporary research on parenting: The case for nature and nurture. *American Psychologist* 55: 218-32.

Commission on Minority Participation in Education and American Life. 1988. *One-third of a nation.* Washington, D.C.: American Council on Education and the Education Commission of the States.

Conchas, G. 2001. Structuring failure and success: Understanding the variability in Latino school engagement. *Harvard Educational Review* 71 (3): 475-504.

Conway, M. 1991. *Political participation in the United States*. 2d ed. Washington D.C.: CQ Press.

Cook, P. and J. Ludwig. 1997. Weighing the "burden of 'acting white'": Are there race differences in attitudes toward education? *Journal of Policy Analysis and Management* 16 (2): 256-78.

Cookson, P. 1994. *School choice: The struggle for the soul of American education.* New Haven: Yale University Press.

Courtney, M. and G. Nobilit. 1994. The Principal as caregiver. In *The tapestry of caring: Education as nurturance*, edited by A. Prillaman, D. Eaker and D. Kendrick. Norwood, NJ: Ablex Publishing.

Crane, J. 1991. The epidemic theory of ghettos and neighborhood effects on dropping out and teenage childbearing. *American Journal of Sociology* 96: 1226-59.

Crawford, J. 1989. *Bilingual education: History, politics, theory and practice.* Trenton, New Jersey: Crane.

Cremin, L., ed. 1957. *The republic and the school: Horace Mann on the education of free men.* New York: Teachers College Press.

Crockett, L., A. Petersen, J. Graber, J. Schulenberg, and A. Ebata. 1989. School transitions and adjustment during early adolescence. *Journal of Early Adolescence* 9: 181-210.

Croninger, R. and V. Lee. 1996. *Social capital and children's development: The case of education.* Madison, Wisconsin: Wisconsin Center for Education Research, Center on Organization and Restructuring of Schools.

Croninger, R. and V. Lee. 2001. Social capital and dropping out of high school: Benefits to at-risk students of teachers' support and guidance. *Teachers College Record*, 103, 548-81.

Crosnoe, R., M. Johnson, and G. Elder. 2004. Intergenerational bonding in school: The behavioral and contextual correlates of student-teacher relationships. *Sociology of Education* 77: 60-81.

Cummins, J. 1981. The role of primary language development in promoting educational success for language minority students. In *Schooling and language minority students: A theoretical framework.* Sacramento, CA: California State Department of Education.

Cusick, P. 1983. *The egalitarian ideal and the American high school.* New York: Longman.

Darder, A., R. Torres, and H. Gutierrez, eds. 1997. *Latinos and education: A critical reader*. New York: Routledge.

Davis, M. 2001. *Magical urbanism: Latinos reinvent the U.S. city*. London: Verso.

De la Campa, R. 2001. Latinos and the crossover aesthetic. Forward to *Magical urbanism: Latinos reinvent the U.S. city*, by M. Davis. London: Verso.

De la Rosa, D. and C. Maw. 1990. *Hispanic education: A statistical portrait.* Washington, D.C.: National Council of La Raza.

Delgado-Gaitan, C. 1991. Involving parents in the schools: A process of empowerment. *American Journal of Education* 100 (1): 20-46.

Delgado-Gaitan, C. and H. Trueba. 1991. *Crossing cultural borders: Education for immigrant families in America.* Bristol, Pennsylvania: Falmer Press.

Delpit, L. 1995. *Other people's children: Cultural conflict in the classroom.* New York: New Press.

Deutsch, M., R. Bloom, B. Brown, C. Deutsch, L. Goldstein, V. John, P. Katz, A. Levinson, E. Peisach, and M. Whiteman. 1967. *The disadvantaged child.* New York: Basic Books.

Dewey, J. [1916] 1966. *Democracy and education.* New York: Free Press.

Dika, S. and K. Singh. 2002. Applications of social capital in educational literature: A critical synthesis. *Review of Educational Research* 72: 31-60.

DiMaggio, P. 1982. Cultural capital and school success. *American Sociological Review* 47: 189-201.

Dishion, T. 1990. The family ecology of boys' peer relations in middle childhood. *Child Development* 6 (1): 874-92.

Doyle, A. 1986. *Sherlock Holmes: The Boscombe Valley Mystery*. Manchester, England: World International Publishing Ltd.

DuBois, D., R. Felner, H. Meares, and M. Krier. 1994. Prospective investigation of the effects of socioeconomic disadvantage, life stress, and social support on early adolescent adjustment. *Journal of Abnormal Psychology,* 103, 511-22.

Du Bois, W.E.B. 1903. *The souls of black folk.* Chicago: A.C. McClurg & Company.

Durán, R. 1987. Hispanics' pre-college and undergraduate education: Implications for science and engineering studies. In *Minorities: Their underrepresentation and career differentials in science and engineering,* edited by L.S. Dix. Washington, D.C.: National Academy Press.

Dusek, J. and G. Joseph. 1983. The bases of teacher expectations: A meta-analysis. *Journal of Educational Psychology* 75: 327-46.

Eckert, P. 1989. *Jocks and burnouts: Social categories and identity in the high school.* New York: Teachers College Press.

Education Week. 2004. Teaching and Learning: NEA foundation focuses giving on closing gap. *Education Week* 23 (39): 11.

Ekstrom, R., M. Goertz, J. Pollack, and D. Rock. 1986. Who drops out of high school and why? Findings from a national study. *Teachers College Record* 87: 356-73.

Epstein, J. 1983. Friends in school: Patterns of selection and influence in secondary schools. New York: Academic Press.

Epstein, J. 1992. School and family partnerships. In *Encyclopedia of educational research*. 6th ed. Edited by M. Alkin.

Erikson, E. 1968. *Identity, youth, and crisis*. New York: W.W. Norton and Co., Inc.

Erickson, F. 1987. Transformation and school success: The politics and culture of educational achievement. *Anthropology and Education Quarterly* 18 (4): 335-55.

———. 1993. Transformation and school success: The politics and culture of educational achievement. In *Minority education: Anthropological perspectives*, edited by C. Jordan and E. Jacob. New Jersey: Ablex Publishing Corporation.

Erickson, F. and G. Mohatt. 1982. Cultural organization of participation structures in two classrooms of Indian students. In *Doing the ethnography of schooling: Educational anthropology in action,* edited by G. Spindler. New York: Holt, Rinehart & Winston.

Etzioni, A. 1993. *The spirit of community: Rights, responsibilities & the communitarian agenda*. New York: Crown Publishers.

Fashola, O., R. Slavin, M. Calderón, and R. Durán. 2001. Effective programs for Latino students in elementary and middle schools. In *Effective Programs for Latino Students*, edited by R. Slavin and M. Calderón Mahwah, New Jersey: Lawrence Erlbaum Associates.

Fehrmann, P., T. Keith, and T. Reimers. 1987. Home influence on school learning: Direct and indirect effects of parental involvement on high school grades. *Journal of Educational Research* 80 (6): 330-37.

Feinman-Nemser, S. and R. Floden. 1986. The cultures of teaching. In *Handbook of Research on Teaching*. 2d ed. Edited by M. Wittrock. New York: Macmillan.

Feldman, S. 1999. Only connect: Professors and teachers with a common mission. *Academe* 85 (1): 22-25.

Fernández, R., R. Paulsen, and M. Hirano-Nakanishi. 1989. Dropping out among Hispanic youth. *Social Science Research* 18: 21-52.

Fernandez-Kelly, P. and R. Schauffler. 1996. Divided fates: Immigrant children and the new assimilation. In *The New Second Generation*, edited by A. Portes. New York: Russell Sage Foundation.

Fine, M. 1991. *Framing dropouts: Notes on the politics of an urban public high school.* Albany: State University of New York press.

Flores-González, N. 2002. *School kids/street kids: Identity development in Latino students.* New York: Teachers College Press.

Fordham, S. and J. Ogbu. 1986. Black students' school success: Coping with the "burden of 'acting White.'" *Urban Review* (18) 3: 176-206.

Frankenberg, E., C. Lee, and G. Orfield. 2003. *A multiracial society with segregated schools: Are we losing the dream?* Cambridge: Harvard University, The Harvard Civil Rights Project.

Fukuyama, F. 1995. *Trust: The social virtues and the creation of prosperity.* New York: Free Press.

Fuller, B. and E. Hannum, eds. 2002. *Schooling and social capital in diverse cultures.* Research in Sociology of Education, vol. 13. Boston: JAI/Elsevier Science.

Furstenberg, F. and C. Nord. 1985. Parenting apart: Problems of childrearing after marital disruption. *Journal of Marriage and the Family* 47 (4): 893-904.

Furstenburg, F. and M. Hughes. 1995. Social capital and successful development among at-risk youth. *Journal of Marriage and the Family* 57: 580-92.

Gamoran, A. 1992. Social factors in education. In *Encyclopedia of educational research*, edited by M.Alkin. New York: Macmillan.

Gamoran, A. and R. Mare. 1989. Secondary school tracking and educational inequality: Compensation, reinforcement, or neutrality? *American Journal of Sociology,* 94: 1146-83.

Gándara, P. 1993. Language and ethnicity as factors in school failure: The case of Mexican Americans. In *Children at risk in America: History, concepts and public policy*, edited by R. Wollons. New York: State University of New York Press.

———. 1994. Language and ethnicity as factors in school failure: The case of Mexican Americans. In *Children at Risk in America: History, Concepts and Public Policy,* edited by R. Wollons. Albany: State University of New York Press.

———. 1996. The challenge of Latino education: Implications for social and educational policy. *In Latino politics in California*, edited by A. Chavez. San Diego: UC San Diego, Center of U.S. Mexican Studies.

———. 2001. *Paving the way to postsecondary education: K-12 intervention programs for underrepresented youth.* Report of the National Postsecondary Education Cooperative Working Group on Access to

Postsecondary Education. National Postsecondary Education Cooperative. Report No. NCES-2001-205. Washington, D.C.: U.S. Department of Education.

Gándara, P., K. Larson, H. Mehan, and R. Rumberger. 1998. *Capturing Latino students in the academic pipeline.* Chicano/Latino Policy Project, Policy Report Vol. 1, No. 1. Berkeley, CA: Univ. of California, Berkeley.

Gándara, P. and M. Gibson. 2004. Peers and school performance: Implications for research, policy and practice. In *School connections: U.S. Mexican youth, peers and school achievement*, edited by M. Gibson, P. Gándara, and J. Koyama. New York: Teachers College Press.

García, E. and A. Wiese. 2002. Language, public policy, and schooling: A focus on Chicano English language learners. In *Chicano school failure and success: Past, present and future*. 2d ed. Edited by R.Valencia. London: RoutledgeFalmer.

Garfinkel, I. and S. McLanahan. 1986. *Single mothers and their children: The new American dilemma*. Washington, D.C.: Urban Institute.

Gewertz, C. 2000. Panel targets Hispanic lag in attainment, *Education Week* 20 (5): 1,13.

Gibson, M., P. Gándara, and J. Koyama, eds. 2004. *School connections: U.S. Mexican youth, peers and school achievement.* New York: Teachers College Press.

Gilbert, J. 1978. Extended family integration among second generation Mexican Americans. In *Family and mental health in the Mexican American community.* Monograph No. 7. Edited by J. Casas and S. Keefe. Los Angeles: UCLA, Spanish Speaking Mental Health Research Center.

Gilroy, P. 2000. *Against race: Imagining political culture beyond the color line.* Cambridge: Harvard University Press.

Gintis, H. 1971. Education and the characteristics of worker productivity. *American Economic Review* 61: 266-79.

Goffman, E. 1974. *Frame analysis: An essay on the organization of experience.* New York: Harper & Row.

González, N., L. Moll, M. Tenery, A. Rivera, P. Rendon, R. Gonzales, and C. Amanti. 1995. Funds of knowledge for teaching in Latino households. *Urban Education* 29: 443-70.

Goodenow, C. 1993. Classroom belonging among early adolescent students: Relationships to motivation and achievement. *Journal of Early Adolescence* 13: 21-43.

Goodlad, J. 1984. *A place called school: Prospects for the future.* New York: McGraw-Hill.

Gotbaum, B. 2002. *Pushing out at-risk students: An analysis of high school discharge figures.* New York: The Public Advocate for the City of New York and Advocates for Children.

Gottlieb, B. 1975. The contribution of natural support systems of primary prevention among four social subgroups of adolescent males. *Adolescence* 10: 207-20.

Granovetter, M. 1982. The strength of weak ties: A network theory revisited. In *Social structure and network analysis*, edited by P. Marsden and N. Lin. Beverly Hills, CA: Sage Publications.

———. 1985. Economic action and social structure: The problem of embeddedness. *American Journal of Sociology* 91: 481-510.

Gray, M. and L. Steinberg. 1999. Unpacking authoritative parenting: Reassessing a multidimensional construct. *Journal of Marriage and the Family* 61: 574-87.

Greeley, A. 1997. The other civic America: Religion and social capital. *The American Prospect* 32: 68-73.

Green, M. and T. Brock. 1998. *Trust, mood, and outcomes of friendship determine preferences for real versus ersatz social capital.* Claremeont, California: Pitzer College, International Society of Political Psychology.

Greene, J. 1997. A meta-analysis of the Rossell and Baker review of bilingual education research. *Bilingual Research Journal* [online], 21. Available: http://brj.asu.edu.

Grogger, J. and S. Trejo. 2002. *Falling behind or moving up? The intergenerational progress of Mexican Americans.* San Francisco: Public Policy Institute of California.

Guerrero, M. 2002. Research in bilingual education: Moving beyond the effectiveness debate. In *Chicano school failure and success: Past, present and future*. 2d ed. Edited by R.Valencia. London: RoutledgeFalmer.

Gumperz, J. 1972. The speech community. In *Language and social context*, edited by P. Giglioli. Chicago: Penguin.

Guthrie, L and G. Guthrie. 2000. *Longitudinal research on AVID 1999-2000: Final Report*. Burlingame, CA: Center for Research Evaluation and Training in Education.

Gutmann, A. 1998. Freedom of association: An introductory essay. In *Freedom of association,* edited by A. Gutmann. Princeton, New Jersey: Princeton University Press.

Hagan, J., R. Macmillan, and B. Wheaton. 1996. New kid in town: Social capital and the life course effects of family migration on children. *American Sociological Review* 61: 368-85.

Hallinan, M. 2001. Sociological perspectives on Black-White inequalities in American schooling. *Sociology of Education Extra Issue*: 50-70.

Hallinan, M. and R. Williams. 1990. Students' characteristics and the peer-influence process. *Sociology of Education* 63: 122-32.

Hansen, K. 1995. Geographical mobility: March 1993 to March 1994. *Current Population Reports (Series P-20, No. 485)*. Washington DC: Government Printing Office.

Harris, F. 1994. Something within: Religion as a mobilizer of African-American political activism. *Journal of Politics* 56:1, 42-68.

Harris, J. 1998. *The nurture assumption: Why children turn out the way they do*. New York: Touchstone.

Hartup, W. 1993. Adolescents and their friends. *In Close friendships in adolescence*, edited by B. Laursen. San Francisco: Jossey-Bass.

Hauser, M. and C. Thompson. 1995. Creating a classroom culture of promise: Lessons from a first grade. In *Children and families "at promise": Deconstructing the discourse of risk*, edited by B. Swadner and S. Lubeck. Albany: SUNY Press.

Haveman, R. and B. Wolfe. 1994. *Succeeding generations: On the effects of investments in children*. New York: Russell Sage Foundation.

Haveman, R., B. Wolfe, and J. Spaulding. 1991. Childhood events and circumstances influencing high school completion. *Demography* 28 (1): 133-57.

Hayes-Bautista, D., W. Schink, and J. Chapa. 1988. *The burden of support: Young Latinos in an aging society*. Stanford: Stanford University Press.

Heinlein, L. and M. Shinn. 2000. School mobility and student achievement in an urban setting. *Psychology in the Schools* 37 (4): 349-57.

Hendrie, C. 2004. In New York City, fast-paced drive for small schools. *Education Week* 23 (41): 1, 22-23.

Herrnstein, R. and C. Murray. 1994. *The Bell Curve: Intelligence and class structure in American life*. New York: Free Press.

Heubert, J. and R. Hauser. 1999. *High stakes: Testing for tracking, promotion, and graduation*. Washington, D.C.: National Academy Press.

Hinojosa, D. and L. Miller. 1984. Grade level attainment among migrant farm workers in south Texas. *Journal of Education Research* 77: 346-50.

Hogue, A. and L. Steinberg. 1995. Homophily of internalized distress in adolescent peer groups. *Developmental Psychology* 31: 897-906.

Holland, J., D. Kaplan, and S. Davis. 1974. Interschool transfers: A mental health challenge. *Journal of School Health* 44: 74-9.

Horvat, E., E. Weininger, and A. Lareau. 2003. From social ties to social capital: Class differences in the relations between schools and parent networks. *American Educational Research Journal* 40 (2): 319-51.

Huberman, A. and D. Crandall. 1982. Fitting words to numbers: Multisite/ multimethod research in educational dissemination. *American Behavioral Scientist* 26 (1): 62-83.

Hudis, P. and P. Rathnam. 1994. *Student mobility*. Mimeo. Berkeley, CA: MPR Associates.

Hurd, C. 2004. "Acting out" and being a "schoolboy": Performance in an ELD classroom. In *School connections: U.S. Mexican youth, peers and school achievement*, edited by M. Gibson, P. Gándara, and J. Koyama. New York: Teachers College Press.

Hurtado, A. and E. García, eds. 1994. *The educational achievement of Latinos: Barriers and successes*. Santa Cruz: University of California Latino Eligibility Study.

Hymel, S., C. Comfort, K. Schonert-Reichl, and P. McDougall. 1996. Academic failure and school dropout: The influence of peers. In *Social motivation: Understanding children's school adjustment*, edited by J. Juvonen and K. Wentzel. Cambridge: Cambridge University Press.

Hymes, D. 1974. On ways of speaking. In *Exploration in the ethnography of speaking*, edited by P. Bauman and J. Sherzer. New York: Cambridge University Press.

Ingersoll, G., J. Scamman, and W. Eckerling. 1989. Geographic mobility and student achievement in an urban setting. *Educational Evaluation and Policy Analysis* 11: 143-49.

Jalongo, M. 1986. When young children move. In *Reducing stress in young children*, edited by J. McCracken. Washington, DC: National Association for the Education of Young Children.

Jarrett, R. 1997. African American family and parenting strategies in impoverished neighborhoods. *Qualitative Sociology* 20: 275-88.

Jason, A., A. Weine, J. Johnson, L. Warren-Sohlberg, L. Filippelli, E. Turner and C. Lardon. 1992. *Helping transfer students: Strategies for educational and social readjustment*. San Francisco: Jossey-Bass.

Jencks, C. and M. Phillips, eds. 1998. *The black-white test score gap*. Washington, D.C.: Brookings Institution Press.

Jencks, C., M. Smith, H. Acland, M. Bane, D. Cohen, H. Gintis, B. Heyns, and S. Michelson. 1972. *Inequality: A reassessment of the effect of family and schooling in America.* New York: Basic Books.

Jencks, C. and S. Mayer. 1990. The social consequences of growing up in a poor neighborhood. In *Inner-city poverty in the United States*, edited by L. Lynn Jr. and M. McGeary. Washington, D.C.: National Academy Press.

Jessor, R. 1993. Successful adolescent development among youth in high-risk settings. *American Psychologist* 48 (2): 117-26.

Jussim, L. and J. Eccles. 1992. Teacher expectations II: Construction and reflection of student achievement. *Journal of Personality and Social Psychology* 28: 281-388.

Kandel, D. 1978. Homophily, selection, and socialization in adolescent friendships. *American Journal of Sociology* 84: 427-36.

Kao, G. 2004. Social capital and its relevance to minority and immigrant populations. *Sociology of Education* 77: 172-83.

Kao, G. and M. Tienda. 1998. Educational aspirations of minority youth. *American Journal of Education* 106: 349-84.

Karabel, J. and A. Halsey, eds. 1977. *Power and ideology in education.* New York: Oxford University Press.

Keefe, S. 1984. Real and ideal extended *familism* among Mexican Americans and Anglo Americans: On the meaning of close family ties. *Human Organization* 43: 65-9.

Keefe, S., A. Padilla, and M. Carlos. 1979. The Mexican-American extended family as an emotional support system. *Human Organization* 38: 144-52.

Keith, T., P. Keith, K. Quirk, J. Sperduto, S. Santillo, and S. Killings. 1998. Longitudinal effects of parent involvement on high school grades: Similarities and differences across gender and ethnic groups. *Journal of School Psychology* 36 (3): 335-62.

Kerbow, D. 1996. *Pervasive student mobility: A moving target for school reform.* Chicago: Chicago Panel on School Policy.

King, G., R. Keohane, and S. Verba. 1994. *Designing social inquiry: Scientific inference in qualitative research.* Princeton, NJ: Princeton University Press.

Kingdon, J. 1995. *Agendas, alternatives and public policies.* 2d ed. New York: Harper Collins College Publishers.

Kirsch, I., A. Jungeblut, and A. Campbell. 1992. *Beyond the school doors: The literacy needs of job seekers served by the U.S. Department of Labor.* Princeton, New Jersey: Educational Testing Service.

Kleiner, B. and C. Chapman. 2000. *Youth service-learning and community service among 6th through 12-grade students in the United States: 1996 and 1999.* Statistics in Brief. Washington D.C.: NCES.

Knack, S. 1992. *Social altruism and voter turnout: Evidence from the 1991 NES Pilot Study*. College Park: University of Maryland.

Kozol, J. 1992. *Savage inequalities*. New York: HarperCollins.

Kroger, J. 1980. Residential mobility and self concept in adolescence. *Adolescence* 15 (winter): 967-77.

Kuhn, T. 1962. *The structure of scientific revolutions*. Chicago: University of Chicago Press.

Kurth, B. 1995. Learning through giving: Using service learning as the foundation for a middle school advisory program. *Middle School Journal* 27 (1): 35-41.

Labov, W. 1963. The social motivation of a sound change. *Word* 19: 273-309. Also published in *Sociolinguistic Patterns* by W. Labov (Philadelphia: University of Pennsylvania Press, 1972).

Lamborn, S., N. Mounts, L. Steinberg, and S. Dornbusch. 1991. Patterns of competence and adjustment among adolescents from authoritative, authoritarian, indulgent, and neglectful homes. *Child Development* 62: 1049-65.

Lamont, M. and A. Lareau. 1988. Cultural capital: Allusions, gaps and glissandos in recent theoretical developments. *Sociological Theory* 6 (2): 153-168.

Lancy, D. 1993. *Qualitative research in education: An introduction to the major traditions*. New York: Longman Publishing Group.

Lareau, A. 1987. Social class differences in family-school relationships: The importance of cultural capital. *Sociology of Education* 60: 73-85.

———. 1989. *Home advantage: Social class and parental intervention in elementary education*. London and New York: Falmer Press.

———. 2002. Invisible inequality: Social class and childrearing in Black families and White families. *American Sociological Review* 67: 747-76.

Larson, R. and M. Richards. 1991. Daily companionship in late childhood and early adolescence: Changing developmental contexts. *Child Development* 62: 284-300.

Lee, V. and T. Bryk. 1988. Curriculum tracking as mediating the social distribution of high school achievement. *Sociology of Education* 61: 78-94.

Lee, V. and J. Smith. 1999. Social support and achievement for young adolescents in Chicago: The role of school academic press. *American Educational Research Journal* 36 (4): 907-45.

Lewin, T. 2003a. Education: the pushouts. *New York Times*, 3 August.

———. 2003b. Schools reduce the number of students they force to leave early. *New York Times*, 24 December.

———. 2004. City resolves legal battle over forcing students out. *New York Times*, 19 June.

Lewin, T. and J. Medina. 2003. To cut failure rate, schools shed students. Pushed out, part 1. *New York Times*, 31 July.

Lewis-Charp, H., H. Yu, and D. Friedlaender. 2004. The influence of intergroup relations on school engagement: Two cases. In *School connections: U.S. Mexican youth, peers and school achievement*, edited by M. Gibson, P. Gándara and J. Koyama. New York: Teachers College Press.

Ligon, G. and V. Paredes. 1992. *Student mobility rate: A moving target.* A paper presented at the annual meeting of the American Educational Research Association, May, San Francisco.

Lin, N. 2001. *Social capital: A theory of social structure and action.* Cambridge: Cambridge University Press.

Lincoln, Y. and E. Guba. 1985. *Naturalistic Inquiry*. Newbury Park, California: Sage Publications.

Lombana, J. 1985. Guidance accountability: A new look at an old problem. *The School Counselor* 32 (5): 340-46.

Los Angeles Unified School District. 2004. Author correspondence with Shirley Kouffman, Director of the Planning Assessment and Research Division, School Information Branch (June, 2004). Los Angeles: Los Angeles Unified School District.

Louis, K. (1982). Multisite/multimethod studies. *American Behavioral Scientist* 26 (1): September/October.

Loury, G. 1977. A dynamic theory of racial income differences. In *Women, minorities and employment discrimination*, edited by P. Wallace and A. Lamond. Lexington, Massachusetts.: Lexington Books.

———. 1987. Why should we care about group inequality? *Social Philosophy and Policy* 5: 249-71.

———. 1992. The economics of discrimination: Getting to the core of the problem. *Harvard Journal of African American Public Policy* 1: 91-110.

———. 2002. *The anatomy of racial inequality*. Cambridge: Harvard University Press.

Lucas, S. 1999. *Tracking inequality: Stratification and mobility in American high schools*. New York: Teachers College Press.

Macías, R. 1993. Language and ethnic classification of language minorities: Chicano and Latino students in the 1990s. *Hispanic Journal of Behavioral Sciences* 15 (2): 230-57.

Madigan, T. 1994. *Parent involvement and school achievement.* A paper presented at the annual meeting of the American Educational Research Association, April, New Orleans.

Mann, H. (1837). The effects of public apathy on education. Horace Mann's first annual report to the Massachusetts Board of Education. In Cremin, L., ed. (1957). *The republic and the school: Horace Mann on the education of free men.* New York: Teachers College Press.

Manno, B., C. Finn, L. Bierlein, and G. Banourek. 1998. Charter schools: Accomplishments and dilemmas. *Teachers College Record* 99: 537-58.

Marjoribank, K. 1995. Parents' involvement in learning as an opportunity structure: A model for evaluation. *Studies in Educational Evaluation* 21: 73-83.

Marsh, H., J. Balla, and K. Hau. 1996. An evaluation of incremental fit indices: A clarification of mathematical and empirical properties. In *Advanced structural equation modeling: Issues and techniques*, edited by G. Marcoulides and R. Schmacker. Mahwah, NJ: Lawrence Erlbaum Associates.

Massey, D. and M. Eggers. 1990. The ecology of inequality: Minorities and the concentration of poverty, 1970-1980. *American Journal of Sociology* 95: 1170-84.

Massey, D., C. Charles, G. Lundy, and M. Fischer. 2003. *The source of the river: The social origins of freshmen at America's selective colleges and universities.* Princeton: Princeton University Press.

Matute-Bianchi, M. 1986. Ethnic identities and patterns of school success and failure among Mexican-descent and Japanese-American Students in a California high school: An ethnographic analysis. *American Journal of Education* 95 (1): 233-55.

Maxim, P. 1999. *Quantitative research methods in the social sciences.* New York: Oxford University Press.

McCann, J. 1998. *Electoral participation and local community activism: Spillover effects, 1992-1996.* A paper presented at the annual meeting of the American Political Science Association, September, Boston.

McClafferty, K., P. McDonough, and A. Nuñez. 2002. *What is a college culture: Facilitating college preparation through organizational change.* A paper presented at the annual meeting of the American Educational Research Association, April, New Orleans.

McDonnell, L. 2000. *From research findings to policy advice: A guide for AERA members*. Washington D.C.: American Educational Research Association, Government Relations Committee

———. 2004. *Politics, persuasion, and educational testing*. Cambridge: Harvard University Press.

McDonnell, L. and P. Hill. 1993. *Newcomers in American schools: Meeting the educational needs of immigrant youth.* Santa Monica: RAND Corporation.

McKown, C. and R. Weinstein. 2002. Modeling the role of child ethnicity and gender in children's differential response to teacher expectations. *Journal of Applied Social Psychology* 32: 159-84.

McLanahan, S. and G. Sandefur. 1996. *Growing Up with a Single Parent: What Hurts, What Helps.* Cambridge: Harvard University Press.

McMurrer, D. and I. Sawhill. 1998. *Getting ahead: Economic and social mobility in America.* Washington, D.C.: The Urban Institute.

McNeal, R. 1999. Parental involvement as social capital: Differential effectiveness on science achievement, truancy, and dropping out. *Social Forces* 78 (1): 117-44.

Medina, J. and T. Lewin. 2003. High school under scrutiny for giving up on its students. Pushed out, part 2. *New York Times,* 1 August.

Mehan, H., L. Hubbard, and I. Villanueva. 1994. Forming academic identities: Accommodation without assimilation among involuntary minorities. *Anthropology and Education Quarterly* 25 (2): 91-117.

Mehan, H., I. Villanueva, L. Hubbard, and A. Lintz. 1996. *Constructing school success: The consequences of untracking low-achieving students.* Cambridge: Cambridge University Press.

Meier, A. 1999. *Social capital and school achievement among adolescents.* CDE Working Paper No. 99-18. A paper presented at the American Sociological Association annual meeting in Chicago.

Melaville, A., and M. Blank. 1991. *What it takes: Structuring interagency partnerships to connect children and families with comprehensive services.* Washington, DC: Education and Human Services Consortium.

Menchaca, M. 1989. Chicano-Mexican cultural assimilation and Anglo-Saxon cultural differences. *Hispanic Journal of Behavioral Sciences* 11: 203-23.

———. 1995. *The Mexican outsiders: A community history of marginalization and discrimination in California.* Austin: University of Texas Press.

Menjivar, C. 2002. Living in Two Worlds? Guatemalan-Origin Children in the United States and Emerging Transnationalism. *Journal of Ethnic and Migration Studies* 28 (3): 531-52.

Merton, R. 1981. Remarks on theoretical pluralism. In *Continuities in Structural Inquiry*, edited by P. Blau and R. Merton. London: Sage Publications.

———. 1987. Three fragments from a sociologist's notebooks: Establishing the phenomenon, specified ignorance and strategic research materials. *Annual Review of Sociology* 13: 1-28.

Metz, M. 1978. *Classrooms and corridors: The crisis of authority in desegregated secondary schools*. Berkeley: University of California Press.

Mickelson, R. 2001. Subverting Swann: First- and second-generation segregation in the Charlotte-Mechlenbury schools. *American Educational Research Journal* 38, 215-52.

Miles, M. and A. Huberman. 1984. *Qualitative data analysis: A sourcebook of new methods*. Newbury Park, California: Sage Publications.

Miller, L. 1995. *An American imperative: Accelerating minority educational advancement*. New Haven, Connecticut: Yale University Press.

———. 1996. *Promoting high academic achievement among non-Asian minorities*. A paper presented at the Princeton University Conference on higher education, Princeton, New Jersey.

Moll, L., D. Amanti, and N. Gonzalez. 1992. Funds of knowledge: Using a qualitative approach to connect homes and classrooms. *Theory Into Practice* 31: 132-41.

Montero-Sieburth, M. and F. Villarruel, eds. 2000. *Making Invisible Latino Adolescents Visible: A Critical Approach to Latino Diversity*. New York: Falmer.

Morgan, S. and A. Sorensen. 1999. Parental networks, social closure, and Mathematics learning: A test of Coleman's social capital explanation of school effects. *American Sociological Review* 64: 661-81.

Morris, A. and C. Mueller. 1992. *Frontiers in social movement theory*. New Haven: Yale University Press.

Muncey, D. and P. McQuillan. 1996. *Reform and resistance in schools and classrooms: An ethnographic view of the Coalition of Essential Schools*. New Haven: Yale University Press.

Munton, A. 1990. Job relocation, stress, and family. *Journal of Organizational Behavior* 11: 401-6.

Narayan, D. 1999. *Bonds and bridges: Social capital and poverty*. Policy Research Working Paper 2167. Washington, D.C.: World Bank, Poverty Reduction and Economic Management Network.

National Assessment of Educational Progress (NAEP). 1997. *NAEP 1996 mathematics report card for the nation and the states*. Washington, D.C.:

U.S. Department of Education, Office of Educational Research and Improvement.

——— 1999. *NAEP 1998 reading report card for the nation and the states.* Washington, D.C.: U.S. Department of Education, Office of Educational Research and Improvement.

———.2000. *NAEP 1999 Long term trend assessment.* Washington, D.C.: U.S. Department of Education, Office of Educational Research and Improvement.

National Association for Bilingual Education (NABE). 1995. *Bilingual education: Separating fact from fiction.* Washington, D.C.: National Association for Bilingual Education.

National Commission on Excellence in Education. 1983. *A nation at risk: The imperative for educational reform.* Washington, D.C.: U.S. Department of Education.

National Research Council. 2004. *Measuring racial discrimination: Panel on methods for assessing discrimination,* edited by R. Blank, M. Dabady, and C. Citro. Washington, D.C.: The National Academies Press, Committee on National Statistics, Division of Behavioral and Social Sciences and Education.

National Research Council and the Institute of Medicine. 2004. *Engaging schools: Fostering high school students' motivation to learn.* Washington, D.C.: The National Academies Press, Committee on Increasing High School Students' Engagement and Motivation to Learn. Board of Children, Youth and Families, Division of Behavioral and Social Sciences and Education.

Noddings, N. 1984. *Caring: A feminine approach to ethics and moral education.* Berkeley: University of California Press.

———. 1992. *The challenge to care in schools: An alternative approach to education.* New York: Teachers College Press.

Noguera, P. 2003. *City schools and the American dream: Reclaiming the promise of public education.* New York: Teachers College Press.

Oakes, J. 1985. *Keeping track: How schools structure inequality.* New Haven: Yale University Press.

Offenberg, R. Forthcoming. Inferring adequate yearly progress of schools from student achievement in highly mobile communities. *Journal of Education for Students Placed at Risk* 9 (4).

Ogbu, J. 1978. *Minority education and caste.* New York: Academic Press.

———. 1989. The individual in collective adaptation: A framework for focusing on academic underperformance and dropping out among involuntary minorities. In *Dropouts from school: issues, dilemmas, and solutions,* edited by L. Weis, E. Farrar and H.G. Petrie. Albany: State University of New York Press.

———. 1992. Understanding cultural diversity and learning. *Educational Researcher* 21 (8): 5-14.

Olsen, L. 1988. *Crossing the schoolhouse border: Immigrant students and the California public schools.* San Francisco: California Tomorrow.

———. 1997. *Made in America: Immigrant students in our public schools.* New York: The New Press.

Orfield, G. 2001. *Schools more separate: Consequences of a decade of resegregation.* Cambridge: Harvard University, The Civil Rights Project.

Orfield, G. and J. Yun. 1999. *Resegregation in American schools.* Cambridge: Harvard University, The Civil Rights Project.

Orr, M. 1999. *Black social capital: The politics of school reform in Baltimore, 1986-1998.* Kansas: University Press of Kansas.

Owen, D. 1981. *High school: Undercover with the class of '80.* New York: Viking Press.

Parcel, T. and E. Menaghan. 1994. Early parental work, family social capital, and early childhood outcomes. *American Journal of Sociology* 99: 972-1009.

Park, E., and G. Palardy. 2004. Impact of parental involvement and authoritativeness on academic achievement: A cross ethnic comparison. In *Advancing Educational Productivity: Policy Implications from National Databases*, edited by S. Paik and H. Walberg. Greenwich, Connecticut: Information Age Publishers.

Paulson, S. 1994. Relations of parenting style and parental involvement with ninth- grade students' achievement. *Journal of Early Adolescence* 14 (2): 250-67.

Pearl, A. 2002. The big picture: Systemic and institutional factors in Chicano school failure and success. In *Chicano school failure and success: Past, present and future*. 2d ed. Edited by R. Valencia. London: RoutledgeFalmer.

Perry, T., C. Steele, and A. Hilliard. 2003. *Young, gifted, and Black: Promoting high achievement among African-American students.* Boston: Beacon Press.

Pettit, B. and S. McLanahan. 2003. Residential mobility and children's social capital: Evidence from an experiment. *Social Science Quarterly* 84 (3): 632-49.

Phelan, P., A. Davidson, and H. Yu. 1998. *Adolescents' worlds: Negotiating family, peers, and schools.* New York: Teachers College Press.

Phillips, M. 2000. Understanding ethnic differences in academic achievement: Empirical lessons from national data. In *Analytic issues in the assessment of student achievement*, edited by D. Grissmer and J. Ross. Washington, D.C.: U.S. Department of Education, National Center for Education Statistics.

Phillips M., J. Brooks-Gunn, G. Duncan, P. Klebanov, and J. Crane. 1998. Family background, parenting practices and the black-white test score gap. In *The Black-White Test Score Gap*, edited by C. Jencks & M. Phillips. Washington D.C.: The Brookings Institution.

Piliavin, J. and H. Charng. 1990. Altruism: A review of recent theory and research. *Annual Review of Sociology* 16: 27-65.

Pittman, R. 1991. Social factors, enrollment in vocational/technical courses, and high school dropout rates. *Journal of Educational Research* 84: 288-95.

Plank, S., K. Schiller, B. Schneider, and J. Coleman. 1993. Effects of choice in education. In *School choice: Examining the evidence*, edited by E. Rasell and R. Rothstein. Washington, D.C.: Economic Policy Institute.

Platt, J. 1973. Social traps. *American Psychologist* 28: 641-51.

Polanyi, K. 1957. *The great transformation.* Boston: Bacon Press.

Pong, S. 1998. The school compositional effect of single parenthood on tenth-grade achievement. *Sociology of Education* 71: 23-42.

Portes, A. 1995. Children of immigrants: Segmented assimilation and its determinants. In *The economic sociology of immigration: Essays on networks, ethnicity, and entrepreneurship*, edited by A. Portes. New York: Russell Sage Foundation.

______. 1998. Social capital: Its origin and applications in modern sociology. *Annual Review of Sociology* 24: 1-24.

Portes, A. and J. Sensenbrenner. 1993. Embeddedness and immigration: Notes on the determinants of economic action. *American Journal of Sociology* 98: 1320-50.

Portes, A. and M. Zhou. 1993. The new second generation: Segmented assimilation and its variants. *Annals of the American Academy of Political and Social Science* 530 (November): 74-96.

Portes, A. and P. Landolt. 1996. Unsolved mysteries: The Tocqueville files II, the downside of social capital. *The American Prospect* 7 (May): 18-21.

Portes, A. and R. Rumbaut, R. 1994. *The educational progress of children of immigrants.* Release No.2. Baltimore, MD: Johns Hopkins University, The children of immigrants project.

Portes, A. and R. Rumbaut. 2001. *Legacies: The story of the immigrant second generation.* Berkeley: University of California Press.

President's Advisory Commission on Educational Excellence for Hispanic Americans. 1996. *Our nation on the fault line: Hispanic American education.* Washington, DC: U.S. Department of Education.

———. 2000. *Creating the will: Hispanics achieving educational excellence.* Washington, D.C.: U.S. Department of Education.

Pribesh, S. and D. Downey. 1999. Why are residential and school moves associated with poor school performance? *Demography* 36 (4): 521-34.

Public Schools of North Carolina. 2004. *North Carolina initiatives: Closing the gap state initiatives.* From www.ncpublicschools.org/schoolimprovement/ Retrieved on 17 June 2004. Raleigh, North Carolina: School Improvement Division, Advisory Commission on Raising Achievement and Closing Gaps.

Putnam, R. 1993. *Making democracy work: Civic traditions in modern Italy.* Princeton: Princeton University Press.

———. 1995. Bowling alone: America's declining social capital. *Journal of Democracy* 6 (1): 65-78.

———. 2000. *Bowling alone: The collapse and revival of American community.* New York: Simon & Schuster.

Rahn, W. and J. Transue. 1998. Social trust and value change: The decline of social capital in American youth, 1976-1995. *Political Psychology* 19: 545-65.

Raley, J. 2004. "Like family, you know?" Schools and the achievement of peer relations. In *School connections: U.S. Mexican youth, peers and school achievement*, edited by M. Gibson, P. Gándara, and J. Koyama. New York: Teachers College Press.

Ramírez, D., S. Yuen, D. Ramey, D. Pasta, and D. Billings. 1991. *Final report: Longitudinal study of structured English immersion strategy, early-exit and late-exit transitional bilingual education programs for language minority children.* San Mateo, California: Aguirre International.

Ream, R. 2003. Counterfeit social capital and Mexican-American underachievement. *Educational Evaluation and Policy Analysis* 25 (3): 237-62.

Ream, R. and R. Rumberger. 1998. *On the move: The impact of mobility on the achievement of Mexican-American and non-Latino White Students.* A paper presented at the annual meeting of the American Educational Research Association, April, San Diego.

Ream, R. and S. Castillo. 2001. *Does peer social capital moderate the impact of student mobility on the mathematics achievement of Mexican-American adolescents across nativity status groups?* A paper presented at the University of California ACCORD invitational conference: Peer influences on the school performance of Mexican-descent adolescents. September, San Jose, California.

Reese, L. 2001. Morality and Identity in Mexican Immigrant Parents' Visions of the Future. *Journal of Ethnic and Migration Studies* 27 (3): 455-72.

Reynolds, A. and J. Temple. 1997. *Predictors and consequences of school mobility for urban black children from low-income families.* A paper presented at the annual meeting of the American Educational Research Association, Chicago.

Rist, M. 1992. Putting services in one basket. *The Executive Educator* 14 (4): 18-24.

Robelan, E. 2000. Budget proposal includes boost for education, *Education Week* 19 (23) 1-25.

Rogler, L., D. Cortes, and R. Malgady. 1991. Acculturation and mental health status among Hispanics. *American Psychologist* 46 (6): 585-97.

Romo, H. 1986. Contrasting perceptions of schooling among the Mexican-origin population. In *Mexican immigrants and Mexican Americans: An evolving relation*, edited by H. Browing and R. de la Garza. Austin: The University of Austin, Texas, CMAS Publications.

Romo, H. and T. Falbo. 1996. *Latino high school graduation: Defying the odds*. Austin: University of Texas Press.

Roof, W. and W. McKinney. 1987. *American mainline religion: Its changing shape and future*. New Brunswick, New Jersey: Rutgers University Press.

Rosenthal, R. and L. Jacobsen. 1968. *Pygmalion in the classroom: Teacher expectations and student intellectual development.* New York: Holt, Rinehart, and Winston.

Rossman, G., and B. Wilson. 1985. Numbers and words: Combining quantitative and qualitative methods in a single large-scale evaluation study. *Evaluation Review* 9 (5): 627-43.

Rothstein, R. 2000. *Improving educational achievement: A volume exploring the role of investments in schools and other supports and services for families and communities*. Washington, D.C. Center on Education Policy.

Ruiz-de-Velasco, J., M. Fix, and B. Clewell. 2000. *Overlooked and underserved: Immigrant students in U.S. secondary schools*. Washington, D.C.: Urban Institute.

Rumbaut, R. 1994. The crucible within: Ethnic identity, self-esteem, and segmented assimilation among children of immigrants. *International Migration Review* 28: 748-94.

Rumbaut, R. 1995. The new Californians: Comparative research findings on the educational progress of immigrant children. In *California's immigrant children: Theory, research, and implications for educational policy*, edited by R. Rumbaut and W. Cornelius. San Diego: University of California, Center for U.S.-Mexican Studies.

———. 1996. *The new Californians: Assessing the educational progress of children of immigrants.* CPS Brief (8), No.3. Berkeley: California Policy Seminar.

Rumbaut, R. and W. Cornelius, eds. 1995. *California immigrant children: Theory, research and implications for educational policy.* San Diego: UC San Diego, Center for U.S./Mexican Studies.

Rumberger, R. 1983. Dropping out of high school: The influence of race, sex and family background. *American Educational Research Journal* 20: 199-220.

———. 1995. Dropping out of middle school: A multilevel analysis of students and schools. *American Educational Research Journal* 32: 583-625.

———. 2003. The causes and consequences of student mobility. *Journal of Negro Education* 72: 6-21.

Rumberger, R. and G. Palardy. Forthcoming. Does segregation (still) matter? The impact of student composition on academic achievement in high school. *Teachers College Record.*

Rumberger, R. and G. Rodríguez. 2002. Chicano dropouts: An update of research and policy issues. In *Chicano school failure and success: Past, present and future,* edited by R. Valencia. 2d ed. London: RoutledgeFalmer.

Rumberger, R. and K. Larson. 1998. Student mobility and the increased risk of high school dropout. *American Journal of Education* 107: 1-35.

Rumberger, R., K. Larson, G. Palardy, R. Ream and N. Schleicher. 1997. *The hazards of changing schools for California Latino adolescents.* Report to the California Policy Seminar. Berkeley, California.

———. 1998. *The hazards of changing schools for California Latino adolescents*. Berkeley: UC Berkeley, Institute for Social Change.

Rumberger, R., K. Larson, R. Ream, and G. Palardy. 1999. *The educational consequences of mobility for California students and schools*. Berkeley: UC Berkeley, Policy Analysis for California Education.

Rumberger, R. and P. Gándara. 2000. The schooling of English learners. In *Crucial issues in California education,* edited by E. Burr, G. Hayward, B. Fuller and M. Kirst. University of California and Stanford University: Policy Analysis for California Education.

Ryan, R., J. Stiller, and J. Lynch. 1994. Representations of relationships to teachers, parents and friends as predictors of academic motivation and self-esteem. *Journal of Early Adolescence* 14: 226-49.

Saint Exupéry, A. 1943. *The Little Prince*. New York: Reynal and Hitchcock.

Salazar, J. 1998. A longitudinal model for interpreting thirty years of bilingual education research. *Bilingual Research Journal* [online]. Available: http://brj.asu.edu.

Sampson, R. 1999. What community supplies. In *Urban Problems and Community Development*, edited by R. Ferguson and W. Dickens. Washington, D.C.: Brookings Institution Press.

Sampson, R. and B. Groves. 1989. Community structures and crime: Testing social disorganization theory. *American Journal of Sociology* 94: 774-802.

Sampson, R. and J. Morenoff. 1997. Ecological perspectives on the neighborhood context of poverty and social organization: Past and present. Chap. 1 in *Neighborhood poverty: Context and consequences for children,* Vol. 2 of *Conceptual, Methodological and Policy Approaches to Studying Neighborhoods*, edited by G. Duncan, J. Brooks-Gunn, and J. Aber. New York: Russell Sage Foundation Press.

Sánchez-Jankowski, M. 1991. *Island in the street: Gangs and American urban society*. Berkeley: University of California Press.

Sandefur, R. and E. Laumann. 1998. A paradigm for social capital. *Rationality and Society* 10: 481-501.

Schneider, B. 2000. Social systems and norms: A Coleman approach. In *Handbook of the sociology of education*, edited by M. Hallinan. New York: Kluwer Academic/Plenum Publishers.

Schneider, B. and D. Stevenson. 1999. *The ambitious generation: America' teenagers, motivated but directionless*. New Haven: Yale University Press.

Schneider, B., K. Schiller, and J. Coleman. 1996. Public school choice: Some evidence from the National Education longitudinal Study of 1988. *Educational Evaluation and Policy Analysis* 18: 19-29.

Schuler, D. 1990. Effects of family mobility on student achievement. *ERS Spectrum* 8 (4): 17-24.

Schultz, T. 1961. Investment in human capital. *American Economic Review* 51 (March): 1-17.

Schumacker, R. and R. Lomax. 1996. *A beginner's guide to structural equation modeling*. Mahwah, New Jersey: Lawrence Erlbaum Associates.

Scott, L., D. Rock, J. Pollack, and S. Ingels. 1995. *Two years later: Cognitive gains and school transitions of NELS:88 eighth graders*. Report No. 95-436. Washington, DC: National Center for Education Statistics.

Sedlak, M., C. Wheeler, D. Pullin, and P. Cusick. 1986. *Selling students short: Classroom bargains and academic reform in the American high school*. New York: Teachers College Press.

Shaw, C. and H. McKay. 1969. *Juvenile delinquency and urban areas*. Rev. ed. Chicago: University of Chicago Press.

Shields, P., C. Esch, D. Humphrey, V. Young, M. Gaston, and H. Hunt. 1999. *The Status of the Teaching Profession: Research Findings and Policy Recommendations*. Santa Cruz, CA: The Center for the Future of Teaching and Learning.

Schumacker, R. and R. Lomax. 1996. *A beginner's guide to structural equation modeling*. New Jersey: Lawrence Erlbaum Associates.

Skocpol, T. 1997. America's voluntary groups thrive in a national network. *The Brookings Review* 15: 16-19.

Skocpol, T. and M. Fiorina. 1999. *Civic engagement in American democracy*. Washington, D.C.: Brookings Institution Press.

Small, M. 2002. Culture, cohorts and social organization theory: Understanding local participation in a Latino housing project. *American Journal of Sociology* 108 (1): 1-54.

Smetana, J. 1988. Concepts of self and social convention: Adolescents' and parents' reasoning about hypothetical and actual family conflicts. In *21st Minnesota Symposium on child psychology*, edited by M. Gunnar. Hillsdale, New Jersey: Lawrence Erlbaum Associates.

Smith, A. and K. Louis, eds. 1982. Multimethod Policy Research: Issues and Applications. *American Behavioral Scientist* 26 (1): 6-144.

Smith, J. 2003. Assimilation across the Latino Generations. *AEA Papers and Proceedings* 93 (2): 315-19.

Smith, J., and L. Heshusius. 1986. Closing down the conversation: The end of the quantitative-qualitative debate among educational researchers. *Educational Researcher* 15 (1): 4-12.

Snyder, J., G. Morrison, and R. Smith. 1996. *Dare to dream: Educational guidance for excellence*. Indianapolis, Indiana: Lilly Endowment.

Soss, J. 1999. Lessons of welfare: Policy design, political learning, and political action. *American Political Science Review* 93 (2): 363-80.

Spillane, J., T. Hallett, and J. Diamond. 2003. Forms of capital and the construction of leadership: Instructional leadership in urban elementary schools. *Sociology of Education* 76: 1-17.

Stanton-Salazar, R. 1997. A social capital framework for understanding the socialization of racial minority children and youths. *Harvard Educational Review* 67 (1): 1-40.

———. 2001. *Manufacturing hope and despair: The school and kin support networks of U.S.- Mexican youth.* New York: Teachers College Press.

Stanton-Salazar, R., O. Vasquez, and H. Mehan. 2000. Reengineering success through institutional support. In *The academic achievement of minority students: Comparative perspectives, practices, and prescriptions*, edited by S. Gregory. Lanham, Maryland: University Press of America.

Stanton-Salazar, R. and S. Dornbusch. 1995. Social capital and the reproduction of inequality: Information networks among Mexican-origin high school students. *Sociology of Education* 68: 116-35.

Steele, C. 1997. A threat in the air: How stereotypes shape intellectual identity and performance. *American Psychologist* 52 (6): 613-29.

Steele, C. and J. Aronson. 1995. Stereotype threat and the intellectual test performance of African Americans. *Journal of Personality and Social Psychology* 69: 797-811.

Steinberg, L. 2001. We know some things: Parent-adolescent relationships in Retrospect and Prospect. *Journal of Research on Adolescence* 11 (1): 1-19.

Steinberg, L., S. Dornbusch, and B. Brown. 1992. Ethnic differences in adolescent achievement: An ecological perspective. *American Psychologist* 47 (6): 723-29.

Steinberg, L., S. Lamborn, N. Darling, N. Mounts, and S. Dornbusch. 1994. Over-time in adjustment and competence among adolescents form authoritative, authoritarian, indulgent, and neglectful families. *Child Development* 65: 754-70.

Stephan, W. and J. Feagin. 1980. *School desegregation: Past, present and future*. New York: Plenum.

Stevenson, D. and D. Baker. 1987. The family-school relations and the child's school performance. *Child Development* 58: 1348-57.

Suarez-Orozco, C., and M. Suarez-Orozco. 1995. *Transformations: Migration, family life, and achievement motivation among Latino adolescents.* Stanford: Stanford University Press.

Suarez-Orozco, M. 1987. Becoming somebody: Central American immigrants in U.S. inner-city schools. In *Explaining the school performance of minority students*, edited by E. Jacob and C. Jordan. *Anthropology and Education Quarterly* 18: 287-99.

Sui-Chu Ho, E. and D. Willms. 1996. Effects of parental involvement on eighth grade achievement. *Sociology of Education* 69 (2): 126-41.

Swanson, C. and B. Schneider. 1999. Students on the move: Residential and educational mobility in America's schools. *Sociology of Education* 72 (January): 54-67.

Tatum-Daniel, B. 1997. *Why are all the Black kids sitting together in the cafeteria? And other conversations about race*. New York: Basic Books.

Teachman, J., K. Paasch, and K. Carver. 1996. Social capital and dropping out of school early. *Journal of Marriage and the Family* 58: 773-83.

Thernstrom, A. and S.Thernstrom. 2003. *No excuses: closing the racial gap in learning*. New York: Simon & Schuster.

Thomas, W. and V. Collier. 1997. *School effectiveness for language minority students*. Washington, DC: National Clearinghouse for Bilingual Education.

Thomspon, L., D. Detterman, and R. Plomin. 1991. Association between cognitive abilities and scholastic achievement: Genetic overlap but environmental differences. *Psychological Science* 2: 158-65.

Tienda, M. 1991. Poor people and poor places: Deciphering neighborhood effects on poverty outcomes. In *Macro-micro linkages in sociology*, edited by Joan Huber. Newbury Park, California: Sage Publications.

Tienda, M. 2001. College admissions policies and the educational pipeline: Implications for medical and health professions. In *The right thing to do, the smart thing to do: Enhancing diversity in the health professions*, edited by B. Smedley, A. Stith, L. Colburn, and C. Evans. Washington, D.C.: The National Academy of Sciences.

Tocqueville, A. [1835] 1969. *Democracy in America*. Translated by G. Lawrence and edited by J. Mayer. New York: Doubleday.

Trejo, S. 1996. *Obstacles to labor market progress of California's Mexican origin workers*. Berkeley: UC Berkeley, Chicano/Latino Policy Project.

———. 1997. Why do Mexican Americans earn low wages? *Journal of Political Economy* 105 (6): 1235-68.

Trueba, E. 1999. *Latinos unidos: From cultural diversity to the politics of solidarity*. Lanham, MD: Rowman and Littlefield.

Trueba, H. 1988. Culturally based explanations of minority students' academic achievement. *Anthropology and Education Quarterly* 19: 270-87.

Trueba, H., G. Spindler, and L. Spindler. 1989. *What do anthropologists have to say about dropouts?* New York: Falmer Press.

Tucker, C., J. Marx, and L. Long. 1998. Moving on: Residential mobility and children's school lives. *Sociology of Education* 71: 111-29.

U.S. Department of Commerce, Bureau of the Census. 1996. *Population projections for states by age, sex, race, and Hispanic Origin: 1995 to 2025,* Population Division, PPL-47. Washington, D.C.: U.S. Government Printing Office.

———. 1998. *Current population survey*, series P20-513. Washington, D.C.: U.S. Government Printing Office.

———. 2000a. *Hispanic population of the United States: March 1999*. Current population reports, series P-20, No. 527. Washington, D.C.: U.S. Government Printing Office.

———. 2000b. *Census 2000 brief: Overview of race and Hispanic origin.* Washington, D.C.: U.S. Government Printing Office.

———. 2000c. *Current population reports: Geographical mobility population characteristics.* Washington, D.C.: U.S. Government Printing Office.

———. 2002a. *Annual demographic supplement to the March 2002 current population survey.* Washington, D.C.: U.S. Government Printing Office.

———. 2002b. *Current population survey,* unpublished data; and U.S. Department of Education, National Center for Education Statistics, *Dropout rates in the United States*. Prepared October 2002. Washington, D.C.: U.S. Government Printing Office.

———. 2003. *The Hispanic population in the United States: March 2002.* Annual demographic supplement to the March 2002 current population survey. Washington, D.C.: Government Printing Office.

———. 2004. *Geographical mobility: 2002 to 2003 population characteristics*. Current population reports, series P-20, no. 549.

U.S. Department of Commerce, Census Bureau News. 2000. *Moving rate among Americans declines, Census Bureau Says.* Press Release 19 January 2000. Economics and Statistics Administration, U.S. Bureau of the Census. Washington, D.C.: U.S. Government Printing Office.

U.S. Department of Education, National Center for Education Statistics (NCES). 1995a. *The condition of education, 1995*. Washington, D.C.: Government Printing Office.

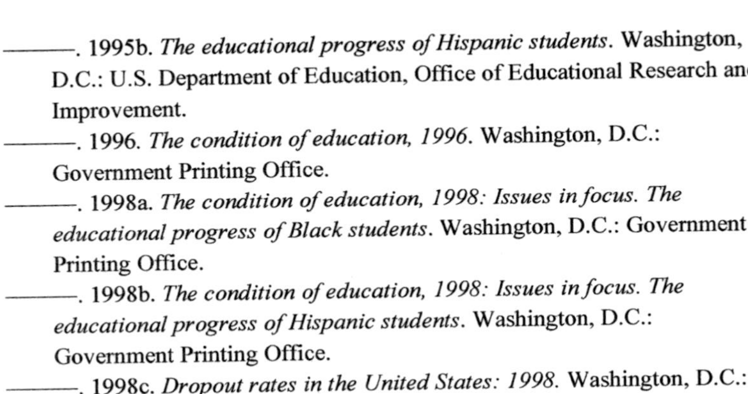

———. 1995b. *The educational progress of Hispanic students*. Washington, D.C.: U.S. Department of Education, Office of Educational Research and Improvement.

———. 1996. *The condition of education, 1996*. Washington, D.C.: Government Printing Office.

———. 1998a. *The condition of education, 1998: Issues in focus. The educational progress of Black students*. Washington, D.C.: Government Printing Office.

———. 1998b. *The condition of education, 1998: Issues in focus. The educational progress of Hispanic students*. Washington, D.C.: Government Printing Office.

———. 1998c. *Dropout rates in the United States: 1998*. Washington, D.C.: Government Printing Office.

———. 2001. *The condition of education: Student effort and educational progress*. Status dropout rates, by race/ethnicity. Table 17-2. October 2001. Washington, D.C.: Government Printing Office.

U.S. General Accounting Office. 1994. *Elementary school children: Many change schools frequently, harming their education*. Washington, D.C.: Government Printing Office.

Valdés, G. 1998. The world outside and inside schools: Language and immigrant children. *Educational Researcher* 27 (6): 4-18.

Valencia, R. 1991. *Chicano school failure and success: Research and policy agendas for the 1990s*. London: Falmer Press.

Valencia, R., ed. 2002. *Chicano school failure and success: Past, present, and future*. 2d ed. London: RoutledgeFalmer.

Valencia, R. and D. Solórzano. 1997. Contemporary deficit thinking. In *The evolution of deficit thinking: Educational thought and practice*, edited by R. Valencia. The Stanford Series on Education and Public Policy. London: Falmer Press.

Valencia, R., M. Menchaca, and R. Donato. 2002. Segregation, desegregation, and integration of Chicano students: Old and new realities. In *Chicano school failure and success: Past, present and future*. 2d ed. Edited by R. Valencia. London: RoutledgeFalmer.

Valenzuela, A. 1990. *Familism and academic achievement among Mexican-Origin high school adolescents*. Ph.D. diss., Stanford University.

———. 1997. Mexican-American youth and the politics of caring. In *From sociology to cultural studies: New perspectives*, edited by E. Long. Boston: Blackwell Publishers.

———. 1999. *Subtractive schooling: U.S.-Mexican youth and the politics of caring.* Albany: State University of New York Press.

Valenzuela, A. and S. Dornbusch. 1994. Familism and social capital in the academic achievement of Mexican-origin and Anglo high school adolescents. *Social Science Quarterly* 75: 18-36.

Velez, W. 1989. High school attrition among Hispanic and non-Hispanic white Youths. *Sociology of Education* 62: 119-33.

Vélez-Ibañez, C. and J. Greenberg. 1992. Formation and transformation of funds of knowledge among U.S.-Mexican households. *Anthropology and Education Quarterly* 23 (4): 313-35.

Vélez-Ibañez, C. 1997. *Border Visions: Mexican Cultures of the Southwest United States*. Tucson: University of Arizona Press.

Vernez, G. and A. Abrahamse. 1996. *How immigrants fare in U.S. education.* Santa Monica: RAND Corporation, Center for Research on Immigration Policy.

Vernez, G. and L. Mizell. 2002a. *Goal: To double the rate of Hispanics earning a bachelor's degree*. Santa Monica: RAND Corporation, Center for Research on Immigration Policy.

———. 2002b. *Monitoring the Education Progress of Hispanics*. DRU-2837-HSF. Santa Monica: RAND Corporation.

Vigil, D. 1997. *Personas Mexicanas: Chicano high schoolers in a changing Los Angeles*. Fort Worth,Texas: Harcourt Brace College Publishers.

Villenas, S. and D. Foley. 2002. Chicano/Latino critical ethnography of education: cultural productions from *la frontera*. In *Chicano school failure and success: Past, present and future*. 2d ed. Edited by R. Valencia. London: RoutledgeFalmer.

Vosk, B., R. Forehand, J. Parker, and K. Rickard. 1982. A multimethod comparison of popular and unpopular children. *Developmental Psychology* 18: 571-75.

Vygotsky, L. 1962. *Thought and language*. Cambridge: MIT Press.

———. 1978. *Mind in society: The development of higher psychological processes*. Edited by M. Cole, V. Steiner, S. Scribner, and E. Souberman. Cambridge: Harvard University Press.

Wall, E., G. Ferrazzi, and F. Schryer. 1998. Getting the goods on social capital. *Rural Sociology* 63 (2): 300-22.

Wehlage, G. and R. Rutter. 1986. Dropping out: How much do schools contribute to the problem? *Teachers College Record* 87 (3): 374-92.

White House Initiative on Educational Excellence for Hispanic Americans. 1998. *Latinos in Education: Early childhood, elementary, secondary, undergraduate, graduate*. Washington, D.C.: U.S. Department of Education.

White, J. and G. Wehlage. 1995. Community collaboration: If it is such a good idea, why is it so hard to do? *Educational Evaluation and Policy Analysis* 17: 23-38.

White, M. and G. Kaufman. 1997. Language usage, social capital, and school completion among immigrants and native born ethnic groups. *Social Science Quarterly* 78 (2): 385-98.

Willis, P. 1981. *Learning to labor: How working class kids get working class jobs.* New York: Columbia University Press.

Wilson, J. and M. Musick. 1997. Who cares? Toward an integrated theory of volunteer work. *American Sociological Review* 62: 694-713.

Wilson, W. 1987. *The truly disadvantaged: The inner city, the underclass & public policy.* Chicago: University of Chicago Press.

Wood, D., N. Halfon, D. Scarla, P. Newacheck, and S. Nessim. 1993. Impact of family relocation on children's growth, development, school function, and behavior. *Journal of the American Medical Association* 270: 1334-38.

Woolcock, M. 1998. Social capital and economic development: Toward a theoretical synthesis and policy framework. *Theory and Society* 27: 151-208.

Wuthnow, R. 1994. *Sharing the journey: Support groups and America's new quest for community.* New York: Free Press.

Zeldin, S. and L. Price. 1995. Community collaboration: If it is such a good idea, why is it so hard to do? *Educational Evaluation and Policy Analysis* 17: 23-38.

Zerkel, 1977. Bilingual education and school desegregation: A case of uncoordinated remedies. *Bilingual Review* 4: 180-88.

Zhou, M. and C. Bankston. 1998. *Growing Up American: How Vietnamese Children Adapt to Life in the United States.* New York: Russell Sage Foundation.

APPENDICES

Appendix A. *NELS:88* Variables Considered in the Development of Composite and Latent Measures of Social Capital

Social Capital Within Families

1. Parents/siblings involved in student's education

student chose school/academic program with parents	F2S12BC
parent talked with student about selecting school courses	F2P49A
parents influence taking science	F2S18BC
student discussed school activities/experiences with parent	F2S99B
parent discussed school activities with student	F2P49B
parent talk with student about things studied in class	F2P49C
parent talked with student about student's grades	F2P49D
parent talked with student about applying to school after H.S.	F2P49F
sibling influences taking science	F2S18BE
sibling helps with homework	F2S26D
parent contacted school re: student's academic performance	F2P44A
parent contacted school re: student's academic program	F2P44B
parent contacted school re: student's after-high-school plans	F2P44C
parent contacted school re: college prep course selection	F2P44D
parent contacted school re: student's attendance	F2P44E
parent contacted school re: student's behavior	F2P44F
parent knows which courses student is taking	F2P46A
parent knows how well student is doing in school	F2P46B
parent worked on homework projects with teen	F2P50B
parent encouraged teen to prepare for SAT	F2P62A
parent encouraged teen to prepare for ACT	F2P62B
parent talked to teen about applying for college	F2P63

2. Parent/student bond

student does things with mother/father	F2S33H
student discussed troubling things with parents	F2S99I
parents discussed troubling things with student	F2P49I
parents trust student to do what they expect	F2S100A
parent talks with student about student's hobbies	F2P49J

parent attended movies/plays/concerts with teen	F2P50C
parent attended non-school-related sports events with teen	F2P50D
parent attended family social functions with teen	F2P50F
parent took day-trips or vacations with teen	F2P50G
parent worked on hobbies with teen	F2P50H
parent went shopping with teen	F2P50I
parent went out to eat with teen	F2P50J
parent spent time just talking together with teen	F2P50K
parent spent time doing something fun with teen	F2P50L

3. Intergenerational closure

student's parents know closest friend's parents	F2S97
parent knows parent of teen's first friend	F2P54B1
parent knows parent of teen's second friend	F2P54B2
parent knows parent of teen's third friend	F2P54B3
parent knows parent of teen's fourth friend	F2P54B4
# of parents teen's parents talks to with kids at teen's school	F2P55
parent discusses happenings at teens school with other parents	F2P56A
parent discusses teen's school plans with other parents	F2P56B
parent discusses teen's career plans with other parents	F2P56C

4. Parents involved in school-related activities

parent attends school activities with teen	F2P50A
parents attend program re: educational opportunities after H.S.	F2P45A
parent attend program re: college financial aid	F2P45B
parent contacted school about doing volunteer work	F2P44G

Social Capital Among Peers

1. Student connected with peers

does things with friends	F2S33G
important having strong friendships	F2S40D
has friends to count on	F2S67J

2. Student friendly with other racial groups F2S7B

3. Student's friends prioritize education

friends think important to take algebra/math	F2S22BD
friends think important to attend class	F2S68A

friends think important to study	F2S68B
friends think important to get good grades	F2S68D
friends think important to continue ed. past H.S.	F2S68H

Social Capital Within the Community

1. Student/parent participates in community

student volunteers in community	F2S37
student volunteers in youth organization	F2S39A
student volunteers in service organization, i.e., Big Brothers	F2S39B
student volunteers with educational group	F2S39G
student volunteers with environmental group	F2S39H
important to do community work	F2S68J
important to help others in community	F2S40F
parent involved in neighborhood	F2P59
parent believes neighborhood to be safe	F2P60

2. Student attends religious services/activities

student attends religious activities	F2S33C
student volunteered with church group	F2S39D
important to participate in religious group	F2S68I
student attends religious services	F2S106
parent attended religious service with student	F2P50E

Social Capital Within Schools

1. Institutional Agent demonstrates caring toward student

teachers interested in student(s)	F2S7D

2. Institutional Agent supports student's academic advancement

teacher helped student with homework	F2S26A
importance of teacher/counselor in taking algebra/ math	F2S22BA
school contacted parent about student's academic program	F2P43B
favorite teacher's desire for student after H.S.	F2S41F

Appendix B. Variable Descriptions, Means, Standard Deviations and Mean Comparisons in the Sample

(NCES Variable Name) Description	Mexican-Americans (N = 1,141)			Non-Latino Whites (N = 10,907)		
	Mean	SD	N	Mean	SD	N
Family Background, 8th Grade						
Socioeconomic Status (BYSES) NCES composite	-.72	.67	1,141	.08	.71	10,907
Immigrant (KIDIMMIG) student born outside U.S. BYP17 = 2,3	.17	.37	975	.01	.12	10,238
Second Generation (GEN2) U.S. - born student/foreign - born parents BYP17 = 1 BYP11 =2,3 or BYP14 = 2,3	.40	.49	975	.05	.21	10,238
Third Generation (GEN3) U.S. - born student/U.S. - born parents BYP17 = 1 BYP11 = 1 or BYP14 = 1	.43	.50	975	.94	.24	10,238
Mobility, Grades K-8						
Never Changed Schools (BYP40) = 0	.47	.50	999	.51	.50	10,340
Changed Schools Once (BYP40) = 1	.22	.42	999	.23	.42	10,340
Changed Schools 2+ Times (BYP40) = 2 thru 5	.31	.46	999	.26	.44	10,340
Academic Achievement, 8th Grade						
Math IRT Score (BY2XMIRR) math estimated number right	30.33	9.25	1,085	38.13	11.57	10,567
Reading IRT Score (BY2XRIRR) reading estimated number right	23.21	6.94	1,085	28.59	8.45	10,561
Science IRT Score (BY2XSIRR) science estimated number right	16.67	3.93	1,087	19.69	4.72	10,562
History IRT Score (BY2XHIRR) history estimated number right	27.51	4.14	1,085	30.30	4.43	10,531

Mobility, Grades 8-12						
Never Changed Schools (F2S103) = 0	.70	.46	818	.79	.41	9,627
Changed Schools Once (F2S103) = 1	.19	.39	818	.15	.36	9,627
Changed Schools 2+ Times (F2S103) = 2,3	.11	.32	818	.06	.24	9,627
Never Changed Residences (F2S102) = 0	.63	.48	820	.69	.46	9,643
Changed Residences Once (F2S102) = 1	.20	.40	820	.19	.39	9,643
Changed Residences 2+ Times (F2S102) = 2,3	.17	.37	820	.12	.33	9,643
Family Social Capital, 12th Grade						
Parents Involved in Student's Education (FSC1)			841			9,917
Parent talks with student about selecting school courses F2P49A	1.38	.66	838	1.54	.57	9,910
Parent discusses school activities with student F2P49B	1.38	.68	838	1.59	.56	9,910
Parent talks with student about things studied in class F2P49C	1.42	.65	839	1.51	.55	9,897
Parents Know Student's Friends' Parents (FSC2)			819			9,668
Parent knows parent of teen's first friend F2P54B1	.76	.43	815	.82	.38	9,625
Parent knows parent of teen's second friend F2P54B2	.63	.48	816	.73	.44	9,618
Parent knows parent of teen's third friend F2P54B3	.48	.50	815	.61	.49	9,612
Peer Social Capital, 12th Grade						
Student Shares Strong Connection with Peers (PSC1)			1,085			11,071

Important for student to have strong friendships F2S40D	1.68	.52	1,084	1.82	.41	11,063
Important to get together among student's close friends F2S68L	1.45	.57	946	1.60	.54	10,513
Chances student will have good friends to count on F2S67J	3.00	.85	934	3.26	.75	10,066
Student's Peers Value Education (PSC2)			953			10,550
Friends think it's important to attend class regularly F2S68A	1.40	.64	953	1.43	.62	10,545
Friends think it is important to study F2S68B	1.22	.61	953	1.21	.64	10,528
Friends think it is important to get good grades F2S68D	1.43	.61	952	1.37	.63	10,515
Friends think it is important to continue ed. past high school F2S68H	1.48	.64	948	1.50	.65	10,506
Community Social Capital, 12th Grade						
Student Volunteers in the Community (CSC1)			1,051			10,947
Student volunteers in community, e.g., scouts, service clubs… F2S37	.35	.48	1,051	.46	.50	10,947
Student Participates in Religious Activities (CSC2)			1,059			10,944
Student attends religious activities F2S33C	.66	.89	1,007	.81	.96	10,281
Student volunteers with religious group F2S39D	.53	.50	360	.48	.50	4,901
Student attends religious services F2S106	2.43	1.65	802	2.22	1.79	10,012

School Social Capital, 12th Grade						
Academically Relevant Teacher/Student Interaction (SSC1)			1,087			11,021
Teachers demonstrate interest in students F2S7D	2.02	.65	1,079	1.96	.65	10,986
Teachers important in student's math course-taking F2S22BA	1.53	1.60	550	1.48	1.50	6,029
Guidance counselor important in student's math course-taking F2S22BB	2.02	1.66	553	1.53	1.58	6,023
Teachers help student with homework F2S26A	.79	.41	1,055	.79	.40	10,861
School-Initiated Interaction with Students' Parents (SSC2)			839			9,935
School contacted parent about student's academic program F2P43B	.56	.80	832	.56	.75	9,906
School contacted parent re: student's plans after high school F2P43C	.48	.80	836	.52	.82	9,893
School contacted parent about college prep. course selection F2P43D	.44	.78	833	.42	.72	9,911
Academic Achievement, 12th Grade						
Math IRT Score (F22XMIRR) math estimated number right	41.47	12.20	901	50.66	13.71	8,805
Reading IRT Score (F22XRIRR) reading estimated number right	29.32	8.81	901	34.62	9.71	8,806
Science IRT Score (F22XSIRR) science estimated number right	20.34	5.30	895	24.65	5.88	8,756
History IRT Score (F22XHIRR) history estimated number right	32.43	4.73	891	35.59	5.23	8,721

Appendix C. Interview Protocols

Parent Interview Protocol

NOTE: Interviews should flow comfortably, like a friendly conversation, so spend a couple minutes, *before* the interview getting to know the interviewee. Once you have established some rapport, remind the parent/guardian of the interview's purpose—we are studying students and former students who have changed schools and/or moved from place to place, to better understand how moving impacts their social relationships and schooling. Lastly, remind parents that the information provided will be held in strictest confidence.

I. Residential Mobility

- A. Since ________ was in eighth grade, have you moved your place of residence or changed houses?
- B. Why did you move?
- C. Has your child ever changed schools without changing residences? Has there ever been a time when you changed residences without your child having to change schools?
- D. How has moving residences impacted your child's school performance? His/her friendships?
- E. Have any community groups ever helped you when you changed residence?
- F. What advice do you have for other parents whose children must attend a new school due to a family move?

II. The School

- A. What could schools do to be more helpful to parents of students that change schools?
- B. What could schools do to be more helpful to the students that change schools?

III. School Mobility

- A. How many high schools has your son/daughter attended?
- B. In what order did he/she attend each of the schools?
- C. For each of the high schools your child attended:
  - * Why did your child leave the school?
  - * Who decided that your child should change schools?

D. Did anyone (school administrator, teacher, principal...) help your child when he/she left an "old" high school or arrived at a "new" high school? If so, how?

E. Did you talk with anyone at your child's new high school about the fact that your son/daughter had just arrived at the new school? If so, how did school personnel respond to your concerns.

F. Did your child have a choice about changing high schools -- did he/she want to leave?

G. How has changing high schools impacted your child's school performance?

H. Has your child ever quit school or dropped out of school for any amount of time?

Note: If the student quit school anytime during their school career, ask the following questions to their parent/guardian:

* Why did your child quit school?
* What did he do when he wasn't in school?
* Why did she go back to school?

Note: If the student is <u>currently not</u> in school, ask the following questions:

* Why isn't your child attending school at this time?
* What do they do when they aren't in school?

IV. Social Capital

A. Families

* How would you characterize your relationship with (insert name of mobile student)?
* Do you discuss school and school activities with ________?
* Does ________ talk with you about things that bother him/her?
* Do you know ________'s friends? Do you know the parents of his/her friend?

B. Peers

* Does _________ have friends that he/she can count on?
* Do ________'s friends think education is important?
* Do his/her friends plan on graduating from high school and going on to college?

* Does ______ have any friends from another race/ethnicity group?

C. Schools
* Do you know any of ________'s teachers?
* Have you ever met with a school counselor concerning your child?
* Are schools helpful to students that move from school to school? If so, how?
* Do teachers show interest in ________ and his/her school work?

D. Community
* Are you involved in any community organizations?
* Are you involved in any religious organizations such as church or a synagogue?
* Do you think it's important to be involved in your community?
* Do you know your neighbors?

V. Family/Personal

A. Employment
* Are you currently employed? If so, where? Is your spouse/partner employed?

B. Education level
* Can you tell me about your educational background? Have you graduated from high school? From college? And your spouse/partner?

C. Immigrant status
* Were you born in the United States? If not, where are you originally from (state, country)?

D. Home language
* What language do you speak at home among family members?

Please include the following information in each interview/transcription:

* Interviewer's name
* Interviewee's name, age (if they don't mind sharing this information!), sex and race/ethnicity (what the parent calls her/himself, i.e., Chicana/o, Mexican American, Mexican, American…)

* The context – where does the interview take place and under what circumstances i.e., who is present, the time and date of the interview…

Parent Interview Protocol (Spanish)

I. Cambio de residencia

A. ¿Desde que ____________ estaba en el octavo grado, se han cambiado de residencia o de casa?
Since ________ was in eighth grade, have you moved your place of residence or changed houses?

B. ¿Por qué se mudaron?
Why did you move?

C. ¿Alguna vez ha tenido su hijo/a que cambiarse de escuela sin haber tenido que cambiarse del lugar donde vivía? Ha habido alguna vez en la que se mudaron sin haber tenido que cambiar de escuela?
Has your child ever changed schools without changing residences? Has there ever been a time when you changed residences without your child having to change schools?

D. Cómo le ha afectado en su rendimiento escolar el haberse cambiado de residencia? Cómo ha afectado a sus amistades?
How has moving residences impacted your child's school performance? Their friendships?

E. ¿Algún grupo comunitario les ha ayudado cuando se han cambiado de residencia?
Have any community groups ever helped you when you changed residence?

F. ¿Qué consejo(s) le daría a otros padres cuyos hijos tienen que asistir a una nueva escuela a causa de una mudanza?
What advice do you have for other parents whose children must attend a new school due to a family move?

II. La Escuela

A. ¿Qué podrían hacer las escuelas para proveerles mejores servicios a los padres de alumnos que cambian de escuelas?
What could schools do to be more helpful to parents of students that change schools?

B. ¿Qué podrían hacer las escuelas para proveerles mejores servicios a los alumnos que se cambian de escuelas?
What could schools do to be more helpful to the students that change schools?

III. Cambio de escuelas

A. ¿A cuántas escuelas prepartorias ha asistido su hijo/a?

How many high schools has your son/daughter attended?

* ¿En qué orden asistió a cada una de las escuelas?
In what order did he/she attend each of the schools?

B. ¿Por cada una de las escuelas a las que ha asistido su hijo/a:
For each of the high schools your child attended:

* ¿Por qué se cambio de escuela su hijo/a?
Why did your child leave the school?

* ¿Quién decidió que su hijo/a debería cambiar de escuela?
Who decided that your child should change schools?

C. ¿Alguien (un administrador, maestro, o director…) le ayudó a su hijo/a cuando se fueron de una escuela o llegaron a otra? Si le ayudaron, cómo lo hicieron?
Did anyone (school administrator, teacher, principal...) help your child when they left an "old" high school or arrived at a "new" high school? If so, how?

D. ¿Habló con alguien en la nueva escuela sobre el hecho que su hijo/a se acababa de matricular? Si habló con alguien, cómo le respondieron a sus necesidades/preocupaciónes?
Did you talk with anyone at your child's new high school about the fact that your son/daughter had just arrived at the new school? If so, how did school personnel respond to your concerns?

E. ¿Su hijo/a tuvo opciónes al tener que cambiarse de la escuela preparatoria? Se quería cambiar de escuela?
Did your child have a choice about changing high schools -- did he/she want to leave?

F. ¿Cómo ha afectado el cambio de escuela en el rendimiento escolar de su hijo/a?
How has changing high schools impacted your child's school performance?

G. ¿Ha dejado su hijo/a de asistir o se ha salido de la escuela por algún tiempo?
Has your child ever quit school or dropped out of school for any amount of time?

Note: If the student quit school anytime during their school career, ask the following questions to their parent/guardian:

* ¿Por qué dejó la escuela su hijo/a?
Why did your child quit school?

* ¿Que hacía su hijo/a cuando dejó de la escuela?

What did he/she do when not in school?

* ¿Por que regresó a la escuela?
  Why did he/she go back to school?

Note: If the student is <u>*currently not*</u> *in school, ask the following questions:*

* ¿Por qué no está asistiendo a la escuela su hijo/a?
  Why isn't your child attending school at this time?
* ¿Qué hace cuando no está en la escuela?
  What does he/she do when not in school?

IV. Capital Social

A. Familias

* ¿Como describiría su relación con ____________________?
  How would you characterize your relationship with (insert name of mobile student)?
* ¿Platica sobre la escuela y las actividades de la escuela con ____________________?
  Do you discuss school and school activities with ________?
* ¿________________ habla con usted sobre cosas qué le molestan?
  Does ________ talk with you about things that bother him/her?
* ¿Conoce a los amigos de ______________? ¿Conoce a los padres de sus amistades?
  Do you know ________'s friends? Do you know the parents of his/her friend?

B. Amigos

* ¿______________ tiene amigos con los que puede contar?
  Does _________ have friends that he/she can count on?
* ¿Los amigos de _____________ piensan que la educación es importante?
  Do _______'s friends think education is important?
* ¿Planean sus amigos graduarse de la preparatoria y asistir a la universidad o al colegio comunitario?
  Do his/her friends plan on graduating from high school and going on to college?

* ¿______________ tiene amigos de otros grupos étnicos o de otras razas?
  Does ______ have any friends from another race/ethnicity group?

C. Escuelas

* ¿Conoce a alguno de los maestros de ___________________?
  Do you know any of ________'s teachers?
* ¿Alguna vez ha tenido una junta con un consejero de la escuela para hablar sobre su hijo/a?
  Have you ever met with a school counselor concerning your child?
* ¿Las escuelas brindan ayuda a los alumnos que se cambian de una a otra escuela? ¿Como?
  Are schools helpful to students that move from school to school? If so, how?
* ¿Muestran interés los maestros en el trabajo escolar de ________________?
  Do teachers show interest in ________ and his/her school work?

D. Comunidad

* ¿Está usted involucrado en alguna organización de la comunidad?
  Are you involved in any community organizations?
* ¿Está involucrado en alguna organización religiosa?
  Are you involved in any religious organizations such as church or a synagogue?
* ¿Cree que es importate involucrarse en su comunidad?
  Do you think it's important to be involved in your community?
* ¿Conoce a sus vecinos?
  Do you know your neighbors?

V. Familia/Personal

A. Empleo

* ¿Está empleado en este momento? ¿Si es así, dónde? ¿Está trabajando su esposa(o)?
  Are you currently employed? If so, where? Is your spouse/partner employed?

B. Nivel de educación

* ¿Me puede decir sobre su nivel de educación? ¿Hasta que año asistió a la escuela? ¿Se graduó de la preparatoria? ¿De la universidad? Y su esposo/a?
* *Can you tell me about your educational background? Have you graduated from high school? From college? And your spouse/partner?*

C. Estado migratorio

* ¿Nació en Los Estados Unidos? ¿Si no nació en los Estados Unidos, de dónde nació (estado, pais)?
  Were you born in the United States? If not, where are you originally from (state, country)?

D. Lenguaje que se habla en casa

* ¿Qué lenguaje hablan en casa o entre familiares?
  What language do you speak at home among family members?

Student Interview Protocol (English)

I. Residential Mobility

A. Since eighth grade, have you lived in the same place or have you ever moved?
B. Do you remember why you moved?
C. Have you ever changed schools without changing the place you lived?
D. Have you ever moved (residence) but stayed at the same school?
E. Has moving affected your grades?
F. Did moving affect your participation in school programs like sports, the school play, or other extracurricular activities?
G. Has moving affected your friendships?
H. How did you make new friends when you entered a new school?

II. The School Setting and Mobility

A. Overall, what impact does changing schools have on a student?
B. Are schools (principals, teachers, counselors…) helpful to students that change schools? If so, how?
C. Did a school counselor ever help you when you changed schools?
D. What could schools (principals, teachers, counselors and students) do to help students who leave for another school?
E. What could schools do to help new students that arrive from another school?

III. Student Mobility

A. Tell me about your experiences changing schools since eighth grade.
    * At which school(s) did you spend ninth grade? Tenth grade? Eleventh grade? Twelfth grade?
    * For each high school you attended, why did you leave that school?
    * Did you have a choice about changing high schools—did you want to leave?
    * Who decided that you should change schools?

B. What is it like to change high schools?

* Can you explain what you do (what is the process) when you move to a new high school?

C. How did your new school know which classes you should attend?

D. Were you able to pick up your schooling pretty much where you left off at the previous school you attended?

E. Did anyone ever help you when your arrived at a new high school? If so, what did they do that helped you?

F. How did teachers react to you as a new student in their classrooms?

G. What are the consequences of changing high schools?
   * How did changing schools impact your social life (friendships, relationships with teachers...)?
   * How did changing schools impact your school performance (grades, school involvement...)?
   * Can you give specific examples?

H. Have you ever stopped attending school for an extended period of time, or dropped out of school? If so, Why?

Note to Interviewer: If the student quit school anytime during her/his school career, ask the following questions:

* Why did you quit school?
* What did you do when you weren't in school?
* How long was it before you returned to school?
* Why did you go back to school?

IV. Social Capital

A. Families
   * Do you live with both your parents?
   * Do you discuss school activities with your parents/guardians?
   * Do you confide in your parents about things that bother you?
   * Do your parents/guardians know the parents of your closest friend?

B. Peers
   * Do you have friends that you can count on?
   * Do your friends think education is important?
   * Do your friends plan on graduating from high school and going on to college?

- * Do you have any friends who are of a different race/ethnicity than you?
- * Are any of your friends recent immigrants from Mexico?

C. Schools

- * Do your teachers show interest in you and your school work?
- * If you have a school-related problem, who is most likely to help you with it?
- * Do the teachers/counselors in your school recommend that you go to college or straight to work after high school?

D. Community

- * Are you involved in any extra-curricular activities or community organizations?
- * Are you involved in any religious organizations or youth groups?
- * Do you think it's important to be involved in your community?
- * Do you know anyone who lives in your neighborhood?

V. Family/Personal

A. How old are you?

B. Where were you born (city, state, country)?

C. What language do you speak at home among family members?

D. Were your parents born in the United States? If not, where are they from (state, country)?

E. Do your parents work?

- * What does your father do for a living?
- * What is your mother's job?

Student Interview Protocol (Spanish)

I. Cambio de residencia

A. ¿Desde el octavo grado, has vivido en el mismo lugar o te has cambiado de residencia?
Since the beginning of eighth grade, have you lived in the same place or have you changed residences?

B. ¿Si te mudaste, recuerdas por qué?
If you changed residences, do you remember why?

C. ¿Alguna vez has tenido que cambiarte de escuela sin haber tenido que cambiarte del lugar donde vivías?
Have you ever changed schools without *changing the place you lived?*

D. ¿Alguna vez has tenido que cambiar de residencia, pero te has quedado en la misma escuela?
Have you ever moved (residence) but stayed at the same school?

E. ¿El haberte mudado afectó tus calificaciones?
Has moving affected your grades?

F. ¿El haberte mudado afectó tu participación en programas escolares tales como deportes, drama, u otras actividades escolares?
Did moving affect your participation in school programs like sports, the school play, or other extracurricular activities?

G. ¿El haberte mudado ha afectado tus amistades?
Has moving affected your friendships?

H. ¿Cómo hiciste nuevas amistades cuando entraste en una nueva escuela?
How did you make new friends when you entered a new school?

II. La locación de la escuela y mobilidad

A. ¿En general, qué impacto tiene el cambio de escuelas en un estudiante?
Overall, what impact does changing schools have on a student?

B. ¿Ayudan las escuelas (directores, maestros, consejeros…) a los estudiantes que cambian de escuelas? Si este es el caso, cómo?

Are schools (principals, teachers, counselors...) helpful to students that change schools? If so, how?

C. ¿Te ayudó un consejero cuando cambiaste de escuela?
Did a school counselor ever help you when you changed schools?

D. ¿Que podrían hacer las escuelas (directores, maestros, consejeros y estudiantes) para ayudar a estudiantes que se cambian a otra escuela?

What could schools (principals, teachers, counselors, and students) do to help students who leave for another school?

E. ¿Que podrían hacer las escuelas para ayudar a los nuevos estudiantes que llegan de otra escuela?

What could schools do to help new students that arrive from another school?

III. Mobilidad del estudiante

A. ¿Dime sobre tus experiencias al cambiar de escuelas desde el empiezo del octavo grado?

Tell me about your experiences changing schools since eighth grade.

* ¿En qué escuelas estuviste en el noveno grado? En el grado 10, 11 y 12?

At which school(s) did you spend ninth grade? Tenth grade? Eleventh grade? Twelfth grade?

* ¿Por cada escuela que asististe, por qué te fuiste de esa escuela?

For each high school you attended, why did you leave that school?

* ¿Tuviste una opción al cambiarte de escuela -- querías cambiar de escuela?

Did you have a choice about changing high schools -- did you want to leave?

* ¿Quién decidió que deberías cambiar de escuela?
Who decided that you should change schools?

B. ¿Cómo se siente tener que cambiar de escuela preparatoria?
What is it like to change high schools?

* ¿Puedes explicar cuál es el procedimiento cuando te cambias a una nueva escuela preparatoria?

* *Can you explain what you do (what is the process) when you move to a new high school?*

C. ¿Cómo supieron en la nueva escuela que clases tenías que tomar?
How did your new school know which classes you should attend?

D. ¿Pudiste continuar con tu educación al mismo nivel en que estabas en la escuela anterior?
Were you able to pick up your schooling pretty much where you left off at the previous school you attended?

E. ¿Alguien te ayudó cuando llegaste a la nueva escuela preparatoria? ¿Si ese es el caso, cómo te ayudaron?
Did anyone ever help you when your arrived at a new high school? If so, what did they do that helped you?

F. ¿Cómo reaccionaron los maestros contigo como un nuevo estudiante en sus clases?
How did teachers react to you as a new student in their classrooms?

G. ¿Cuáles crees que son las consecuencias de cambiarse de escuela preparatoria?
What are the consequences of changing high schools?

* ¿Cómo afectó tu vida social (amistades, relaciones con maestros…) el haberte cambiado de escuela?
How did changing schools impact your social life (friendships, relationships with teachers...)?
* ¿Cómo afectó tu rendimiento escolar (calificaciones, participación en actividades de la escuela…) el haberte cambiado de escuela?
How did changing schools impact your school performance (grades, school involvement,...)?
* ¿Puedes dar ejemplos específicos?
Can you give a specific examples?

H. ¿Has dejado de asistir a la escuela por un largo tiempo, o te has salido por completo (dropped out) alguna vez? ¿Si ese es el caso, por qué?
Have you ever stopped attending school for an extended period of time, or dropped out of school? If so, Why?

Note to Interviewer: If the student quit school anytime during her/his school career, ask the following questions:

- ¿Por qué te saliste de la escuela?
  Why did you quit school?
- ¿Qué hiciste o hacías cuando no estabas asistiendo a la escuela?
  What did you do when you weren't in school?
- ¿Cuánto tiempo tardaste para regresar a la escuela?
  How long was it before you returned to school?
- ¿Por qué regresaste a la escuela?
  Why did you go back to school?

IV. Capital Social

A. Families

- ¿Vives con tus dos padres?
  Do you live with both your parents?
- ¿Discutes tus actividades escolares con tus padres o las personas encargadas de ti?
  Do you discuss school activities with your parents/guardians?
- ¿Confías o hablas con tús padres sobre cosas que te molestan?
  Do you confide in your parents about things that bother you?
- ¿Conocen tus padres o encargados a tus mejores amigos?
  Do your parents/guardians know the parents of your closest friend?

B. Amigos

- ¿Tienes amigos con quienes puedes contar?
  Do you have friends that you can count on?
- ¿Piensan tus amigos que la educación es importante?
  Do your friends think education is important?
- ¿Planean tus amigos graduarse de la preparatoria y asistir a la universidad o al colegio?
  Do your friends plan on graduating from high school and going on to college?
- ¿Tienes amigos que pertenecen a un grupo étnico o raza diferente de la tuya?

Do you have any friends who are of a different race/ethnicity than you?

* ¿Tienes algún amigo que sea un reciente inmigrante?
  Are any of your friends recent immigrants?

C. Escuelas

* ¿Demuestran interés en ti y en tu rendimiento escolar tus maestros?
  Do your teachers show interest in you and your school work?
* ¿Si tienes problemas relacionados con la escuela, quién es la persona que crees que te puede ayudar?
  If you have a school-related problem, who is most likely to help you with it?
* ¿Te recomiendan tus maestros/consejeros que asistas a la universidad o que vayas derecho a trabajar después de la preparatoria?
  Do the teachers/counselors in your school recommend that you go to college or straight to work after high school?

D. Comunidad

* ¿Estás involucrado en actividades después de la escuela o en organizaciónes de la comunidad?
  Are you involved in any extra-curricular activities or community organizations?
* ¿Estás involucrado en alguna organización religiosa o algún grupo juvenil?
  Are you involved in any religious organizations or youth groups?
* ¿Crees que es importante involucrarte en actividades de tu comunidad?
  Do you think it's important to be involved in your community?
* ¿Conoces a alguién que viva en tu comunidad?
  Do you know anyone who lives in your neighborhood?

V. Familia/personal

A. ¿Cuantos años tienes?
   How old are you?

B. ¿Donde nacíste (ciudad, estado, pais)?
   Where were you born (city, state, country)?

C. ¿Qué lenguaje hablas en casa con tus familiares?
What language do you speak at home among family members?

D. ¿Nacieron tus padres en los Estados Unidos? Si no es así, de dónde nacieron (estado, país)?
Were your parents born in the United States? If not, where are they from (state, country)?

E. ¿Trabajan tus padres?
Do your parents work?

* ¿En qué trabaja tu papá?
  What does your father do for a living?
* ¿En qué trabaja tu mamá?
  What is your mother's job?

School Counselor Protocol

I. Background

- A. How long have you been a counselor?
- B. What degrees do you hold?

II. Student Mobility

- A. Is the issue of children moving in and out of your school one that has come to your attention?
- B. How does mobility impact your students?
- C. Does student mobility impact school morale? If so, how?
- D. When a new student arrives on your campus, how does the school decide where to place that student?
- E. Why do students move from your school?
- F. How are cumulative files exchanged between your school and the school from which a new student has arrived? How long does this process typically take?
- G. How does mobility impact a student's social adjustment? Their adjustment to school?
- H. Are there positive aspects of mobility for school children?
- I. What are the negative aspects of school mobility for kids?
- J. Have you ever had any formal training designed to assist you in counseling mobile students?
- K. Can you distinguish student mobility between Whites and Latinos in terms of its causes and consequences or do both groups change schools for similar reasons and with similar effects?
- L. If you could make one recommendation to education policymakers about how to better deal with the issue of student mobility/transience, what would it be?

Teacher Interview Protocol

I. Background

A. How long have you been teaching?
B. What grade do you teach?
C. What degrees do you hold?
D. Do you have a teaching credential?

II. Student mobility

A. What is it like to teach a class that changes composition (students) throughout the school year?
B. What are your strategies for integrating newcomers into your classroom?
C. In a typical month, how many students withdraw from your classroom? How many new students enter your classroom in a typical month?
D. Have you ever taught in a school that evidenced more mobility than the school where you are now teaching?
E. What do you need to know about a new student entering your class? How do you get that information?
F. How do you integrate the new student into the normal routine of the class?
G. Are there tactics that you use to help the new student adjust socially to his/her new classroom setting?
H. Are there certain times of the year that make it difficult to accommodate new students in your classroom?
I. Do you receive advance notice that a new student will enter your classroom?
J. Are there special problems associated with student mobility in your classroom?
K. Are there any benefits to student mobility in your classroom?
L. Can you distinguish student mobility between Whites and Latinos in terms of its causes and consequences or do both groups change schools for similar reasons and with similar effects?
M. If you could make one recommendation to education policymakers about how to better deal with the issue of student mobility/transience, what would it be?

School Administrator Protocol

I. Background

A. How long have you been an administrator?

B. What degrees do you hold?

II. Student Mobility

A. Is the issue of children moving in and out of your school one that has come to your attention?

B. In general, what percentage of the children who start the year in your school actually finish the school year at your school?

C. When a new student arrives on your campus, how do you decide in which classes to place that student? Who at your school is responsible for securing that information?

D. Does student mobility impact classroom instruction in your school? How?

E. Does student mobility impact school morale? If so, how?

F. What are some of the reasons that students move from your school?

G. Can you distinguish student mobility between Whites and Latinos in terms of its causes and consequences or do both groups change schools for similar reasons and with similar effects?

H. What are the implications of student mobility in light of the statewide movement toward school accountability? Should schools be held accountable for the test scores of transient students?

I. If you could make one recommendation to education policymakers about how do better deal with the issue of student mobility/transience, what would it be?

Appendix D. Logistical Information

Who will be interviewed for this study?

Sixteen middle to low-income Mexican Americans (including immigrants, second and third+ generation participants) and sixteen non-Latino Whites with similar socioeconomic profiles will be included in the interviews. An equal number of boys and girls will be interviewed. Their parents/guardians will also be interviewed.

Who will identify the student informants that we will interview?

Bob Ream and the rest of the interview team.

Who will conduct the interviews?

Recognizing that race/ethnicity is one interviewer characteristic that may exert a biasing effect, Bob Ream plans to pair interviewers with student informants who are of the same gender, race/ethnicity, generation status and language preference. Table 1 below highlights the interviewer positions for which Bob is hiring (4 Mexican Americans and 2 non-Latino Whites).

	Mexican Americans			Non-Latino Whites	
	Immigrant	*Second or 3+ generation*		*Immigrant*	*Second or 3+generation*
Men	1	1		Bob Ream will conduct these interviews	
Women	1	1		1	1

How many interviews will each interviewer conduct?

Each interviewer will conduct 8 interviews -- four student interviews and four more (separate) interviews with the students' parent/guardian. Altogether, the study consists of 64 interviews (8 Mexican-American girls, 8 Mexican-American boys, 8 Whites girls, 8 White boys, and the parent/guardian of each student).

How much will the interviewer be paid for each interview?

$25.00

How much will each informant be paid for participating in an interview?

$20.00

How much will be paid for transcribing each interview into English?

$50/interview

Reminder:

Please include the following information in each interview/transcription:

1. your name
2. student's name, age, sex and race/ethnicity (what the students call themselves)
3. the context – where does the interview take place and under what circumstances, i.e., who is present, what time of day…
4. the date and time of the interview

Appendix E. Parent/Student Permission Forms

Parent Permission Form (English)

Parent(s)
I grant my daughter/son permission to participate in an interview to discuss her/his experiences associated with changing schools and/or residences.

Parent Signature:______________________________________

Please print your name: _________________________________

Home
address:____

Telephone
number:____

Date:____________________________

Student
I agree to participate in an interview regarding my experiences associated with changing schools and/or residences.

Student Signature:_____________________________________

Please print your name:_________________________________

Home
address:____

Telephone
number:____

Date:___________________________

** Although highly unlikely, if our interview revealed information about sexual or physical abuse involving someone who isn't yet 18 years old, I would be required by law to report that information to Social Services.

Parent Permission Form (Spanish)

Padre(s)
Permito que mi hijo/a participe en una entrevista para que discuta sus experiencias relacionadas con el cambio de residencia o de escuela.

Firma del
padre/madre:____

Escriba su nombre en letra de molde:___________________________

Escriba su
dirección:____

Número de
teléfono:____

Fecha:______________________________

Estudiante
Estoy de acuerdo a participar en una entrevista para hablar sobre mis experiencias al cambiarme de residencia o de escuela.

Firma del
estudiante:____

Escriba su nombre en letra de
molde:________________________________

Escriba su
dirección:____

Número de
teléfono:____

Fecha:______________________________

** Como una medida de precaución, le quiero informar que si durante la entrevista se observara alguna señal de abuso físico o sexual que incluya un menor de 18 años de edad, yo tendría la obligación de reportar este caso a la oficina de Servicios Sociales.

INDEX